Frontiers of Evangelization

FRONTIERS OF EVANGELIZATION

Indians in the Sierra Gorda and Chiquitos Missions

Robert H. Jackson

UNIVERSITY OF OKLAHOMA PRESS : NORMAN

Some material in this volume was previously published in article and book form and is used here by permission of the respective publishers:

"The Chichimeca Frontier and the Evangelization of the Sierra Gorda, 1550–1770," Estudios de Historia Novohispana 47 (July–December 2012), 46–91.

Conflict and Conversion in Sixteenth Century Central Mexico: The Augustinian War on and beyond the Chichimeca Frontier (Leiden: Brill Academic Publishers, 2013).

All photographs in this volume are by the author.

Library of Congress Cataloging-in-Publication Data

Name: Jackson, Robert H. (Robert Howard), author.
Title: Frontiers of evangelization : Indians in the Sierra Gorda and Chiquitos missions / Robert H. Jackson.
Description: Norman : University of Oklahoma Press, 2017. | Includes bibliographical references and index.
Identifiers: LCCN 2016056645 | ISBN 978-0-8061-5772-6 (hardcover)
ISBN 978-0-8061-9458-5 (paper)
Subjects: LCSH: Indians of Mexico—Missions—Mexico—Sierra Gorda—History. | Guarani Indians—Missions—Bolivia—Chiquitos (Province)—History. | Franciscans—Missions—Mexico—Sierra Gorda—History. | Jesuits—Missions—Bolivia—Chiquitos (Province)—History. | Evangelistic work—Mexico—Sierra Gorda—History. | Evangelistic work—Bolivia—Chiquitos (Province)—History. | Indians of Mexico—Colonization—Mexico—Sierra Gorda—History. | Guarani Indians—Colonization—Bolivia—Chiquitos (Province)—History. | Sierra Gorda (Mexico)—Ethnic relations—History. | Chiquitos (Bolivia : Province)—Ethnic relations—History.
Classification: LCC F1219.3.M59 J323 2017 | DDC 266/.27245—dc23
LC record available at https://lccn.loc.gov/2016056645

The paper in this book meets the guidelines for permanence and durability of the Committee on Production Guidelines for Book Longevity of the Council on Library Resources, Inc. ∞

The manufacturer's authorized representative in the EU for product safety is Mare Nostrum Group B.V., Mauritskade 21D, 1091 GC Amsterdam, The Netherlands, email: gpsr@mare-nostrum.co.uk

Copyright © 2017 by the University of Oklahoma Press, Norman, Publishing Division of the University. Paperback published 2025. Manufactured in the U.S.A.

All rights reserved. No part of this publication may be reproduced, stored in a retrieval system, or transmitted, in any form or by any means, electronic, mechanical, photocopying, recording, or otherwise—except as permitted under Section 107 or 108 of the United States Copyright Act—without the prior written permission of the University of Oklahoma Press. To request permission to reproduce selections from this book, write to Permissions, University of Oklahoma Press, 2800 Venture Drive, Norman, OK 73069, or email rights.oupress@ou.edu.

Contents

List of Illustrations	vii
Acknowledgments: The End of a Journey	ix
Introduction	3
1. The Geography of Colonization and Evangelization	15
2. Creating Utopia	59
3. Birth, Family Formation, and Death: Indigenous Demographic Patterns	97
Conclusion	134
Appendix A. Demographic Indicators of the Jesuit Missions of Lowland South America	145
Appendix B. Demographic Indicators of the Sierra Gorda Missions	157
Notes	163
Selected Bibliography	185
Index	195

Illustrations

Figures

1. The Augustinian doctrina San Pedro y San Pablo Yuririapúndaro	23
2. Chichimeca archer on façade of a church at Yuririapúndaro	24
3. The Augustinian doctrina Los Reyes Metztitlán	27
4. The Augustinian doctrina at Xilitlán	28
5. The Dominican mission Santo Domingo de Guzmán Soriano	33
6. The Franciscan doctrina San Pedro Tolimán	37
7. The Franciscan doctrina San Pedro y San Pablo de Cadereyta	39
8. The Franciscan church at Pachuca	41
9. San Fernando church in Mexico City	43
10. The Jesuit church at San Luis de la Paz	45
11. Santiago Xalpa	62
12. San Miguel de Fuenclara	62
13. Agua de Landa	63
14. Tancoyol	64
15. N.S.P. San Francisco del Valle de Tilaco	64
16. A mural in the Metztitlán tecpan depicting an eagle grasping a scorpion	72
17. Detail of the upper façade of the tecpan in Tlayacapan	72
18. Tezcatlipoca depicted as a Tepeyollotl, or jaguar	73
19. Mural detail of an eagle and two Tepeyollotl in church San Miguel Ixmiquilpan	74

20. Mural detail of a jaguar in the Franciscan doctrina
    San Gabriel Cholula ... 74
21. Mural detail of an eagle and jaguar in the Franciscan
    doctrina San Juan Bautista Cuauhtinchán ... 75
22. Detail of the atrial cross at San José Taximaroa ... 77
23. Mural detail of the Augustinian doctrina Divino Salvador Malinalco ... 78
24. Capillas posa at Tilaco mission ... 89

Tables

1.1. The Chiquitos missions, 1691–1760 ... 55
2.1. Communions recorded on the Chiquitos missions ... 79
2.2. The population of the Chiquitos missions, 1713 ... 83
2.3. Income and expenses of the Chiquitos missions ... 92
2.4. Livestock reported on the Chiquitos missions ... 93
3.1. Fugitive tributaries recorded in the 1735 tribute censuses ... 103

Graphs

3.1. The population of San Francisco Xavier mission, 1710–1833 ... 120
3.2. Baptisms and burials registered at San Francisco Xavier mission,
    1712–1768 ... 121

Maps

1. The Sierra Gorda missions ... 26
2. The Chiquitos and Moxos missions ... 53

Acknowledgments

The End of a Journey

I consider this inquiry to have begun nearly forty years ago when I was first encouraged to conduct primary research on missions in northern colonial Mexico, but the first sparks of interest in frontier missions date back to my days in the fourth grade in public schools in Alameda, California. Between atomic bomb drills and playing in a bomb shelter built in the yard of a friend's home, we dutifully studied California history and the story of Junípero Serra, O.F.M., and the twenty-one missions the Franciscans administered. I was not satisfied with the answers to many questions I asked about the missions, and it was at this point that my parents drove me up and down California to visit the mission sites. Although I did not realize it at the time, this taught me a sense of the importance of place in the writing of history.

In more than thirty years of scholarly inquiry, my interests have shifted. But one common theme appears in my research, namely, a focus on indigenous experiences in missions and in particular on how these experiences are reflected in historical demography. I first researched missions on the northwestern frontier of Mexico (northern Sonora, Baja California, and California). Over the years I have also written about missions in Coahuila-Texas, the Chiquitos region of eastern Bolivia, the Rio de la Plata region, and finally central Mexico and the sixteenth-century Chichimeca frontier. It has been a stimulating and rewarding intellectual odyssey.

With this volume I bring closure to my research on the subject of colonial frontier missions and evangelization. I have been fortunate in being able to publish books and articles over the years and to have expressed my views and presented my interpretations. I will now leave it to other scholars who may be interested to present new and engaging interpretations regarding frontier missions, and perhaps to prove me wrong. This is not to say that I will completely abandon intellectual inquiry, but in the future I may explore different subjects.

I would like to express two personal debts of gratitude at this point. Over the last nine years I have dedicated considerable time to visiting small towns across Mexico. My companion on many of these trips has been my wife and life companion Laura Diez de Sollano Montes de Oca. She has tolerated both my propensity to wander and my many hours spent writing at the computer. The second debt I owe to my friend César Cortés Cortés, who has joined me on weekend trips to *pueblear* to visit small towns outside of Mexico City. He shares a love of photography and has a keen interest in colonial architecture, in particular the Sierra Gorda and Querétaro. We have explored the Sierra Gorda and other scenic corners of Mexico, and we will probably continue to do so. These two individuals have made this intellectual journey interesting and meaningful.

Frontiers of Evangelization

Introduction

The Spanish Crown sponsored a program of evangelization of the native populations of its American territories, which included sedentary peoples that lived in stratified societies and hierarchical state systems, agriculturalists that lived in tribal or clan-based societies, and nonsedentary peoples that lived in small bands and collected wild plant foods and hunted game in well-defined territories. The challenge for the Crown was to create policies and institutions that would integrate the indigenous populations living at different levels of social, economic, and political organization, and to impose a new set of religious beliefs. To accomplish this last goal the Crown supported the establishment of missions by different Catholic orders that included the Franciscans, Dominicans, Augustinians, and Jesuits. The challenge for the missionaries was to develop methods of evangelization and organizational structures that would attempt the religious conversion of sedentary and nonsedentary peoples on different mission frontiers.

In this study, I compare the historical experiences of nonsedentary and sedentary native peoples brought to live in missions on two frontiers in distinct parts of Spanish America. They are the nonsedentary Pames and Jonaces that inhabited the Sierra Gorda region of Mexico, which was a part of the sixteenth-century Chichimeca frontier, and the sedentary clan-based natives brought to live on the Chiquitos missions of what today is eastern Bolivia. I build the conceptual organization of this study on the different levels of social, economic, and political organization between sedentary and nonsedentary indigenous populations. In an effort to understand the historical experiences of sedentary and nonsedentary populations brought to live on missions, I ask several basic questions throughout this work. I focus in particular on the outcomes of the evangelization campaigns and social engineering that sought to create stable communities and to integrate the natives into the new Spanish colonial order as laborers and tribute payers.

One question I address is whether or not the organizational strategies and evangelization methods were a key factor in the different outcomes in the Sierra Gorda and Chiquitos missions. Missionaries from four religious orders attempted to evangelize the nonsedentary Pames and Jonaces over a period of nearly two-hundred years with limited success. In an effort to finally integrate the band members into colonial society, royal officials brought in Franciscans from the apostolic college of San Fernando (Mexico City) to resettle the natives in stable communities, a job the other missionaries had failed to accomplish. Was the mission organization and the methods of evangelization employed by the Franciscans similar or different from those of the Jesuits that staffed the Chiquitos missions? The Jesuits brought sedentary agriculturalists that lived in clan groups to the Chiquitos missions, and like the Franciscans in the Sierra Gorda, they created new communities from whole cloth. Did the methods employed for sedentary populations have the same appeal to nonsedentary peoples? The hypothesis is that there were differences that determined the outcome of the mission programs in the two regions.

Alternatively, did other factors contribute to different outcomes in the creation of stable communities in the Sierra Gorda and Chiquitos mission frontier? In this study, I analyze demographic patterns as a key factor in the formation of stable communities, and in particular I analyze the differences in demographic patterns between sedentary and nonsedentary populations settled on missions. What differences were there between sedentary and nonsedentary populations, and did these differences contribute to the outcome of the mission programs? The hypothesis is that there were differences in demographic patterns, and that nonsedentary populations proved to be demographically fragile. Furthermore, this difference proved to be an important factor that contributed to the failure of mission programs. I attempt in this study to understand the development of missions by focusing on the similarities and differences between sedentary and nonsedentary populations and by exploring the questions posed above. My approach in the study has a foundation in the literature on frontier missions but also suggests different comparative approaches that may prove useful in future studies.

Historical studies of Spanish colonial missions have documented the experiences of the native peoples in the context of Spanish colonialism using different conceptual frameworks, methodological approaches, and paradigms. Twenty years ago, I published a collection of essays with Erick Langer titled *The New Latin American Mission History*.[1] The essays in the volume were case studies of missions on different frontiers of Spanish America, and the volume explored paradigms for understanding mission history and in particular the experiences of the indigenous peoples missionaries attempted to evangelize. The volume also suggested ways to conceptualize the history of the missions and of native responses to directed social, cultural, and religious change. One of the topics considered was the demographics of indigenous populations brought to live on the missions.

Over the past several decades, the study of missions on the fringes of Spanish America has evolved beyond the institutional focus and self-study by members of the same religious orders that administered the missions. There are studies of discrete mission groups that place them into their larger historical context and consider a range of issues, including economics, ethnohistory, cultural and religious change and persistence, indigenous accommodation and resistance, and demographics. Most studies concentrate on the colonial period, but there are also monographs that document missions following independence.[2] There are also comparative studies that document differences and similarities between missions on different frontiers.[3]

One example of the latter is the 2005 monograph written by Cynthia Radding. Radding brought a comparative approach to the study of mission communities in Sonora in northern Mexico and the Chiquitos mission frontier, one of the regions examined in this study. Radding brought to her comparative study a social-history focus as well as her previous study of the native peoples of Sonora.[4] This present study differs from Radding's approach. For one, it relies on a broader range of sources, including documents that Radding did not consult such as the *cartas anuas* and individual mission reports. Moreover, this present study analyzes the effort by the missionaries to evangelize the native peoples and the difficult question of changes in religious beliefs. In additional, this study more fully examines the organization of mission communities within the broader context of evangelization in Spanish America beginning with one of the first missionary frontiers in central Mexico. Finally, Radding compared native societies that were similar, namely, the peoples of the Chiquitos mission frontier, who practiced swidden agriculture supplemented by hunting and gathering, and the native peoples of Sonora, who practiced agriculture in river flood plains and hunted and collected wild plant foods. The distinction Radding made was between two different ecological zones. This study focuses on two different comparisons—between sedentary and nonsedentary peoples, on the one hand, and between peoples who lived in dry regions and peoples who lived in tropical rain forests, on the other.

My own research over the past three decades has examined different frontiers, time periods, and topics, but in general I have focused on the experiences of indigenous peoples. This present study builds on my previous research. My initial interest was the northern frontier of colonial Mexico, and my publications explored demographics and the social-economic and cultural context of the missions in northern Sonora, Baja California, California, and Texas.[5] In recent years I have studied sixteenth-century missions in central Mexico and Jesuit missions in lowland South America.[6] These lines of research analyzed demographics and the social-cultural context of demographic change, as well as analyzing what I have characterized as the cultural war in sixteenth-century Mexico that was evidence of the persistence of traditional religious beliefs in the face of evangelization and repression. I have also discussed the first frontier in colonial Mexico, the porous cultural border between sedentary and nonsedentary indigenous populations known as the Chichimeca frontier.

In this current study I build on and refine a point of analysis I have previously examined, namely, the importance of the factors discussed above that can be employed to conceptualize outcomes in mission programs. The discussion of evangelization on the missions in this study considers three separate points: mission organization and tools of evangelization; how the missionaries presented doctrine and if it was adjusted to take into consideration native cultural norms; and how native peoples chose to interpret and incorporate the content of Catholic doctrine into their world view and to what extent. It tests the hypothesis that there were few substantial differences in the organization or methods of the missionary orders active in Spanish America.

A closely related issue is the interaction between missionaries and civil officials, and how the missionaries modified their programs of directed social-cultural change and evangelization in response to shifts in government policy over time, such as the implementation in the later eighteenth century of the so-called Bourbon Reforms during the administration of Charles III (1759–1788). Reform-minded royal officials questioned the traditional role of the Catholic Church in Spanish dominions and of the continuing reliance on missions as a frontier colonial institution. However, the Crown decided to continue to rely on missions, but with an eye to promoting policy objectives such as those aiming to more fully integrate natives into colonial society. This played out in a number of ways on different frontiers, such as in the decision to remove the Augustinians from the Sierra Gorda and replace them with Franciscans, who were given a mandate to congregate and evangelize the Pames, or in the decision to expel the Jesuits in 1767. The mild anticlericalism of late eighteenth-century royal reformers later gave way to the more radical liberal ideas of the nineteenth century that seriously challenged the role of the Catholic Church in society.[7]

The second issue pertains to the differences in the demographic profiles of sedentary and nonsedentary indigenous populations brought to live on the missions. I have previously suggested that when brought to live on missions, nonsedentary indigenous populations experienced demographic collapse.[8] Moreover, there are examples of resistance to the transition to a sedentary lifestyle. Examples included the equestrian Abipones in the Chaco region of South America and the groups collectively known as the Karankawas that lived on the Texas Gulf Coast.[9] The missionaries failed to convince or force the Abipones and Karankawas to adopt a sedentary way of life and the shifts in gender labor roles and the social changes it implied. The hypothesis tested here is that the differences in the demographic profiles of nonsedentary and sedentary indigenous peoples made a difference to their outcomes on missions.

Demographic differences between sedentary and nonsedentary populations first developed in the wake of the so-called "Neolithic Revolution," which was the emergence of agriculture in the Middle East some 10,000 years ago and the resulting shift to a sedentary life style.[10] The cost of raising children dropped with a sedentary way of life. The families of sedentary populations tend to be larger for practical reasons. When children reached a certain age, they could be put to work in agriculture, whereas young children having to be carried from place to place could be a burden for highly mobile populations. Studies also suggest higher survival rates among children of sedentary populations owing, in part, to a more reliable supply of food.[11] The families of nonsedentary populations could be expected to be smaller. On the other hand, sedentary populations became exposed to more infections, and in particular to pathogens that evolved from domesticated animals. Measles is closely related to canine distemper and rinderpest that infects livestock, and smallpox most likely evolved from cowpox among livestock, perhaps in India.[12] Is there evidence of differences in family formation and family sizes between sedentary and nonsedentary populations brought together on the missions?

I offer in this study detailed case studies of missions on the frontiers of colonial Spanish America established among sedentary and nonsedentary indigenous populations. My goal is to evaluate the importance of these two factors in explaining the trajectory of the development of mission communities. The first case study is of the missions established by Franciscans from the apostolic college of San Fernando (Mexico City) in the Sierra Gorda region (Querétaro). The Sierra Gorda was a part of the Chichimeca frontier and one of the points of conflict in the frontier war that began around 1550 as bands of nomadic hunters and gatherers resisted Spanish intrusion into their territory, and in particular the intrusion of cattle and sheep that competed for and destroyed plant foods that the natives collected.

Missionaries from four orders (Franciscan, Dominican, Augustinian, and Jesuit) established missions and attempted to evangelize the band members from the mid-sixteenth century to the early nineteenth century. Their efforts led to mixed results, with the missionaries experiencing considerable frustration and the native groups, such as the Pames and Jonaces, resisting to the pressures to change their way of life. Assigning missionaries from the apostolic colleges of San Fernando and Pachuca to the region, royal officials in the 1740s attempted to accelerate the integration of the Pames and Jonaces into colonial society. This study examines the methods used in the new missions and the demographic consequences of congregation.

The second case study is of the Chiquitos missions located in the lowlands of eastern Bolivia. Jesuits established the first Chiquitos mission in 1691 among sedentary populations that lived in clans and practiced shifting swidden agriculture. The Jesuits employed different methods in the creation and administration of mission communities, and I compare their approach to that of the Franciscans in the Sierra Gorda. I suggest that the two groups of missions displayed distinct demographic patterns, and my analysis shows not only the trajectory of change but also the profile of the mission population. Moreover, information on the demographic patterns of the Jesuit-administered Paraguay missions are included and evaluated to provide additional context and comparison. Epidemics of highly contagious crowd disease such as smallpox and measles shaped the demographic evolution of the mission communities studied here, and the inclusion of data on the Paraguay missions allows for a discussion of the propagation of epidemics on a different frontier. Relatively rapid river transportation and integration into a larger regional economy facilitated the spread of epidemics within the larger Rio de la Plata region, whereas geographic isolation buffered the Chiquitos mission populations from the effects of catastrophic epidemic mortality.

The context is critical for understanding the development of mission communities and demographic patterns. The first chapter of this study sets the stage for the analysis of the Sierra Gorda and Chiquitos missions. It discusses the first missions in sixteenth-century central Mexico in terms of their organization and urban plan. The missionaries who first evangelized along and beyond the Chichimeca frontier introduced methods and modes of organization based on their experiences in the missions among the sedentary populations. In order to understand the first missions beyond the Chichimeca frontier, it is necessary to describe the first Mexican missions. This is followed by a summary of the efforts to evangelize beyond the Chichimeca frontier. These efforts began in the sixteenth century and extended to the arrival in the Sierra Gorda of the Franciscans from the apostolic college of San Fernando. The chapter highlights the difficulties inherent in the attempts to change the way of life of the Jonaces, Pames, and other Chichimeca groups. The last part of the chapter briefly describes the different missions the Jesuits established in the larger jurisdiction known as the Paraguay Province, as well as the Moxos missions established by Jesuits from the Peru Province and located in the lowlands of eastern Bolivia north of the Chiquitos missions. The Moxos missions were similar to the Chiquitos establishments and provide an additional point of comparison.

Chapters 2 and 3 constitute the core of this study, and the analysis of the Sierra Gorda and Chiquitos missions. In chapter 2, I discuss three elements of the mission programs. The first element addresses mission construction and urban planning. This is important for understanding demographic patterns and the mobilization of native labor. The missionaries created compact nucleated communities, but bringing the native populations to live cheek by jowl on the missions also facilitated the spread of contagion. The second element involves the methods of evangelization and the native responses to the efforts to impose a new religion. The third element concerns mission economics and the missionaries' attempts to organize and administer the missions while controlling the native populations brought to live there.

In chapter 3, I analyze the missions' demographic patterns, and I include data from the Paraguay missions. I first discuss epidemics, followed by case studies of the demographic patterns of Paraguay, Chiquitos, and the Sierra Gorda missions. With the goal of evaluating the profile of sedentary and nonsedentary populations through the analysis of detailed censuses recording the sizes of individual families, I document overall trends as well as differences in family formation and family structure. I show that there were measurable differences in the families of the sedentary natives brought to live on the Chiquitos missions, and the nonsedentary Pames. Concluding this study, I summarize my findings before offering final statements about my research into this subject.

Sources and their Limitations

The sources used in this study were written by the missionaries and contain obvious biases. These biases, which we perceive only fleetingly, limit the native voice in the discussion of the history of the missions. The historian's task is to decipher the rhetoric and Eurocentric bias of the missionaries and colonial officials and thereby to arrive at an approximation of the realities of native life on the missions.

Historical demography generally relies on different sources that include censuses drafted with varying degrees of detail and registers or records of baptisms (births), marriages, and burials. Censuses prepared for different purposes provide a snapshot at one point in time of the structure of a population, but they also suffer from deficiencies depending on the purpose of the population count and the method or methods used in the collection of data. Many early modern censuses were prepared for tax purposes or to identify males for military service. People avoided being counted, and even today modern national censuses miss people. This study analyzes detailed censuses of mission populations. When the Franciscans from the apostolic college of San Fernando arrived in the Sierra Gorda in the spring of 1744, royal officials brought Pames to settle on the missions and enumerated the populations in detailed counts broken down into family groups. In enumerating native populations, however, the census takers demonstrated their own cultural bias by conceptualizing the family using European norms. Later Franciscan reports on the Sierra Gorda missions provided minimal demographic information. They reported only total population, the number of families, and the totals of baptisms, marriages, and burials over a number of years.

The Jesuits stationed on the missions in lowland South America similarly enumerated the mission populations in several formats. Their annually prepared censuses summarized the total population, which was broken down into broad age categories, and also reported total numbers of baptisms, marriages, and burials. In the absence of complete runs of sacramental registers, these censuses are used to reconstruct vital rates. The Jesuits also prepared more detailed tribute censuses that enumerated the population by family group. The natives congregated on the Jesuit missions had to pay tribute to the Crown. However, the Jesuits generally used communal resources to pay the tribute. Unlike in the Andean region, where many natives left their communities to avoid tribute and in particular labor obligations, the Jesuit system on the missions limited flight to avoid tribute and labor services. This is not to say that there were no instances of flight from the Jesuit missions. In the 1730s, for example, natives fled the Paraguay missions in the face of subsistence crisis, recurring epidemics, and mobilization for military service. Fugitives from the Paraguay missions established a community on the edge of mission territory. They organized their new community along the same lines as the missions they were fleeing.[13] Following the Jesuit expulsion from Spanish dominions (1767), a large-scale diaspora from the Paraguay missions occurred.[14]

Registers of baptisms, marriages, and burials provide detailed information that can be used to calculate vital rates and trends over time. Baptisms of newborn children are used as a source for calculating birth rates. Family reconstitution is one method used to reconstruct demographic patterns.[15] It entails reconstructing the life history of families over time from the point of family formation, procreation, and death. However, complete sets of sacramental registers have not survived for the Sierra Gorda, Paraguay, and Chiquitos missions. Baptismal registers exist for two of the Sierra Gorda missions. Fragments of baptisms and burials survive for several of the Paraguay missions. A baptismal register also exists for one of the Chiquitos missions. In the absence of the companion registers, the record is incomplete, but the existing registers do provide important clues to demographic patterns on the missions. The majority of baptisms recorded at the Sierra Gorda missions of Tilaco and Tancoyol were of recently born children, although the Franciscans did baptize small numbers of adults. The missionaries continued to relocate Pames to the missions.[16] The Jesuits stationed on the Chiquitos mission San Francisco Xavier baptized both adults and children. The Chiquitos missions had open populations, meaning that the Jesuits relocated and settled non-Christians on the missions.[17] Finally, baptisms for the Santa Rosa mission in Paraguay showed the opposite. The Jesuits baptized only children born on the mission.[18]

The Jesuits periodically baptized small numbers of non-Christians, but the Paraguay missions were closed populations. Demographers who have analyzed sacramental registers to reconstruct European demographic patterns have shown that some people did not get married in the church because of the fees the priests recorded, did not have their children baptized, or did not have a church burial. This was not a factor on the missions, since the missionaries did not charge fees for administering the sacraments.

What information do the baptismal registers contain? The amount of information varies from site to site and depending on what each missionary chose to record. A baptismal entry from 1763 from the Sierra Gorda mission Tancoyol was typical. The translation of the entry reads as follows:

> On the eighth day of the month of February of One Thousand, Six Hundred and Sixty-Three in the Church of the Holiest Virgin of the Light of Tancoyol I solemnly baptized a *Párvulo* [young or newborn child] who was born at about twelve at night, legitimate son of Diego Lucas Ojeda and of Maria Ana Ojeda his legitimate wife, Pame Indians of this Mission of the barrio of Soyapilca. The said *Párvulo* was named Juan Tomas Ojeda; his Godparents were Martin Pirineo and his Wife Maria Agustina, both Pame Indians of this Mission of the New barrio here, who I admonished of the Spiritual Relationship and Obligation they had contracted, and to attest I signed it in this [Mission] of Tancoyol on the referenced day, month, and year.
> Fr. Antonio Paterna[19]

The baptismal entry identified the parents of the newborn child, their residence in one of the barrios or neighborhoods of the mission community, the approximate time of birth, and the names of the godparents that can be used to reconstruct social relationships in the missions. A perusal of the sacramental registers can also be used to establish the tenure of the missionaries, since they signed each entry. The Tancoyol baptismal register also records the transition in 1770 from the Franciscan missionaries to the administration of secular parish priests.

Documenting religious conversion is a much more difficult proposition because of the nature of the sources and the near impossible task of deciphering the unknowable, namely, the real religious beliefs of natives who had been "converted" to the new faith. The written sources reflect the perceptions of the missionaries and contain inherent biases since the missionaries wrote most reports on the missions for their superiors and colonial officials to describe conditions in the missions. A decided tone of Christian triumphalism pervades the reports. A handful of reports surviving from the Sierra Gorda missions described the material status of the mission communities and provide some observations on what the Franciscans believed to be indications of the religious conversion of the Pames. The Jesuits wrote periodic narrative reports on individual missions that similarly noted what they considered to be the spiritual progress of the natives. The Black Robes also wrote longer narrative documents, known as *cartas anuas*, that provided a broader overview of conditions on the missions.

The missionaries played a numbers game that employed the number of sacraments administered as a surrogate marker for religious conversion. In other words, these numbers indicated to them the acceptance of Catholicism by the natives living on the missions. The Franciscans in the Sierra Gorda and the Jesuits stationed on the missions in lowland South America reported, for example, total numbers of communions, a sacrament administered when a neophyte confessed. In the annual summary censuses of both the Paraguay and Chiquitos missions, the Jesuits recorded the total number of communions.[20] The Franciscans and Jesuits also made general comments in the reports about what they believed to be evidence of the spirituality of the neophytes. This included being able to repeat prayers in Latin (learned through rote memorization) and attendance at mass and catechism, which the missionaries considered to be obligatory. The missionaries punished neophytes who did not attend and, on the Chiquitos and Paraguay missions, appointed native officials to go through the mission villages to round up those natives who missed mass and catechism.

Useful comparisons can be made between the sixteenth-century central Mexican missions and the later frontier missions. The missionaries used similar techniques, and as I discuss below, the first missionary impulse beyond the Chichimeca frontier in Mexico relied on the methods employed among the sedentary populations of central Mexico. The missionaries came to the table with certain assumptions about what religious conversion entailed, but these assumptions frequently proved to be flawed. Moreover, they approached the conversion of native populations with little or no information about pre-Hispanic religious beliefs. Much of what we know about pre-Hispanic religious practices comes from the pen of a handful of missionaries who wrote about these beliefs, but the rank and file missionaries did not have access to this information.

Written documents and iconography show the persistence of pre-Hispanic religious beliefs in central Mexico, and these sources are employed to place the later frontier missions in a broader context. The works of several scholars are important in going beyond the missionary rhetoric and getting closer to the reality of native responses to evangelization. Louise Burkhart analyzed both the doctrinal content of what the missionaries taught natives in central Mexico as well as the resources used, such as visual guides.[21] David Tavárez analyzed records of what the missionaries considered to be idolatry in central Mexican and Oaxaca communities. These records show that what the missionaries and rank-and-file secular parish priests believed to be the reality of native religious beliefs was far from the truth.[22] The natives created an alternative worldview that incorporated Catholic beliefs, but not exclusively as the missionaries believed and hoped. Art historian Eleanor Wake documented the persistence of pre-Hispanic religious beliefs through an analysis of iconography incorporated into sixteenth-century churches and convents, atrial crosses, and murals.[23] My own 2014 study built on the research of these scholars to offer my own views on the persistence of pre-Hispanic religious beliefs.[24] These studies provide a broader context for the limited information the missionaries left regarding the methods of evangelization on the frontier missions.

CHAPTER ONE

THE GEOGRAPHY OF COLONIZATION AND EVANGELIZATION

This chapter outlines the expansion and organization of missions established to attempt to evangelize native populations beyond the Chichimeca frontier in Mexico and in lowland South America, the area of Jesuit activity. It begins with a discussion of central Mexican missions established among sedentary populations, which is crucial for understanding later efforts to establish missions beyond the Chichimeca frontier. The missionary orders adapted the existing social-political structure in central Mexico as the basis for their own organizational structure. The missionaries who ventured beyond the Chichimeca frontier attempted to use this same structure to organize their missions as well as evangelization methods. What worked for the sedentary populations did not work beyond the frontier.

The chronology and discussion of the organization of missions beyond the Chichimeca frontier is complicated because the missionaries attempted to place the proverbial round peg in a square hole. In other words, the social-political structure employed in central Mexico did not work well with the nonsedentary populations beyond the frontier. Franciscans, Augustinians, Dominicans, and Jesuits attempted to impose the central Mexican model, but with limited success. To understand the context of the missions established in the 1740s by Franciscans from the apostolic college of San Fernando, it is first necessary to discuss the previous evangelization campaigns.

The final section of this chapter outlines the establishment of missions by the Jesuits in the Province of Paraguay, which included the Chiquitos missions. The Jesuits also implemented the same social-political structure among different native groups in lowland South America. The outcome was similar to what happened beyond the Chichimeca frontier, and Spanish-Portuguese colonial rivalry in the larger Rio de la Plata region influenced the outcome. The Guaraní, for example, pressured by slave traders from Sao Paulo, found common cause with the Jesuits and settled on the missions by the thousands. Natives on other frontiers, such as the Guaraní-speaking Chiriguanos, on the other hand, did not universally opt to settle on the missions the Jesuits established.

Sixteenth-Century Central Mexican Missions

Members of three orders arrived in central Mexico in the first decade following the collapse of the Culhua-Mexica tribute state to initiate the evangelization of the large native populations. In the first decades following the Spanish conquest of central Mexico, relatively small numbers of Spaniards created a system of indirect colonial rule on the existing matrix of indigenous political structures. The new colonial order in central Mexico also had a basis in the construction of two corporate societies, the *República de Españoles* and the *República de Indios*. The Spanish imposed their rule on the existing native political structure of the *altépetl* and granted native rulers autonomy as long as they complied with tribute and labor demands and remained loyal to the new colonial order. The altépetl itself was a jurisdiction that consisted of a main town known to the Spaniards as the *cabecera* and subject towns known as *sujetos*. The political leaders of the altépetl collected tribute and labor services from the subject communities and in turn paid tribute to the dominant polity in the region, be it the Culhua-Mexica or later the Spaniards. The Franciscan, Dominican, and Augustinian missionaries who arrived in central Mexico after 1524 grafted their mission organization onto the existing social-political structure.

The first generation of Spanish adventurers who subjugated central Mexico divided the altépetl into *encomienda* grants of jurisdiction over tributaries that enabled them to accumulate wealth through tribute collection and labor demands. At the same time, the Crown attempted to limit the political and economic power of the encomienda grant holders and, when possible, escheated private encomienda grants to Crown jurisdiction.[1]

The Culhua-Mexica had dominated altépetl in central Mexico, making tribute demands in a loosely knitted political system that also lent itself to fragmentation and resistance, something seen following the arrival of the first

Spaniards in 1519. The Spanish eliminated the Culhua-Mexica and adapted the existing tribute and political system as the basis for their system of indirect rule. For example, the Culhua-Mexica had subjugated the region known today as Oaxaca and established centers from which to control and direct tribute collection. One such site was Inguiteria, located near the modern town of Coixtlahuaca in the Sierra Mixteca.[2] Culhua-Mexica tribute collectors based in Inguiteria collected tribute from eleven head towns in the tribute province.

Tribute reports from the mid-sixteenth century provide the earliest information on communities in central Mexico. The *suma de visitas,* a summary of tribute reports prepared around 1550, provides details regarding the political organization of communities and altépetl, and in particular their tribute obligations. Several communities in the Sierra Mixteca region of Oaxaca where the Dominicans later established missions were typical. The report on Yodzocahi (Yanhuitlan) noted that sixteen other towns were subject to Yodzocahi, and the town with its different barrios had a population of some 12,007 above the age of three. The tribute obligation paid to the *encomendero* Gonzalo de las Cabras consisted of 782 gold pesos in gold dust and planted wheat as a part of their obligation. Moreover, they provided four birds from local species and two from Europe (chickens?) daily, as well as a small jug of honey, wax, corn, cacao, corn tortillas, eggs, salt, chile, tomato, firewood, and *yerba* (herbs?). In additional, ten natives had to provide labor services.[3]

Yucundáa (Teposcolula) had escheated to the Crown. The report of circa 1550 noted that the town had six barrios and a population of 9,387 people above the age of three. As a Crown jurisdiction, the tribute obligation had been set at an annual money payment of 832 pesos.[4] Disinuu (Tlaxiaco) was held in encomienda to Francisco Vázquez. It was an important polity that counted thirty-one subject communities identified by the term estancia as well as other towns with independent ruling lineages: Santa María, which had a church; Choquistepeque; Chilapa; Tepusutepeque; and Comaltepeque. The population of Disinuu and its estancias was reported to be 1,851 men, 1,356 women, 433 boys between the age of 12 and 17, and 379 girls of the same age. The tribute payment totaled 45 gold pesos in gold dust, corn supplied every forty days, and other items. The ruling lineage at Santa María had nine subject estancias and counted 380 tributaries, 507 boys between the age of 12 and 17, and 102 girls. The tributaries of Santa María paid 13 gold pesos in gold dust every sixty days. Choquistepeque had six subject estancias and a population of 455 male tributaries, 280 women, and 233 boys above the age of seven. Its tribute was 11 gold pesos in gold dust paid every sixty days. Chilapa had five subject estancias and a population of 340 married men and 247 boys. The tribute obligation was 10 gold pesos in gold dust paid every sixty days. Tepusutepeque had twenty-two subject estancias, and a population of 1,322 married men and 507 boys. The tribute was 33 gold pesos in gold dust paid every sixty days. Finally, Comaltepeque had six subject estancias and a population of 540 men, 280 women, 140 boys, and 130 girls. The tribute obligation was 20 gold pesos paid in gold dust every sixty days.[5] The importance of these jurisdictions explains why the Dominicans selected them as sites for missions.

The Dominicans established permanently staffed *doctrinas* in the three head towns of Yodzocahi, Yucundáa, and Disinuu, and they designated the subject communities of the three altépetl as visitas that did not have resident missionaries and that the missionaries visited only periodically. The tributary province of Huaxtepec (Oaxtepec) in the northern part of the modern state of Morelos provides a second example of the social-political organization of missions.

The tributary province consisted of seven cabeceras. They were Huaxtepec, Yacapichtlan (Yecapixtla), Totolapan, Tepoztlán, Yautepec, Atlatlauhca, and Tlayacapa. Each of the seven head towns in turn had sujetos. Moreover, there was a hierarchy of political authority within the region that defined the relationship between the head towns. For example, the ruling lineages of Atlatlauhca and Tlayacapa were subject to that of Totolapan, which was one of the dominant polities within the region.[6] Dominicans and Augustinians shared responsibility for the evangelization of the native populations of the tributary province of Huaxtepec and established doctrinas in each of the seven head towns.

The Franciscan mission province of Tepeaca (Puebla) provides another example. Tepeaca was an important and populous jurisdiction, and the Franciscans established five doctrinas in the province: San Francisco Tepeaca (1530); Asunción de Nuestra Señora Tecamachalco (1541); Santa María Magdalena Cachulac (modern Quecholac) (ca. 1550); Señor Apóstol Tecali (1554); and San Juan Evangelista Acacingo (modern Acatzingo) (1558).[7] The suma de visita report for Tepeaca reported a population of 9,878 in the cabecera and sujetos, which included Acacingo. This suggests a population of about 49,000. This figure did not include the populations of Cachulac, Tecali, and Tecamachalco.[8] The 1580 *relación geográfica* report on Tepeaca reported a population of 8,000 native heads of household including Acacingo, or some 45,000 people. There were 7,000 heads of household in Tecamachalco and its sujetos, or some 35,000 people. Tecali counted 5,000 heads of household, or some 25,000 people.[9]

The Franciscans grafted the structure of their missions on the existing political-administrative structure. Several of the main towns in Tepeaca province were still held in encomienda in the early 1580s. Tepeaca itself had escheated to the Crown, but Tecamachalco was jointly held in encomienda by Rodrigo de Bierro and Melchora de Aberucha. Tecali was held in encomienda by Jusepe de Ovduña. Cachulac was held in encomienda by Gonzalo Coronado and Nicolása de Villanueva. Spaniards had also begun to settle in several of the head towns. Sixty Spaniards reportedly lived in Tepeaca and were involved in raising livestock in the region, and another one hundred Spaniards reportedly lived in Tecamachalco. As noted above, the Franciscans established their doctrinas in the head towns and designated subject towns as visitas. In the 1580s, Tepeaca counted seventy-three sujetos, which included Acacingo. Tecamachalco had twenty-nine subject communities, Cachulac had thirty-four, and Tecali had nineteen.[10]

The Franciscans also introduced a new urban plan to the native communities in Tepeaca province, and they relocated communities to new sites. For example, the Franciscans relocated Tepeaca to a new site in 1543. Similarly, they relocated Tecamachalco to a new location at about the same time, in 1541.[11] The Franciscans directed the construction of the new sacred complex: the church and convent, located at the center of Acacingo. Kubler reported that the construction of the church and convent San Juan Evangelista began around 1558.[12] Antonio de Ciudad Real, O.F.M., reported that construction of the church and cloister had been concluded prior to his visit in the mid-1580s.[13] The Franciscan noted, "The convent is completed, with its church, cloisters, dormitories and orchard. Two friars reside there."[14] The Franciscan reported that the construction of the new sacred complexes at the other missions in Tepeaca province had also been completed by the same period.

The arrival of the Spaniards led to processes of demographic change that included shifts in settlement patterns as well as population decline. The introduction of diseases such as smallpox and measles was an important cause of demographic decline, and the late sixteenth-century relaciones geográficas reports referenced the lethal consequences of epidemic.[15] The report for Tepeaca (Puebla) noted that "today, of the people that were [here] when the

Spanish entered [the country], out of ten nine [are missing]."[16] The report on Teitipac (Oaxaca) also estimated the degree of population decline: "This town of Teticpaque used to be a town with many natives [*naturales*], and there was something like two thousand Indians [*yndios*], and now a thousand; the cause for there being fewer now are the diseases and pestilences they have had."[17]

Periodic epidemics killed thousands of natives. The report for Coatzacualco, also located in Oaxaca, provides additional details on the chronology and effects of contagions: "What they have reports on about the reduction [in number] of these people was smallpox that broke out in the year one thousand five hundred and thirty-four, and measles that broke out in the year one thousand five hundred and forty-five. And it is clearly seen that they are becoming fewer [in number] every day."[18]

Civil and religious officials instituted a policy known as *congregación* to shift and resettle population because of population decline. Some communities disappeared as a result of depopulation or population shifts to new settlements. Population decline, however, was not the only motive for congregación. In some instances, civil officials or the missionaries relocated existing towns from hilltops to valley locations, where they were easier to manage when trying to organize labor drafts, collect tribute, or enforce attendance at catechism or mass. An example was Yucundáa (Teposcolula), located in the Sierra Mixteca of Oaxaca and the site of an early Dominican mission established around 1529 or 1530.[19] The Dominicans directed the construction of a primitive church and convent at the hilltop site of Yucundáa. Archaeological excavations at the site uncovered the remains of the primitive church and convent, as well as burials associated with epidemics in the first half of the sixteenth century. The primitive church, built of stone taken from pre-Hispanic buildings, measured thirty-three by twelve meters, and the convent measured fifty-seven by eighteen meters.[20]

The Dominicans later had the population of Yucundáa relocated to the valley and established the new mission San Pedro y San Pablo Teposcolula at a new site around 1552.[21] The Dominicans directed the construction of a new complex that included an open chapel, church, and cloister, as well as a hospital for the native population. The ruling lineage had a complex known today as the *Casa de la Cacica*, built a short distance from the new religious complex. It was an *aniñe* or residence of a Ñudzahui ruling couple. The complex was the residence of doña Catalina de Peralta, who took up residence there in the mid-1560s with her husband don Diego de Mendoza.[22]

THE CENTRAL MEXICAN MISSION SETTLEMENT PLAN AND URBAN DEVELOPMENT

The 1579 relación geográfica for the jurisdiction of Nexapa in what today is Oaxaca included details regarding the urban development of a community where Dominicans had established a mission. Nexapa was a jurisdiction with a population of Be'ena'a, Mixes, and Chontales located in the Isthmus of Tehuantepec.[23] The Dominicans established a doctrina there in 1556. The report noted that "there is nothing more than a monastery, and there is no other town in the province that can suffer more, because they are poor, there is no hospital in the entire district if not one in this Villa [Nexapa] that his Excellent Lord don Martín Enriquez, viceroy and Captain General of this kingdom, ordered built."[24] The fact that Nexapa did not have a hospital was important enough to note in the 1579 report and points to the practice of including hospitals in the urban plan of mission communities.

The new or existing communities modified under the Spanish-missionary urban plan incorporated different types of buildings. At the center of the community was the new sacred complex built under the direction of the missionaries and in different stages. In many cases the first structures built were primitive convents with residences for the missionaries and an open chapel that functioned as the church until the completion of a permanent church. Open chapels exist at several Dominican missions in Oaxaca, including Yucundáa (Teposcolula) and Yodzocoo (Coixtlahuaca). At other sites, such as Yodzocahi (Yanhuitlan), the Dominicans directed the construction of the new sacred complex on a temple platform and had the pre-Hispanic temple demolished. This was the temple that figured in the Yodzocahi inquisition case in the 1540s.

The Dominicans directed the construction of other elements in the new sacred complexes. They included the cloister, which served not only as the headquarters of the missionaries but also as their habitations, communal dining hall, and store rooms; and the permanent church generally built on a monumental scale. A large open space enclosed by walls known as the atrium fronted the sacred complex, and within the atrium there generally were small chapels known as *capillas posa* located at the four corners or four cardinal points. The missionaries used the capillas as stopping points to explain points of Catholic doctrine during the processions that were an important element in ritual life, in particular during Easter week.[25] The urban plan also contained structures for the native populations. Examples of these non-religious structures still exist at the site of Yucundáa (Teposcolula). One is the so-called *casa de la cacica,* mentioned above. The second was the hospital built to isolate sick natives. The practice in the sixteenth century was to quarantine or isolate those infected with contagious diseases, as well as those who had been exposed to the infected. The treatment of those infected was rudimentary, and death rates in the hospitals were high.

Missions beyond the Chichimeca Frontier

With the onset of the conflict known as the Chichimeca War (1550–1600), missionaries expanded their evangelization campaign beyond the porous frontier between sedentary and nonsedentary peoples in an effort to convert and control the Chichimecas. They used the central Mexican social-political model for their missions beyond the frontier, which proved to be an approach that did not work well among nonsedentary peoples. The native groups collectively known as the Chichimecas may have adopted a nomadic life style in response to climate change at the point of transition from the classic to the post-classic around 1000 a.d. The climate in northern Mexico became drier and hotter, forcing a contraction of the Mesoamerican frontier. Native groups that previously practiced agriculture were forced into hunting and gathering. One hypothesis based on the analysis of linguistic evidence suggests that the Pames and Jonaces practiced agriculture before the climate change. The languages of both groups, which are related, contain words that refer to agriculture and domesticated plants such as corn.[26]

Missionaries from four orders—the Augustinians, Franciscans, Dominicans, and Jesuits—established missions beyond the Chichimeca frontier from the sixteenth to the early nineteenth centuries. This section briefly outlines the trajectory of the efforts at evangelization beyond the Chichimeca frontier from around 1550 to when the Franciscans from the apostolic college of San Fernando arrived in the Sierra Gorda in 1740. It first discusses the Augustinian missions.

Augustinian Missions on and beyond the Chichimeca Frontier

In the 1550s, the Augustinians established a chain of missions along the frontier. One of the first was San Pedro y San Pablo Yuriripúndaro, which was

Fig. 1. The Augustinian doctrina San Pedro y San Pablo Yuririapúndaro, located beyond the Chichimeca frontier in what today is southern Guanajuato.

located beyond the frontier northeast of Laguna Cuitzeo (see figure 1) and administered visitas inhabited by sedentary and also nonsedentary natives. The nature of the frontier and its pattern of economic development can be seen in the circa-1580 map prepared for the relación geográfica report of that year. The map shows the church and convent, which have not physically changed for more than 400 years, and small visita chapels. The landscape, however, is shown as being dominated by cattle and mounted and armed Spaniards, as well as the already-noted environmental changes such as the destruction of food-producing plants that contributed to the outbreak of the Chichimeca conflict. The map illustrates a frontier space very different from the well-ordered urban plan in sedentary central Mexico. The report also noted that the district counted a native population that spoke two languages (P'urépecha and the local Chichimeca language) living in the cabecera and twenty-seven subject communities.[27] The Spanish strategy in dealing with the nonsedentary Chichimecas was to encourage or direct the settlement of sedentary natives beyond the frontier.

Fig. 2. Design element on the façade of the church at Yuriripúndaro depicting a Chichimeca archer.

A design element on the church façade highlighted the status of the community located beyond the volatile and dangerous Chichimeca frontier. It depicts two Chichimeca archers with their bows loaded and ready to fire (see figure 2). The territory surrounding Yuririapúndaro was the scene of active warfare as late as the 1580s, and there is one documented Chichimeca attack on the mission complex. The design element is one of several examples of the incorporation of war-related iconography in Augustinian doctrinas established along the frontier. The enigmatic battle mural program in the church at Ixmiquilpan (Hidalgo) is another example.

In 1550, the Augustinians established two other missions along the frontier in northern Michoacán. They were Santa María Magdalena Cuitzeo, established on the edge of the lake of the same name, and San Nicolás Tolentino Huango, located northwest of Laguna Cuitzeo on a particularly exposed section of the frontier. Augustinian chronicles documented several Chichimeca attacks on Huango, and Guillermo de Santa María, O.S.A., who wrote an important description of the Chichimecas, died in 1585 during one such attack. The Augustinians completed the mission frontier with the establishment of Ucareo, Charo, and Jacona.[28]

The Augustinians organized their missions on the Chichimeca frontier along the same lines as in central Mexico. The missionaries stationed on the doctrinas periodically visited the visitas, although as the conflict escalated this became more dangerous. Initially, the Augustinians directed the construction of small freestanding open chapels. They later replaced these with more substantial structures. The organization of Santa María Magdalena Cuitzeo typified the Augustinian missions along and beyond the Chichimeca frontier.

The Augustinians used the doctrina at Cuitzeo to evangelize the native population living around Laguna Cuitzeo. The urban plan of Cuitzeo paralleled that of other central Mexican mission communities discussed above. The Augustinians directed the construction of a new sacred complex that consisted of the cloister and open chapel, later adding the large monumental church. Other elements that still exist include the hospital chapel and a barrio chapel. With limited numbers of missionary personnel, the Augustinians initially could staff only the doctrina at Cuitzeo. As more missionaries arrived from Spain, they elevated two visitas to independent doctrina status. They were Copándaro (1566) and Chucándiro (ca. 1576).[29]

The missionaries stationed on Cuitzeo directed the construction of small chapels in the smaller communities designated as visitas. In 1579, the missionaries at Cuitzeo administered twelve visitas, and those at Copándaro administered four. As the native population declined, the Augustinians reduced the number of visitas. In the mid-seventeenth century, the missionaries at Cuitzeo administered only four visitas.[30] The first visita structures were small, freestanding open chapels. The chapel at Taramequaro, a visita of Copándaro, is a surviving example of this. The Augustinians had an open chapel built. Later, in the seventeenth century, they built a larger enclosed chapel. The chapel at Onxao (Huacao) may also have been initially built as an open chapel before being converted later into an enclosed structure. Other surviving Augustinian visita chapels on the shores of Laguna Cuitzeo were built using the same architectural plan, and this most likely was unique to Cuitzeo. Within the town itself the hospital chapel and the barrio chapel of San Pedro are examples. The visita chapels at Jerúco and San Agustín del Pulque are identical, and that of Capamucireo is very similar. The architectural similarity suggests that the Augustinians may have erected the chapels as part of a major building campaign directed by one missionary-architect.

The Augustinians established missions along the Chichimeca frontier in three areas (see map 1). They were in what today are known as the Sierra Alta

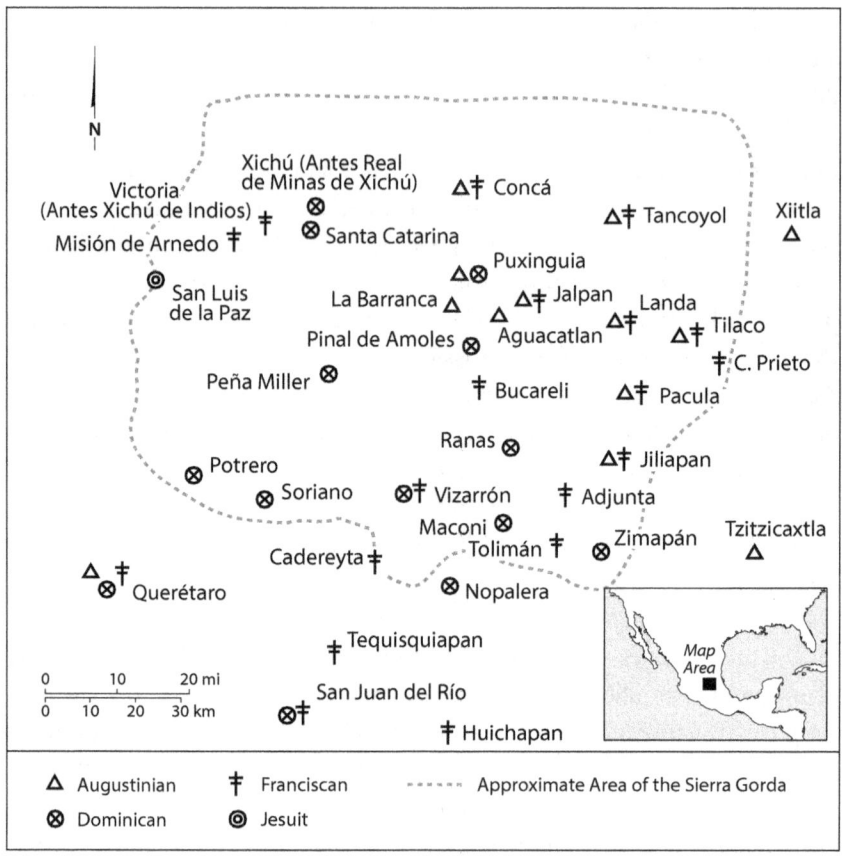

Map 1. The Sierra Gorda missions.
Map by Bill Nelson. Copyright © 2017 by the University of Oklahoma Press.

in the modern state of Hidalgo; the Mezquital Valley, also in Hidalgo; and in northern Michoacán and southern Guanajuato.[31] The doctrina established at Metztitlán (see figure 3) around 1539 played an important role in the first attempt to evangelize the groups collectively known as the Chichimecas living beyond the frontier. The Augustinians staffed the mission at Metztitlán with four or five missionaries who also visited numerous visitas across a large territory that extended as far north as what today is southern San Luis Potosi. At the end of the sixteenth century, the Augustinians stationed there administered 120 visitas.[32] As more missionary personnel became available, the Augustinians elevated selected visitas to the status of independent mis-

Fig. 3. The Augustinian doctrina Los Reyes Metztitlán (Hidalgo).

sions with resident missionaries, including Chichicaxtla (alternative spelling Tzitzicaxtla) (Hidalgo), Chapulhuacán (Hidalgo), and Xilitlán (Xilitla, San Luis Potosí). These three establishments were important in the first efforts to evangelize the Chichimecas.

A report written around 1571 described the doctrina at Chichicaxtla. Francisco de Mérida and Isabel de Barrios held Chichicaxtla's jurisdiction in encomienda. As many as three Augustinians staffed the mission, although at the time of the drafting of the report there were only two. They administered another eleven communities as visitas. The Augustinians assigned missionaries to frontier missions based on their language skills. One of the missionaries stationed at Chichicaxtla reportedly spoke Náhuatl, and the other the local Chichimeca language. This detail in the report also indicates that the mission district contained a mixed population of Náhuas and Chichimecas and was an example of the existence of small colonies of sedentary natives living beyond the Chichimeca frontier. However, Chichimecas constituted the majority, and the evangelization program focused its efforts on them. The report also noted that the Chichimecas had begun to comply with the Catholic sacraments, and in particular with confession. A total of 849 natives reportedly confessed, and most also received the sacrament of communion.[33]

In the late sixteenth century, two missionaries staffed Chapulhuacán, and the mission district reportedly consisted of twenty-one communities.[34] A report

Fig. 4. The Augustinian doctrina at Xilitlán (San Luis Potosi).

on Xilitlán (Tastoloxilitlán) (see figure 4) prepared around 1571 noted that the prior stationed there spoke Otomí and also visited Chapulhuacán. This indicates that Chapulhuacán was also an example of a community of sedentary Otomí speakers living in Chichimeca territory.[35] Xilitlán was the third of the three doctrinas established beyond the Chichimeca frontier, and it served as the base of operations for the first evangelization campaign among the Chichimecas living in the Sierra Gorda. It was another example of a colony of sedentary natives living in Chichimeca territory, and in this case, there were Náhuatl and Otomí speakers settled on the cabecera and eight visitas. Xilitlán itself had a mixed population of Náhuatl and Otomí speakers, and the other communities either had Náhuas or Otomí populations. Two Augustinians staffed the mission. One spoke Náhuatl and the other Otomí, and the assignment of missionaries to a given doctrina depended on their linguistic abilities in one or more of the indigenous languages spoken there. Tilaco, the site of one of the five Franciscan missions established in the 1740s, was also a community of Otomí speakers, and the report noted that "[Tilaco] has fifteen tributaries, all Otomís, and is nine leagues from this town [Xilitlán], because it borders [the territory] of the Chichimecas." At the time of the report, some 1,518 natives in the mission district already confessed. The report, however, did not indicate that the Augustinians attempted to evangelize Chichimecas; they focused their attention instead on the colonies of sedentary natives.[36]

The Augustinians administered other doctrinas along the Chichimeca frontier in the Sierra Alta of Hidalgo, but most focused on populations of Náhuas, Otomí, or Huastecos. Toward the end of the sixteenth century, the Augustinians stationed on the doctrina at Metztitlán reportedly spoke either Náhuatl or Otomí, and none spoke a Chichimeca language. The reorganization of the missions in the region with the elevation of the status of former visitas to independent doctrinas shifted responsibility for the evangelization of Chichimecas primarily to the missionaries stationed on Chichicaxtla.[37] The Augustinians at Molango and Huejutla also spoke languages of the sedentary Náhuas and Hustecos.[38] At Tlachinoltipac the missionaries reportedly spoke Náhuatl, Serrano (a generic term for natives that lived in mountainous areas), and Ocuilleco, which is an Otopame language also known as Tlahuica or Matlazinca.[39] With the exception of Chichicaxtla, the missionaries stationed on the Augustinian doctrinas in this frontier zone did not attempt to evangelize groups identified as Chichimecas.

In the 1560s, the Augustinians established a mission at Xalpa (modern Jalpan de Serra, Querétaro). Xalpa was also a community of sedentary Náhuatl-speaking natives living in Chichimeca territory. The circa-1550 report on Xalpa from the suma de visitas provides the earliest details on the community. One Francisco Barrón held Xalpa in encomienda, and the tribute obligation consisted of clothing, honey, and birds. It reportedly had a population of 212 sedentary natives (heads of household?) in addition to an unremunerated number of Chichimecas. The report also noted the potential for establishing cattle ranches and some wheat production, although it also characterized the district as having broken terrain.[40]

An uprising in 1568–69 ended the first Augustinian mission at Xalpa, and the rebels also attacked Xilitlán and Chapulhuacán. Luis de Carvajal received a commission to suppress the uprising, and he reestablished the Augustinian mission and built a small fort at Xalpa. The Augustinians had their mission inside of the fort, which reportedly was built of stone.[41] The remains of the fort now form a part of a local museum dedicated to the history of the Sierra Gorda region, and the structure has been used for different purposes during its long history, including as a prison.

The Augustinians continued to administer the mission at Xalpa until the early 1740s, although there may have been periods in which the mission did not have resident missionaries. The names of some Augustinians stationed there exist in Augustinian records. The last was Lucas Cabeza de Vaca, O.S.A. The report prepared on conditions in the Sierra Gorda in the early 1740s by José de Escandón enumerated the populations of Xalpa and the visitas administered by the Augustinians, as well as the ethnic group of the natives. Xalpa, for example, reportedly had a population of 122 Náhuas. The report documents a shift in the focus of the Augustinian missionaries. In the mid- and late sixteenth century, the missionaries targeted the populations of the colonies of sedentary natives living in Chichimeca territory. The Augustinians later attempted to congregate and convert the Pames, the most important Chichimeca group in the eastern Sierra Gorda. However, as Lucas Cabeza de Vaca, O.S.A., wrote in a report on the mission at Xalpa in the early 1740s, the Pames resisted evangelization. Moreover, they preferred to live in small communities in the mountains and refused to settle on larger mission communities. Only fifteen Pames families lived at Xalpa out of a native population that Cabeza de Vaca estimated to number around 6,000.[42]

The inability to congregate the Pames became a point of criticism that Escandón noted in his 1743 report. The mission at Pacula typified the failure to convince the natives to resettle at a single site and the failure of the central Mexican model as applied beyond the frontier. The report enumerated a population of 1,234 living at the mission and three other sites, including one former mission. The report also noted that the natives should be made to relocate to larger mission communities.[43] Escandón later recommended the removal of the Augustinians from their missions in the Sierra Gorda; he advised that they be replaced by Franciscans who were to be given a mandate to congregate the Pames.

The Augustinians also approached the Chichimeca frontier from what today are northern Michoacán and southern Guanajuato. As hostilities escalated beyond the Chichimeca frontier, the Augustinians established a chain of doctrinas along and just beyond the frontier. They used these missions as bases of operations for new missions beyond the frontier. Guillermo de Santa María, O.S.A., stationed at the doctrina at Huango, visited Chichimeca bands along the Lerma River as far west as what today is Ayo el Chico (Jalisco), where the missionary also established a visita of Huango. In 1550, he congregated Guamares at Pénjamo along with sedentary P'urépecha colonists from further south. It was a common strategy to settle sedentary natives along with Chichimecas.[44]

In 1553, the Franciscans established a mission at Villa de San Felipe in the territory of the Guamares, located in what now is northern Guanajuato close to the border with San Luis Potosi. However, they abandoned the mission following the murder of Bernardino de Cosín, O.F.M. The Augustinians reestablished the mission in 1566 or 1568, and in 1571 three missionaries resided there, including Guillermo de Santa María, O.S.A. The Augustinians abandoned the mission in 1575 following a raid by hostile Chichimecas.[45] A report written in 1571 provided some details on the organization of the evangelization campaign among the Guamares. The prior served as the preacher and confessor for the local Spanish population, which totaled some thirty heads of household (*vecinos*). A small number of P'urépecha lived at San Felipe and worked as laborers for the Spaniards. They reportedly lived in a separate barracks.[46]

The other two Augustinians dedicated their attention to the attempt to convert the Guamares. Guillermo de Santa María already had more than twenty years of experience as a missionary along and beyond the frontier in Michoacán. The procedure used in teaching Church doctrine was awkward and points to the inherent difficulty of trying to translate culturally embedded religious concepts into terms understandable in different cultures. Santa María spoke P'urépecha, and there reportedly were Guamares who spoke the same language. The Augustinian translated the doctrine into P'urépecha and explained the concepts to the Guamares translators, who in turn attempted to translate the doctrinal points to the Guamares living on the mission.[47] The Augustinian had no way to verify what the Guamares translators actually told the other neophytes, or what the Guamares actually understood.

The Villa de San Felipe was an important way station on the supply route to northern mining centers, and caravans and large numbers of people passed through the community.[48] This activity attracted hostile Chichimecas, who raided the community and forced the Augustinians to abandon the mission there. The continuing violence of the Chichimeca War materially limited the evangelization campaign beyond the frontier.

Dominican Missions beyond the Chichimeca Frontier

The Dominicans arrived in Mexico two years following the Franciscans. They established doctrinas in communities surrounding Mexico City, such as Tepetlaoxtoc, Azcapotzalco, Tacubaya, Coyoacán, and Mixcoac, and in

Morelos, Oaxaca, Chiapas, and Tabasco.[49] Their main mission frontiers were in Oaxaca and Chiapas-Tabasco, where they enjoyed a monopoly on evangelization. The Dominicans did establish a group of missions in the larger Sierra Gorda region, and later in 1774 they assumed responsibility for the missions in Baja California. However, with the exception of these two groups of missions, the Dominicans did not actively participate in the northern missions, and it was the Franciscans and Jesuits who were involved in the evangelization of this region.

In the late seventeenth century, the Dominicans staffed a mission at Zimapán (Hidalgo), and this may have been the first of their missions in the Sierra Gorda region. A 1579 report described Zimapán, which is located north of Ixmiquilpan in the mountains that border the Valle de Mezquital. In about 1575, the Spanish established a mining camp that exploited silver that also reportedly had a high lead content. Surrounding the mining camp, there were three native communities. With a total population of about 400, these communities were populated by Chichimecas that had been gradually congregated there. The report identified the natives by the generic term Chichimeca, but they may have been Jonaces. Later in the eighteenth century a mission populated by Jonaces existed close to Zimapán. Each of the three communities reportedly had its own church.[50] The report did not specify that the Dominicans staffed the mission at Zimapán, but they were there at the end of the seventeenth century and dedicated the mission to Nuestra Señora de los Dolores (see appendix B.1).

At the end of the seventeenth century, the Dominicans administered a group of seven missions in the Sierra Gorda region, including Zimapán. Felipe Galindo, O.P., promoted the establishment of new missions, and in 1688 the Crown approved his plan and provided *sinodos* (subsidies) for six missionaries. By 1689 the Dominicans had begun to establish missions at Zimapán, Nuestra Señora del Rosario (La Nopalera), San Buenaventura Maconi, San José del Llano (later Vizarrón), Santo Domingo Soriano San Miguel de Palmillas, Nuestra Señora de Guadalupe Ahuacatlán, and Santa Rosa de las Minas de Xichú.[51] One document shows that Dominicans had already replaced the Franciscans at San José del Llano by 1688 and were at La Nopalera as early as 1686. The document noted that a jacal functioned as a chapel at La Nopalera. The same document also reported the visit of the archbishop of Mexico Francisco de Agiar y Sejas, who confirmed many Jonaces in an act of public theater.[52] The Dominicans targeted their evangelization campaign on the Jonaces. Although

The Geography of Colonization and Evangelization 33

Fig. 5. The Dominican mission Santo Domingo de Guzmán Soriano (Colón, Querétaro).

the Dominicans had a convent in Querétaro City, Galindo also established a doctrina in San Juan del Río (Querétaro) that served as their base of operations for their missions and prepared missionaries for the Sierra Gorda missions.[53]

The missions were located east of Querétaro City in three zones. Santo Domingo de Guzmán Soriano (modern Colón, Querétaro) was located in a watered valley in a hilly region a short distance from the city (see figure 5). Soriano was also close to the Franciscan convent San Pedro Tolimán. Galindo was at Soriano by 1691, if not earlier, and it served as the headquarters for the Dominican missions.[54] It still operated in 1743 and had a mixed population of 32 Spaniards, 160 Otomí, and 171 Chichimecas (Jonaces?). Six Otomí families descended from a group settled at Soriano to assist the missionaries, and other families later came to settle there.[55] The Dominicans administered three missions in the semiarid region of eastern Querétaro. This is the area located between Cadereyta and the Sierra Gorda massif. There were other ephemeral Dominican missions or visitas in the semiarid region. In his study of the Sierra Gorda in the eighteenth century, Gerardo Lara Cisneros published a map of the missions in the region in which the author also identified Ranas, Peña Miller, and Pinal de Amoles as Dominican missions.[56] The three missions were San José del Llano, which had been the site of a short-lived Franciscan mission San José de Vizarrón (1739–1748); San Miguel Palmillas (modern San Miguel de Palmas, Querétaro, located on the Xichú River); and La Nopalera. San Buenaventura Maconi and Ahuacatlán were in the Sierra Gorda massif. Xichú was located in what today is Guanajuato close to its border with Querétaro on the Xichú River. The Dominicans reportedly staffed Santa Rosa until 1728 or 1729, at which time the owners of the *haciendas de minas* Diego Navarijo and María Valdés assumed responsibility for the evangelization of the Jonaces.[57]

The effort to evangelize the Jonaces proved to be difficult. Resistance by rebel Jonaces in 1703 led to the destruction and abandonment of San José del Llano. The Dominicans abandoned the mission, requesting that Spaniards from Cadereyta be settled at the site of the former mission and that a fortified house be built for defense.[58] The Dominicans continued to staff La Nopalera until 1713, but by the late 1730s they had abandoned the mission, which became a private hacienda owned by one Joachín de Villapando from Toluca, who also had connections to Gerónimo de Labra, who held the title of *protector de indios* of the Sierra Gorda.[59] In 1713, a group of soldiers participating in a campaign against hostile Jonaces demolished the mission because they believed the natives living there collaborated with rebels. The action taken by soldiers without orders from their commander ended an active mission program, and the mission residents fled the mission site.[60]

According to the report prepared by Escandón in 1743, the Dominicans still administered three missions in the Sierra Gorda. They were Soriano, Ahuacatlán, and San Miguelito (San Miguel de Palmas). All were populated by congregated Jonaces. The largest population was at San Miguelito. The Dominicans did not participate in the expansion of the Sierra Gorda mission frontier organized by Escandón. A diary of a military inspection of the Sierra Gorda from the late 1780s reported on conditions in the region and described the missions, which by that time had been significantly reduced in number. The Dominicans reportedly staffed only one mission, San Miguel de las Palmas. It had a population of fifty-three families and some two-hundred people.[61] The others presumably had been secularized as the Crown deemphasized the mission program in favor of more fully integrating natives into colonial society.[62]

Franciscan Missions on and beyond the Chichimeca Frontier

The Franciscans also established missions on and beyond the Chichimeca frontier in the sixteenth century. Their approach to the frontier came from two directions, and missionaries from two Franciscan provinces established doctrinas. Franciscans from the Province of the Santo Evangelio responsible for central Mexico established several missions on the frontier in the Mezquital Valley in what today are the modern states of Hidalgo and México. The Franciscans had already established several doctrinas in the southern part of the Valley, including at Tula in 1529. Their missions on the frontier included Xilotepec, also founded in 1529, and Hueychiapa (Huichapan), established in 1531 or 1532. They later elevated several visitas to the status of independent doctrinas. They included Tepexi del Rio in 1552, Alfaxayuca in 1569, and Tepetitlán in 1571.[63] The doctrina at Tecozautla, located north of Hueychiapa at the edge of the Sierra Gorda massif, was a seventeenth-century establishment.[64] In the 1550s, missionaries from the Santo Evangelio visited places such as Tancoyol, and by the end of the century they established short-lived missions at Tonatico, Xalpa, and Jiliapan.[65]

Antonio de Ciudad Real, O.F.M., described the building complexes at the frontier doctrinas in the mid-1580s, and in one case he noted modifications to one complex to take into account the Chichimeca threat. Ciudad Real accompanied Fr. Alonso Ponce, O.F.M., on a general inspection of the Franciscan establishments in Mexico and Central America and described most of the Franciscan establishments. Of Xilotepec, Ciudad Real noted, "The convent is completed with its cloister, church, dormitories and orchard. Next to the convent there is a large and sumptuous ramada [open chapel] where the Indians are gathered and they preach to them and say mass. Four friars usually reside there."[66]

The church and cloister still exist, but the open chapel has largely disappeared. However, it was depicted in the sixteenth-century Codex Xilotepec. Open chapels were an architectural feature common to sixteenth-century Mexican convents and played an important role in the evangelization strategy of the missionaries. Ciudad Real also described the complex at Hueychiapa (Huichapan). He wrote that "the convent is completed with its church, cloister, dormitories and orchard. The structure of the convent is [of] good [quality] and four friars lived there."[67]

Franciscan missionaries from the Province of San Pedro y San Pablo (Michoacán) also approached and established missions beyond the Chichimeca frontier. Around 1540, they established a doctrina at Acámbaro in what today is Guanajuato, located just beyond the frontier.[68] Acámbaro was typical of the mixed ethnic communities formed along the frontier. It had a native population of P'urépecha, Mazahua, Otomí, and Chichimecas, who supported themselves primarily through agriculture. The P'urépecha reportedly were the most numerous. A 1580 report on Acámbaro Province, however, highlighted that the community was located in a war zone and noted the important role played by sedentary native allies in the Chichimeca conflict. It noted that "the Otomis and Chichimecas don't serve for any other thing than to be on the frontier with the enemy, and thus if they win any booty of textiles [*mantas*] or prisoners in their encounters, they go with all of it to said Lord."[69]

The suma de visitas written around 1550 provides details regarding the early political organization of Acámbaro. One Herman Pérez de Bocanegra held the jurisdiction in encomienda. Acámbaro itself had thirteen barrios and a total of 1,048 people above the age of three living in 183 households. There were four other cabeceras (head towns) subject to Acámbaro. They were Yrameo, which had a population of 360 people above the age of three and provided 13 native laborers as a part of its tribute obligation; Amocotin, which had a population of 980 over the age of three and provided 13 laborers; Atacorin, which had a population of 494 over the age of three and provided 13 laborers; and Emenguaro, which had a population of 190 over the age of three and a tribute obligation of 33 native workers to tend livestock, 26 for textile production, and 20 native servants to tend the encomendero's house. Other tribute obligations included wheat and corn production, the provision of hay, twenty-eight cakes of salt, eight pairs of hemp sandals, and twenty-four pairs of leather sandals. The report also noted that crops grown included cotton in addition to the cereals already mentioned.[70]

The urban development of Acámbaro took into account the different ethnic groups settled there. One example was the foundation of two hospitals, one for the P'urépecha and the second for the Otomí. Fr. Juan de San Miguel, O.F.M., reportedly founded the two hospitals in 1550.[71] The natives most likely lived in separate barrios, and the hospitals would have been located in the two neighborhoods. A hospital complex and chapel still exists on one side of the Franciscan doctrina, but it is not clear which community it served.

The Geography of Colonization and Evangelization 37

Fig. 6. The Franciscan doctrina San Pedro Tolimán (Tolimán, Querétaro).

The Franciscan mission in Acámbaro served as a base of operations for the establishment of new doctrinas beyond the frontier, a strategy that was also one aspect of the Chichimeca pacification campaign. Viceroy Martin Enriquez ordered the settlement of Celaya beyond the frontier, and around 1570 the Franciscans established a doctrina there. Similarly, in about 1574 the Franciscans elevated the visita of Apatzeo, located between Celaya and Querétaro, to the status of an independent mission. Two Franciscans staffed the new mission.[72] Antonio de Ciudad Real described the Franciscan mission in Acámbaro in 1586. He wrote that "the convent was completed with its cloister, dormitories, church and orchard. It is of middling quality built of masonry, and seven missionaries lived there."[73] The number of missionaries stationed on the mission showed its importance in the evangelization campaign along the frontier.

The Franciscans from the Province of San Pedro y San Pablo also established one doctrina in the Sierra Gorda, and most likely it was the first Franciscan establishment in the region. This was San Pedro Tolimán (not to be confused with the later mission named Tolimán established near Zimapán), located in a watered valley not very far from the Dominican mission at Soriano discussed above (see figure 6). It already existed in the 1580s at the time of the inspection tour by Alonso Ponce; O.F.M. Ponce had the Guardian at Pátzcuaro report on Tolimán. The convent itself was "small and built of adobe," but a church had already been built. Two Franciscans staffed the mission.[74] A much larger complex exists at the site today. The Franciscans also established a doctrina in the northern Sierra Gorda at San Juan Bautista Xichú de Indios that probably also dated to at least 1580, although Franciscans first attempted to establish a doctrina there in 1540.[75] Ciudad Real described Xichú de Indios in the following terms:

> Xichú is a small town of Otomí Indians placed among the war-like Chichimecas (*Chichimecas de Guerra*), in which there normally are four Spanish soldiers in garrison (*de presidio*) . . . the church of the convent, which is also of adobe walls covered with straw . . . The convent was not finished, and is nothing more than a small adobe structure (*casita*), its designation is San Juan Bautista and two missionaries (*religiosos*) resided there, and live in great danger like the residents of the town.[76]

The Franciscan doctrinas established along the Chichimeca frontier had a basis in the organization and methods employed in the first stages of the evangelization among the sedentary native populations of central Mexico. The approach taken with the sedentary natives was not particularly successful with the nomadic populations living beyond the Chichimeca frontier. Groups that did not practice agriculture had a different gender division of labor and social values based on male skills as hunters and warriors. They did not respond well to missionary social engineering that envisioned radical changes in their way of life, and incorporation into the Spanish Colonial system also frequently included labor demands made by Spaniards.

As the Spanish advanced northward, there were a number of causes for conflict with the nomadic hunters and gatherers. One was the competition for food resources with the growing number of livestock the Spanish introduced into their territory. The 1580 report on Acámbaro touched on this. It noted that the seeds from the mesquite constituted an important food source for the natives.[77] However, Spanish cattle also consumed the mesquite bean. Spanish livestock also drove off animals that the nomadic groups hunted. When Chichimecas killed Spanish livestock as an alternative to the animals they had hunted, the Spanish retaliated. This contributed to an escalating cycle of violence.

The Geography of Colonization and Evangelization

Fig. 7. The Franciscan doctrina San Pedro y San Pablo de Cadereyta. The church dates to the 1720s.

Missions established beyond the frontier often proved to be ephemeral. The Franciscans congregated groups of Chichimecas, but they frequently remained for only a short time and then returned to their traditional way of life. The Spaniards classified this as an act of rebellion. The Franciscan missions established in the Custodio de Rio Verde in what today is the southern part of San Luis Potosi in the first decades of the seventeenth century are an example. Santa María del Río occupied several sites. In 1622, the Guachichiles living on the mission "rebelled" because of labor demands made by Spaniards. Six years later, in 1628, the Guachichiles fled to the mountains.[78] Similarly, in 1629 Guachichiles fled from the mission at Valle de Maiz, but the Spanish returned them to the mission by force.[79]

The same occurred with many missions the Franciscans established in the Sierra Gorda region. In 1640, the Franciscans established San Pedro y San Pablo mission at Cadereyta (see figure 7).[80] This doctrina proved to be stable, but others did not. For example, in 1682 and 1683 Pero Gerónimo de Labra, who held the position of protector de indios, promoted a plan to establish a group of missions in the Sierra Gorda, in particular in the semiarid region.

Two Franciscans from the Province of the Santo Evangelio named Francisco de Aguirre, O.F.M., and Nicolás de Ochoa, O.F.M., established San Buenaventura Maconi, San Nicolás Tolentino Ranas, Nuestra Señora de Guadalupe de Deconi, San Juan de Tetlá, San Francisco Tolimán, La Nopalera, Santiago del Palmar (modern Santa María del Palmar, Querétaro—the Dominicans later staffed this mission), and San José del Llano. Labra had jacal-like churches built at the sites of all of the new missions.[81] However, as already discussed above, the Dominicans assumed responsibility for several of the new missions, and others such as Ranas and Deconi lasted only a short period of time because of resistance by the Jonaces that undermined this missionary initiative.

From 1713 to 1715, one Gabriel Guerrero de Ardilla led a military campaign against the Jonaces who continued to resist Spanish authority, and he scored a notable victory in February of 1715. In 1718, the Augustinian Felipe Medrano, O.S.A., was brought in to congregate 281 Jonaces at a new mission at Maconi that was given the designation of Santa Teresa de Valero de Maconi. Different sources give conflicting versions of what happened to the new mission at Maconi. A 1739 report by the Commissary General of the Province of the Santo Evangelio noted that the mission lasted only eight months. He attributed the demise of the mission to the labor demands ("extortion") of Joachín de Villapando, the Spaniard who held the concession to the mines at Maconi and later owned the hacienda established at the site of the suppressed Dominican mission La Nopalera.[82] Another document reported that a Franciscan named Pedro de la Fuente, O.F.M., was at the mission from at least 1721 until his death in 1726. However, following his death the Jonaces abandoned the mission and fled back to the mountains.[83] It is likely that the first group of missionaries abandoned Maconi after eight months, but then De la Fuente arrived and attempted to revive the mission. The Jonaces remained at the mission most likely because of the person of the missionary, but they returned to their way of life following his death.

Franciscan Mission Reorganization: The Apostolic Colleges

In the late seventeenth century the *Propaganda Fide* in Rome promoted the reinvigoration of overseas missions through the foundation of apostolic colleges. The idea was to train missionaries, and the colleges were also to administer missions. The first apostolic college established in Spanish America was Santa Cruz de Querétaro, founded in the early 1680s.[84] The missionaries

Fig. 8. The Franciscan church at Pachuca (Hidalgo). In 1727, the Province of San Diego established an apostolic college there.

from Santa Cruz de Querétaro staffed missions on the north Mexican frontier, primarily in Coahuila and Texas. However, they were not involved in the Sierra Gorda missions.

Franciscans from two apostolic colleges established during the first decades of the eighteenth century were involved in the Sierra Gorda mission frontier. The first were Franciscans affiliated with the apostolic college at Pachuca (Hidalgo), founded by the Province of San Diego de México in 1727 (see figure 8). These were the so-called "barefoot" ("descalzos") Franciscans who established the province in 1599. The apostolic college remained a dependency of the province until 1772.[85] Following his inspection tour in 1743, Escandón removed the Augustinians from Pacula and assigned the mission to Pachuca. In his report, Escandón noted of the Jonaces living in the Pacula mission district that "the Mecos Indians [of Pacula] are found dispersed living in the hills and forests [wilderness], almost with the same barbarity, that they had in the gentility [before the arrival of the Christians]."[86]

Escandón wanted the Jonaces congregated in a single mission community and properly catechized, and he criticized the Augustinians for not having done more.[87] For the Spanish the way of life of the Jonaces was contrary to the ideal that linked "civilization" to urban life. The Jonaces could not be civilized until they lived in proper towns. The Augustinians had failed to accomplish this, so now he handed the job over to the Franciscans.

The Pachuca Franciscans also established several new missions in their assigned district, which was around Zimapán. The first was established at a site known as Las Adjuntas on July 20, 1741, but the mission lasted only three months. The Franciscans relocated the mission to Tolimán, a short distance from Zimapán. When Escandón visited the new mission, he noted that it had a population of twenty-four families and 67 people. In 1743, the Franciscans founded the mission San José de Fuenclara at Xiliapa, which had been a visita of Pacula. The population of Xiliapa was 372 when Escandón visited the community. They also founded Nuestra Señora de Guadalupe, also known as Cerro Prieto.[88]

The Franciscans from the apostolic college of San Fernando (Mexico City) also played an important role in the Sierra Gorda. San Fernando initially (1731) was a hospice located in Mexico City, but it later attained the status of an independent apostolic college in 1733 (see figure 9).[89] Missionaries from San Fernando first staffed missions in the Sierra Gorda, in Baja California (1768–1773), and later in California (1769–1834). The Sierra Gorda missions were the first experiences in the field for several Franciscans who later were involved in the California missions, including Junípero Serra, O.F.M., Francisco Palou, O.F.M., and Fermín Francisco Lasuen, O.F.M. The Sierra Gorda missions also became a testing ground for social and economic policies and methods later implemented on the Baja California and California missions.

José Ortés de Velasco, O.F.M., founded the first mission administered by San Fernando in the Sierra Gorda. It was San José de Vizarrón, established in 1740 at the site of the earlier Dominican mission San José del Llano. The Franciscans settled Jonaces on the mission, and in 1743 Escandón reported a population there of 67. Between 1740 and 1743, the Franciscans reportedly congregated 225 Jonaces on the mission, but many died and others fled. Between 1740 and 1746, the Franciscans baptized 94 *párvulos* (children under age nine). Deaths totaled 30 young children and 11 adults.[90] The new mission lasted only eight years, and the Franciscans closed it following the flight of the Jonaces. A small garrison of soldiers was still at the site, as were settlers from Cadereyta who

Fig. 9. San Fernando church (Mexico City), which was a part of the complex of the apostolic college of San Fernando founded in 1733.

settled there in 1705. One can speculate that there were frictions between the natives and the soldiers and settlers. In 1742, a group of 53 Jonaces fled to the mission at Tolimán, which perhaps also suggests nonconformity with the methods of the Franciscans from San Fernando.[91] Soldiers hunted down the fugitive Jonaces and consigned them to work in *obrajes* (textile mills) in Santiago de Querétaro.

Escandón was also critical of the Augustinians stationed at Xalpa, and he petitioned to have them replaced by Franciscans from San Fernando. His intention was very clear. He wanted the Pames congregated at Xalpa, and he wanted a group of new missions to be established to accelerate the integration of the natives into colonial society. The Augustinians had staffed Xalpa as well as Pacula for more than a century, and they had made little progress in conversion or the development of stable mission communities. He expected that the Franciscans would be able to use different methods to achieve their conversion and change in their way of life.

In April of 1744, ten Franciscan missionaries left Mexico City to staff the five missions that Escandón assigned to them. The Franciscans took possession of the former Augustinian mission at Xalpa on April 20. They established the mission San Miguel de Fuenclara at Concá on April 26, which had been a visita of the Augustinian mission at Xalpa. They established the mission at Landa on April 30, the mission at Tilaco on May 2, and finally the mission at Tancoyol on May 3.[92] The Franciscans initially congregated 402 families and a total of 1,445 Pames at Xalpa, 144 families and 449 people at Concá, 193 families and 564 at Agua de Landa, 218 families and 574 people at Tancoyol, and 184 families and 749 people at Tilaco.[93] The Franciscans continued to congregate Pames on the missions, and by early 1746 the total number resettled reached 7,406 people.[94] The following chapters examine the Franciscan missions in more detail.

The Jesuits in the Sierra Gorda

The Society of Jesus (Jesuits) was the last missionary order to arrive in Mexico, but they assumed an important role in missions on the northern frontier in Nueva Vizcaya (Durango, Chihuahua), Sinaloa, and Sonora. They also administered several missions in the Sierra Gorda region. The Jesuits established several missions beyond the Chichimeca frontier at the end of the sixteenth century, including San Luis de la Paz (Guanajuato), founded in 1590 (see figure 10).[95] When Escandón visited the Sierra Gorda in 1743, the Jesuits still administered San Luis de la Paz, which had a population of 245 Jonaces in 66 families. The Jonaces reportedly were well instructed in Christian doctrine, and they knew basic prayers.[96]

The earliest references to the mission at San Luis de la Paz show that the missionaries used methods similar to those employed later by the Franciscans in the Sierra Gorda. This included providing food rations to enhance economic dependence and so that the natives would not have to leave the mission to collect food.[97] The baptismal registers from the end of the sixteenth century recorded the names of different Chichimeca groups. They included the Guaxabanes, Guachichiles, Copuces, Jonaces, and Pames in addition to Otomí. In addition, two generic terms appeared in the record. They were Serranos, or natives from the mountains, and Chichimeca. The first baptism of a Chichimeca reportedly took place in 1594.[98]

The mission formed part of a more complex community and district. The central town itself was inhabited by natives—Jonaces and other groups—

Fig. 10. The Jesuit church at San Luis de la Paz (Guanajuato).

organized into distinct barrios that each had a small chapel. In the rural areas surrounding the town, there were private properties classified as *labores* (smaller farms), *ranchos* (larger properties), and haciendas. The majority of natives were Otomís settled at the site when the Jesuits established the mission toward the end of the Chichimeca war.[99] There were also Náhuas and P'urépechas. The rural population was predominately nonindigenous and classified as Spaniards and *castas,* or people of mixed ancestry as defined in the Spanish colonial social matrix.[100] By the eighteenth century, the region surrounding San Luis de la Paz had evolved from being an isolated mission outpost beyond the Chichimeca frontier to a more fully developed sedentary rural society. However, evangelization of the natives classified as Chichimecas had not been completed.

Jesuit Missions in Lowland South America

The Spanish and Portuguese encountered clan-based sedentary agriculturalists and nomadic hunters and gatherers in the lowland region of South America that today encompasses what are parts of Argentina, southern Brazil, Uruguay,

Paraguay, and eastern Bolivia. This was the region the Jesuits classified as their Province of Paraguay. The native groups inhabiting the region did not live in stratified and hierarchical states, so the Spanish devised other modes of colonization and exploitation. At the same time, Jesuit social engineering in the missions sought to convert them to a fully sedentary way of life along the model of central Mexico discussed above. The Jesuits encountered the same type of resistance from nonsedentary natives as did the missionaries beyond the Chichimeca frontier. The Portuguese enslaved natives, whereas the Spanish used the encomienda to organize what amounted to forced labor. It was also a contested frontier, as the Spanish and Portuguese struggled during several centuries for control of land and native labor, even during the period of the union of the Crowns (1580–1640).

The Franciscans were the first to attempt to evangelize the different native groups living in the region. The Jesuits entered the region in 1607, establishing the missionary Province of Paraguay in 1607. The discussion here outlines the establishment of missions not only on the Chiquitos frontier but also in the other parts of the Jesuit province. The initiative came from Jesuits stationed on the Jesuit College at Cordoba, and two years later the missionaries established the first mission at San Ignacio Guazú, in what today is southern Paraguay. The initial thrust of their evangelization campaign was to evangelize the groups collectively known as the Guaraní, who lived in a huge territory that stretched from southern Brazil to Uruguay, parts of northern Argentina, and Paraguay. The Jesuit strategy was to establish missions among populations not held in encomienda and as far from Spanish settlement as possible. San Ignacio Guazú was a community partially held in encomienda, but the other missions established among the Guaraní were not. Over the next two decades, the Black Robes expanded to Guairá (Modern Paraná State, Brazil), Tape (modern Rio Grande do Sul State, Brazil), Itatín (northern Paraguay), and what became the core territory located between the Paraná and Uruguay Rivers. Between 1610 and 1632, the Jesuits established and administered fourteen missions in Guairá. They were San Ignacio Miní (1610), Nuestra Señora de Loreto (1610), San Francisco Xavier (1624), San José (1625), Nuestra Señora de Encarnación (1625), Santa María (1626), San Pablo del Inaí (1627), San Antonio (1627), Los Ángeles (1627), San Pablo (1627), Nuestra Señora de Guananas (1627/1628), Santo Tomás (1628), Emida de Nuestra Señora de Copacabana (1628), and Jesús María (1628). The *bandeirantes* destroyed this group of missions in 1632.[101]

Raids by bandeirantes, slave traders from Sao Paulo, also forced the Jesuits to abandon Guairá and Tape in the 1630s, and after that the Jesuits focused their evangelization campaign on the region between the Paraná and Uruguay Rivers. As a part of the geopolitics of control over the disputed borderlands in the Rio de la Plata region, the Jesuits established new missions in the late seventeenth century east of the Uruguay River in what today is modern Rio Grande do Sul. In 1680, the Portuguese established Colonia do Sacramento in what today is Uruguay. The Jesuit expansion east of the Uruguay River served to assert Spanish territorial claims and to geographically isolate the Portuguese settlement. By the early eighteenth century, the missions among the Guaraní numbered thirty, and in 1732 they had a total population of more than 140,000.[102]

The history of Los Santos Cosme y Damián mission was typical of the Paraguay missions. The Black Robes established the mission in 1634 at a site in Tape known as Ibití mire.[103] In 1636, the mission had a population of 1,200 families and some 6,000 people.[104] Raids launched by bandeirantes from 1636 to 1640 forced the relocation of the Tape missions. The Jesuits abandoned Santos Cosme y Damián in May of 1638, and some 2,500 Guaraní joined the exodus. However, not all reached the new site of the mission on the Paraná River approximately five kilometers from Candelaria.[105] In 1647, nine years following the relocation, the population of the mission was 1,075, much lower than it had been in Tape. The Jesuits relocated the mission three more times, and the last move was in 1760 to a site in what today is southern Paraguay.

The process of community formation took different forms on the Paraguay missions. The case of Los Santos Reyes de Yapeyú, established on the west bank of the Uruguay River in 1627, typified the process. The Jesuits initially congregated Guaraní speakers known as Charrúa, but in later years they resettled non-Christians from non-Guaraní groups.[106] For example, in the years 1665–66 the Jesuits congregated some 250 non-Christians, and in 1701 some 500 Yaros.[107] By the early years of the eighteenth century, the Paraguay missions were largely closed communities, meaning that they received few or no migrants and population growth resulted from natural reproduction. However, there were sporadic instances of the resettlement of non-Christians, mostly small bands encountered during expeditions sent to collect yerba mate from wild stands. In 1702, for example, an expedition from Corpus Christi brought 109 non-Christians to the mission. However, 21 of the recently congregated natives died shortly after their arrival.[108] A census prepared in the same year recorded a total of 6,750 baptisms of newborn children on the Paraguay missions in addition to 73 baptisms of non-Christians. The Jesuits baptized 46 non-Christians at Corpus Christi, 10 at Loreto, 7 at San Ignacio Miní, 4 at Jesús, 3 at Santa Ana, 2 at Ytapúa, and 1 at San José.[109]

The Jesuits did establish new missions in the late seventeenth and early eighteenth century, but they did so by relocating Guaraní from existing missions. This occurred, for example, in the case of Santa Rosa de Lima mission. The Jesuits established the mission in 1698 at a site close to San Ignacio Guazú in what today is southern Paraguay, with natives originally from the Itatín region northeast of Asunción who resided at Nuestra Señora la Fe mission.[110] The population of Santa Rosa grew robustly in the first three decades of the eighteenth century owing to high birth rates, and the vital rates were typical of the Paraguay missions that were high fertility and high mortality populations. Death rates were high, but in non-epidemic years birth rates were higher. The crude birth rate (CBR) was 82.1 per thousand population in 1702, and 74.1 in 1724. In 1702, four years following the establishment of the mission, 2,879 natives lived at Santa Rosa, and this number increased to 6,093 in 1731, making Santa Rosa one of the most populous of the Paraguay missions.

Following the establishment by the Portuguese of Colonia do Sacramento in what today is modern Uruguay in 1680, the Jesuits transferred several existing missions and established new communities in the region east of the Uruguay River to assert Spanish claims to the disputed borderland in the *Banda Oriental* (modern Uruguay).[111] The Jesuits relocated San Nicolás and San Miguel missions east of the river and elevated San Francisco de Borja to the status of an independent mission. They also established four new missions with populations from existing missions: San Luis Gonzaga, San Lorenzo Mártir, San Juan Bautista, and Santo Ángel Custodio.

While most of the Paraguay missions were closed communities, the Jesuits stationed on San Francisco de Borja congregated numbers of new converts as late as the 1730s, most likely from groups in the *Banda Oriental*. Sacramental registers do not exist for the mission during this period, but reports summarized the total number of baptisms of adults and children. Between 1687 and 1707, for example, the Jesuits baptized 250 adults (new converts), and another 120 in the years 1721 to 1732. In contrast, the record for Santo Ángel Custodio, established in 1707 as the easternmost of the Paraguay missions, shows no baptisms of adults, indicating that the Jesuits at this mission did not congregate non-Christians and formed the new mission community from populations at older establishments.

The Jesuits also shifted population between missions, particularly following epidemics. This occurred at Yapeyú following a lethal smallpox epidemic that reduced the mission population. The Jesuits shifted 500 families and around 2,200 people from San Francisco Xavier to Yapeyú.[112] In 1717, Yapeyú had a population of 2,873, but this number dropped to 1,886 in 1720 as a result of smallpox mortality. The population of San Francisco Xavier, on the other hand, was 5,600 in 1717 and dropped to 5,280 in 1720. Despite smallpox mortality, it was one of the most populous of the Guaraní missions. Moreover, San Francisco Xavier was one of a group of five missions located west of the Uruguay River, with large populations within a relatively small area and the missions located in close proximity to each other. The five missions were San Francisco Xavier, Apóstoles, Concepción, Santa María la Mayor, and Los Santos Mártires del Japón. The Jesuits tapped the population of this group of five missions to shift Guaraní to less populous communities. In 1717, the five missions counted a combined population of 20,181 Guaraní. The numbers dropped to 18,922 in 1720 but then increased to 19,276 in 1724.[113] Following the relocation, Yapeyú had a population of 4,360, while that of San Francisco Xavier dropped to 3,409 and 775 families (down from 1,271 families reported in 1717 and 1,244 in 1720). The families from San Francisco Xavier were organized politically and socially into *cacicazgos* (the clan based social-political unit) that were distinct from those of the original population of Yapeyú.[114]

In 1715, the governor of Paraguay, Juan Gregorio Bazan de Pedraza, visited the Paraguay missions to prepare detailed tribute censuses and to report on conditions in the missions. His reports included details on social control in the missions and levels of military preparation. The mission militia was an important element of royal policy in the Rio de la Plata region. The armories had muskets and pistols with shot and gunpowder, lances, clubs with stone heads, swords, pikes, and bows and arrows. The natives had a government structure organized around the *cabildo,* but they also had a separate military hierarchy.[115] The Jesuits assigned cabildo officials responsibility for punishing violations of mission social norms. The mission complexes contained a jail stocked with shackles and stocks for prisoners. Bazan de Pedraza also described the different buildings in the mission complexes. The report on Santa Rosa noted, for example, that the mission had a decent church, but that a new one was nearly ready and needed only to be dedicated. The natives lived in houses built of *tapia* (walls of compressed soil) with tile roofs. The report also mentioned the jail and cabildo structure.[116]

In the seventeenth and eighteenth centuries, the Jesuits established missions among other sedentary and nonsedentary native populations in the larger region. One area was in the Chaco. The missions established in the Chaco operated for short periods of time.[117] The Jesuits were unable to convince the nonsedentary native groups that inhabited the region to permanently settle on the missions and change their way of life to become sedentary agriculturalists. One reason for this failure was the unwillingness of men to engage in sustained agricultural work, which was similar to the collection of wild plant food and thus considered gendered work for women. Men obtained status from their skills as hunters and warriors, and in their ethos doing work they associated with the proper role of women would have been demeaning. The Jesuits established one group of Chaco missions among the bands collectively known as the Abipones. The gender division of labor among the Abipones was similar to the problems missionaries encountered beyond the Chichimeca frontier in Mexico.

The Jesuits established four missions among the Abipones in the late 1740s and early 1750s: San Jerónimo, San Fernando, Concepción, and San Carlos.[118] Several reports enumerated the populations of the Abipone missions. In a 1758 census of San Jerónimo, the Jesuits divided the mission population between "Christians" (those already baptized) and those still receiving religious training prior to being baptized. The population of the first group totaled 341 persons divided between fifty-six families. The second group totaled 250 persons divided between seventy-four families. The total population of the mission was 591.[119] The 1762 anua similarly divided the population between those already baptized and those receiving religious instruction. The first group totaled 363 people divided between fifty-five families, and the second group 207 in sixty-five families. During 1761, the Jesuits baptized five adults and twenty-nine young children. Five died without receiving extreme unction, and eight children and two adults received a church burial. The census also listed nine categorized as captives (*cautibos y cautivas*).[120] The carta anua for the years 1756–62 recorded the population of the Chaco missions in 1762, and by that year the Jesuits had abandoned several missions. Two Abipone missions (San Jerónimo and San Fernando) had a population of 875.[121] The other Chaco missions were San Esteban de Lules with a population of 703,

San Juan Bautista de Isistines with 647, and San Ignacio de Tobas with 314.[122] A 1764 census of San Ignacio de Tobas recorded a population of 357, plus another 135 people resettled from a recently closed mission.[123] San Francisco Xavier de Mocobis is an example of one of the ephemeral Chaco missions. In 1755, the mission had a population of 969, including 826 Christians and 143 non-Christians. Each group lived in their own community.[124] The Jesuits did not list San Francisco Xavier as an active mission in 1762. Several of the Chaco missions continued to operate following the Jesuit expulsion in 1768, but they dissolved with the collapse of authority during the period of the independence movement.

In the 1740s, the Jesuits established two missions north of Asunción, in the Tarima region. The first was San Joaquín, established in 1746, and the second was named San Estanislao and established in 1749.[125] The populations of San Joaquín and San Estanislao were high-fertility and high-mortality populations. Moreover, the evidence suggests that the Jesuits continued to settle hundreds of non-Christians on the missions, in particular at San Estanislao. The number of baptisms recorded at San Estanislao was higher than would be expected from normal birth rates, even from a high-fertility population. The population of San Estanislao nearly doubled between 1759 and 1766, increasing from 1,090 recorded in the first year to 1,930 seven years later. The carta anua reported populations of 1,415 and 1,182 for San Joaquín and San Estanislao, respectively.

The last area where the Jesuits from the Province of Paraguay established missions was in the lowlands of what today is eastern Bolivia among groups collectively known as Chiriguanos and Chiquitos. Jesuits from the Province of Peru also established missions in the Moxos, close to the Chiquitos missions. The Chiriguanos spoke Guaraní and lived in clan-based communities in what today is southeastern Bolivia. Different groups of missionaries, including the Jesuits, attempted to evangelize the Chiriguanos but with mixed results. In the 1720s, the Jesuits established a mission in the Valle de las Salinas, but in 1727 a group of Chiriguanos killed the missionary and the Jesuits abandoned the mission.[126] The Jesuits attempted again in 1733, and they established two missions in the Valle de las Salinas with the designation of Concepción and Rosario.[127] Some Chiriguano clan leaders supported the Jesuit missions, whereas others did not and instead sought to defend their traditional way of life. In 1735, groups not aligned with the Jesuits conspired to destroy the recently established missions. The initiative came from a group of seven communities located in the Valle de Yngre. On May 16, 1735, Chiriguano warriors surrounded Concepción and captured and killed missionary Julian Lizardi, S.J., and several other Chiriguanos who sided with the Jesuits. The Chiriguanos failed to destroy Rosario, but they did disperse the mission community at San Jerónimo. This was a mission established by Jesuits from the Province of Peru.[128]

The Jesuits continued to administer Rosario mission up to the time of their expulsion in 1768. As was the case with many establishments in the region, including the Chiquitos missions discussed below, Rosario occupied six different sites over the next thirty years.[129] The carta anua reported a population of sixty families and 268 people in 1762.[130] The evangelization of a larger part of the Chiriguano population occurred only in the nineteenth century, following Bolivian independence. Conditions on the frontier changed, and the Chiriguano communities felt more pressure from settlers who competed for land and attempted to impress Chiriguanos into labor. Under these changed conditions life on the missions became more attractive than in the previous century.[131]

The Jesuits opened the Chiquitos mission frontier after 1691 among native groups that practiced seasonal swidden agriculture, occupied shifting homesteads, and supplemented their economy by hunting and the collection of wild plant foods. They were also organized in clans, a social-political structure the Jesuits preserved on the missions. The Jesuits congregated hundreds of natives on the Chiquitos missions, and they were open populations, which meant that the Jesuits continued to relocate non-Christians up to the point of their expulsion in 1767. A 1715 incident related to recruitment and exploration efforts highlights the ambiguity that some native groups felt toward the Jesuits. The vice provincial sent José de Arce, S.J., and Bartolome de Blende, S.J., to explore a river route between Asunción and the Chiquitos missions. On an Island in the Paraguay River, a group of Payaguaes killed Blende and the neophytes that accompanied him, cutting off his head. José de Arce, S.J., later found the bodies.[132]

The Chiquitos missions were multiethnic and multilingual communities, which complicated the effort to communicate the basic elements of Christian doctrine. There always existed a problem with explaining culturally embedded religious concepts from the Judeo-Christian tradition. A European Christian generally understood doctrinal points, but it was a problem to explain these same points to individuals from a different cultural background with different religious concepts.

The Jesuits established ten missions between 1691 and 1760 (see map 2). They created communities from whole cloth by congregating non-Christians on new

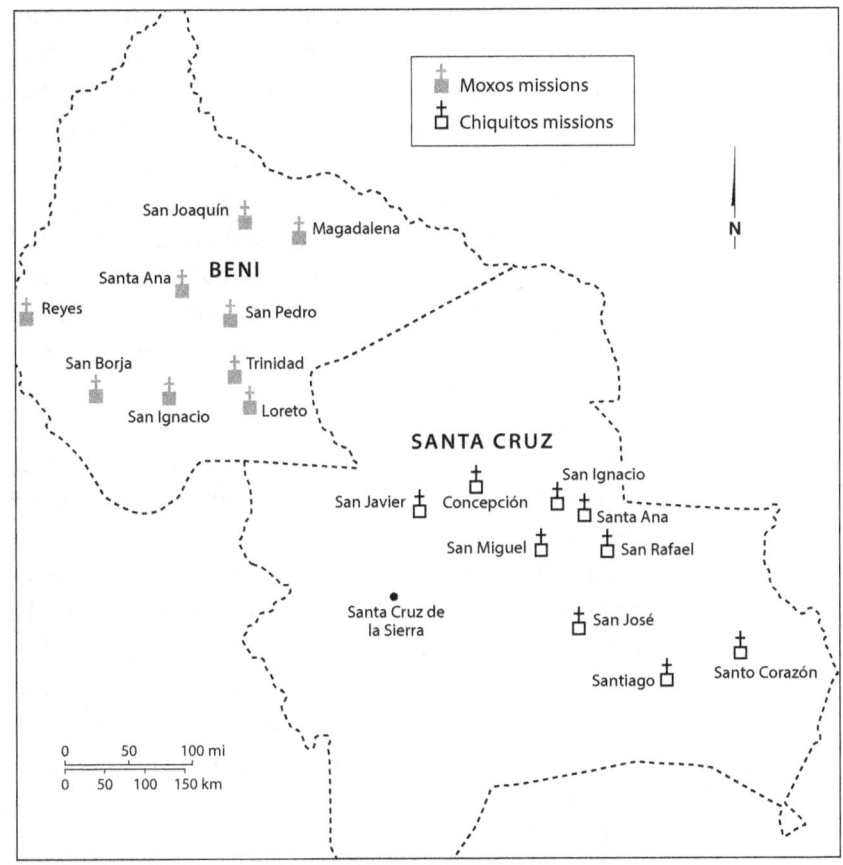

Map 2. The Chiquitos and Moxos missions.
Map by Bill Nelson. Copyright © 2017 by the University of Oklahoma Press.

mission communities. They also shifted populations from existing missions to establish new ones. The expansion of the mission frontier depended on the availability of missionaries, and there were periods in which few Jesuits were available to staff the existing establishments, let alone found new missions. For example, there was a shortage of missionaries during the War of Spanish Succession (1701–13). The Jesuits temporarily abandoned San Juan Bautista in 1709, reestablishing the mission only in 1716, although it most likely was a community periodically visited by Jesuits stationed at other missions until the number of available missionaries increased. In 1709, the Black Robes established Concepción.[133]

Several of the missions occupied multiple sites and were relocated for different reasons. For example, the Jesuits relocated San Francisco Xavier in 1696 because of the threat of Portuguese raids.[134] The Jesuits established San Ignacio de Boacocas in 1707 but later combined it with Concepción (see table 1.1). In 1745, they abandoned San Ignacio de Zamucos (established 1723) as a consequence of actions by the native residents of the mission. The three ethnic groups settled on the mission, the Zamucos, Zatienos, and Cutades, reportedly abandoned the mission and migrated to San Juan Bautista, where they were settled. The first reports on the abandonment of the mission suggested that the natives wanted to be at a site closer to the other mission communities.[135] However, three years later, in 1748, the Jesuits established a new mission San Ignacio. In 1748, the new mission reportedly had a population of 1,655.[136]

There was instability in the mission program as a consequence of a shortage of missionaries during the War of Spanish Succession (1701–13). As discussed above, the Jesuits temporarily abandoned San Juan Bautista in 1709 and reestablished the mission only in 1716. At the same time, the Black Robes established Concepción in 1709[137] and founded several new missions in the 1720s as more personnel was available, including San Miguel (1721) and San Ignacio de Zamucos (1724). Two decades later, in 1744, the Jesuits abandoned San Ignacio but established a new mission with the same designation at a site closer to the other Chiquitos missions.[138] The final expansion of the Chiquitos mission frontier occurred between 1754 and 1760. The Jesuits established three new missions: Santiago, with natives from San José and San Juan Bautista missions (1754); Santa Ana (1755); and Santo Corazón de Jesús, with population from San Miguel and San Juan Bautista (1760).[139]

To recruit new converts, the Jesuits organized expeditions they called *excursiónes*, which often lasted for months. Sometimes the Jesuits themselves went, accompanied by native converts, and sometimes they sent groups of neophytes. The narrative reports the Jesuits prepared, the *Littre Annuae*, dedicated considerable space to describing the recruitment expeditions, which were important in the Chiquitos mission program since they reflected efforts to evangelize non-Christians. In 1702, for example, two Jesuits accompanied by forty natives visited different groups.[140] On other occasions, the Jesuits sent mission residents to visit non-Christian villages. Typical was an *excursión* from San Rafael that left the mission on August 1, 1711, and went toward the Paraguay River. The expedition returned to San Rafael with 24 non-Christians that spoke a language distinct from Chiquita.[141] A second example was the

TABLE 1.1

The Chiquitos missions, 1691–1760

Mission	Founded	Missionary	Relocations
San Francisco Xavier	1691	José de Arce	Four relocations
San Rafael	1696	Juan Zea/ Francisco Hervas	1701, 1705
San José	1698	Felipe Suarez/ Dionisio Avila	
San Juan Bautista	1699	Juan Zea/ Juan Fernandez	1706, 1716
San Ignacio de Zamucos	1723	Agustín Contanares	Abandoned 1745
Concepción	1699/1707	Lucas Caballero	1711, 1722
San Ignacio de Boacocas	1707	—	Combined with Concepción
San Miguel	1721	Felipe Suarez	—
San Ignacio	1748	Miguel Streicher	—
Santiago	1754	Gaspar Troncoso/ Gaspar Campos	—
Santa Ana	1755	Julian Knogler	Relocated following Jesuit expulsion
Santo Corazon	1760	Antonio Guasp/ José Chucca	—

Source: Alcides Parejas Moreno and Virgilio Suarez Salas, *Chiquitos: Historia de una utopia* (Santa Cruz de la Sierra: CORDECRUZ, 1992), 67–71, 189–90.

1735 expedition that left San Miguel mission on July 1, 1735, and consisted of 112 natives from the mission. The expedition visited a group known as the Guarapes and returned to San Miguel on December 12 of the same year with 282 non-Christians.[142] Some expeditions ended violently, as was the case in 1715 discussed above that ended with the death of Bartolomé Blende, S.J., and the natives who accompanied him. Payaguaes killed the group on an Island in the Paraguay River.[143] Many expeditions met little or no resistance and often returned with new converts. Others were not successful at all.

As Daniel Santamaría points out, the natives on the Chiquitos and Moxos mission frontier practiced seasonal migration, leaving established village sites to hunt and collect wild plant foods during the rainy season (December–April).[144] The Jesuits documented expeditions sent out in search of potential recruits that returned empty handed. In 1740, for example, the Black Robes sent expeditions from all of the missions. Two sent from San Miguel returned with no new recruits and reported that the one that visited the Guarayos found their villages "deserted."[145] These expeditions failed largely because the Jesuits sent them out during the rainy season. Nevertheless, during the entire period of Jesuit administration of the missions, the Black Robes settled hundreds of natives from different ethnic groups. One consequence of the congregation of natives from different ethnic groups was linguistic diversity among the Chiquitos mission populations. In 1745, for example, the missions counted a total population of 14,706. The majority of this population spoke Chiquita (9,625 people or 65.5 percent), 1,617 spoke Arawak (11 percent), 1,341 spoke Otuqui (9.1 percent), 1,160 spoke Zamuca (7.9 percent), 649 were spoke Chapacura (4.4 percent), and 314 spoke Guaraní (2.1 percent).[146]

Jesuits from the Province of Peru established a chain of missions north of the Chiquitos establishments in the Amazon Basin in what today is Beni, Bolivia. The Moxos missions shared characteristics in common with the Chiquitos missions, both in terms of social, political, and economic organization as well as in architecture and the development of a similar urban plan. The Moxos missions were also multilingual communities.[147] The Moxos missions were similar to the Chiquitos missions in terms of demographic patterns. Some of the Moxos missions had open populations, meaning that the Jesuits congregated non-Christians on the mission communities. The 1748 Moxos mission census enumerated the number of natives baptized as well as those who had not been baptized. Two missions, San Nicolás and San Miguel, still had large numbers of unbaptized residents. At San Nicolás the number of baptized totaled 1,374 as against 442 unbaptized, and it was 2,822 and 622, respectively, for San Miguel. Both missions already existed in 1732, so the 1748 census data shows that the Jesuits continued to congregate non-Christians, as did the missionaries stationed on the Chiquitos missions. Five other missions reported non-Christian residents, but the total was 149. Deposorios de la Virgen María had the largest number with 80. The Jesuits also established new missions in the Moxos region. In 1748, for example, the census noted that Santa Rosa and San Simón were recently established missions only in the first stages of organization (see appendix A.10).[148] As already noted above, the Jesuits on the Paraguay missions sporadically congregated non-Christians, but the mission populations generally were closed populations.

CACIQUES AND CABILDOS

The Jesuits instituted a system of shared governance on the Paraguay and Chiquitos missions. The missionaries and royal officials recognized the status of the traditional clan chiefs, which they identified by the term *cacique,* and they organized the mission populations socially and politically by cacicazgos, the jurisdiction of the cacique. The caciques enjoyed special privileges, such as exemptions from tribute and the use of special symbols of status. When the Jesuits on the Paraguay missions registered the baptism of newborn children, they identified the cacicazgo the parents belonged to. This practice continued as late as the 1840s in some ex-mission communities, such as Santa Rosa. The cacicazgos on the Chiquitos missions were organized along ethnic lines, as seen in a detailed 1745 tribute census that recorded the population by ethnic cacicazgo.[149] The cacicazgos on the Paraguay missions, on the other hand, were generally organized on the basis of descent from clan chiefs who settled on the missions. This is not to say that there were exceptions where groups were differentiated from the general population. One example is on Corpus Christi mission, where Guananas clans settled as separate cacicazgos.[150] Similarly, when the Jesuits transferred population from San Francisco Xavier to Yapeyú around 1720, the new residents continued to be organized in cacicazgos distinct from those indigenous to Yapeyú.[151]

The Jesuits also introduced the Iberian municipal form of government based on the town council or cabildo. In a recent study, Julia Sarreal argued that the caciques on the Paraguay missions retained their status but not their political authority as other community members held positions on the cabildo. Sarreal characterized the caciques as placeholders who maintained status as petty indigenous nobility, but who did not exercise effective political authority on the cabildos. Moreover, Sarreal argued that rules of primogeniture undermined their political position, although the author does not adequately explain the relationship between rules of inheritance and the exercise of political power.[152] What is clear is that there was a difference in the political organization on the Paraguay and Chiquitos missions. The Paraguay missions were organized for war and maintained a military structure that paralleled the political structure.

In the mission political structure there were political offices and militia offices.[153] The Chiquitos missions did not have a similar military organization.

The cabildos exercised real authority, and the Paraguay and Chiquitos missions were among the few examples of frontier missions that approached the ideal of autonomous self-government, as in the *pueblos de indios* in the Andean Highlands and central Mexico. Missions on other frontiers did not develop similar levels of shared governance, even though some civil officials insisted on elections for mission government positions.[154] Charles Gibson documented a similar loss in political authority by the central Mexican indigenous nobility.[155] One important factor was demographic, or more precisely the extinction of some lineages during periods of heavy epidemic mortality. Sarreal documented instances of lineal descent over several generations at two missions, but a more meaningful analysis would have examined the family history of more cacique families over a longer period of time and at missions that experienced catastrophic epidemic mortality, such as San Lorenzo Mártir in 1739 or Santa Rosa in 1764. Sarreal based her analysis on tribute censuses prepared in 1735 and 1759 at Corpus Christi and Santa Ana. The Jesuits prepared the 1735 tribute census in the midst of the second of three epidemics that decimated the mission populations.[156] However, mortality differed between missions. Corpus Christi and Santa Ana lost population during the epidemics, but not on the scale of others such as those mentioned above. The demographic factor in the decline of the caciques requires more detailed genealogical analysis.

Did the Franciscans share effective authority with indigenous leaders on the Sierra Gorda missions? The process of the establishment of the five missions also included the election of indigenous officials. The process was presided over by royal officials, including Escandón. The election took place at Tilaco, for example, on May 2, 1744. The indigenous officials elected included a governor, an *alcalde de primer voto*, an *alcalde de segundo voto*, an *alguacil mayor*, a *regidor*, and a *topil*. The Franciscan Pedro Perez de Mezquia, O.F.M., also named a fiscal mayor, which was an assistant to the missionaries. The Spaniards gave the civil officials a staff (*vara*) that symbolized their authority.[157] The way the Franciscans described conditions on the Sierra Gorda missions and their later practice in the California missions, however, suggests that the missionaries viewed indigenous officials as subordinate to their authority with no room for independent actions, as in the Jesuit missions in lowland South America.

CHAPTER TWO

Creating Utopia

In the previous chapter, I outlined the expansion of missions in the Sierra Gorda and the Jesuit Paraguay province. In this chapter I examine the organization of the mission programs, what I call "the creation of utopia." I examine three topics. The first encompasses the creation of a mission urban plan from whole cloth and its associated construction techniques. The second topic pertains to the evangelization of the native populations, and in particular the methods employed and the measures used by the missionaries to document what they believed to be acceptance of the new faith by the natives. The final topic includes aspects of economics, and in particular agriculture and ranching.

Urban Planning and Construction

Architecture and Urban Plan on the Chiquitos Missions

A mural depicted the urban plan of the fully developed San José mission building complex as it existed toward the end of the Jesuit period.[1] The church and *colegio* occupied one side of the main square and were the largest structures in the community. On either side of the church were a freestanding bell tower, colegio, and mortuary chapel. The colegio contained the residence of the Jesuit missionaries, offices, and storerooms. The neophytes lived in small apartments in long structures that contained multiple apartments and occupied three sides of the main square. The mural does not show the use of tiles as the roofing material for the neophyte housing, and thatch most likely was the material used.[2] The creation of new communities from whole cloth required substantial investments of labor. Moreover, the mission urban plan of having large numbers of neophytes living cheek by jowl in compact villages helped facilitate the spread of contagion.

Recent restoration projects at the Chiquitos missions provide detailed information on construction techniques. The German Jesuit Martin Schmid was responsible for directing the construction of several mission churches, including the one at San Rafael that he described in a 1761 letter:

> It [the church at San Rafael] has two rows of columns, eight on each side. These columns are well worked large and thick trees like the columns of Solomon. The walls also have their columns, capitals, and pedestals, cornices, etc... They are built of crude [adobe] bricks, but have a lovely appearance because of the lovely paintings [murals] in various colors, like all of the [other] churches and altars... The floor is covered with tiles and the roof with tiles, that we had made and burned for the first time for this church, and then for our entire house [colegio]. Up to that point we had roofed [buildings] only with straw and grass [thatch]. I have built a new and large organ for this new and beautiful church.[3]

The Jesuits directed the construction of the mission complex at San José using stone. The freestanding bell tower and the church façade reportedly were completed in 1748. Actual work on the church may not have been completed until shortly following the expulsion of the Jesuits, around 1770. Work on the mortuary chapel reached completion in 1750, and the colegio with its vaulted roof was completed in 1754.[4] The Jesuits employed other techniques and materials in the construction of the other Chiquitos and Moxos missions, and there is some information on the chronology of church construction. The construction of the church at San Francisco Xavier concluded in 1752, that of San Juan Bautista between 1755 and 1759, the church at Concepción was built between 1753 and 1760, and the churches at San Ignacio and Santiago were completed in 1761 and 1767, respectively. The information regarding the construction of other churches is less precise—that of San Miguel dates to the 1740s, of Santo Corazón to the 1760s, and of Santa Ana to some time after the Jesuit expulsion.[5]

The construction process employed in the other missions first entailed planting large wooden columns in the ground without stone foundations. The building walls rested on the ground, which had been flattened and compressed. The next step was to construct a temporary roof to protect the adobe walls from the torrential rains during the rainy season. The adobe bricks were laid in between the columns. The permanent roof was extended to form a covered walk to protect the adobe walls from the rains and to provide artificial shade. The roof was a structure built of wood sections and beams joined by joints; it required few iron nails.[6] As Schmid noted in his 1761 letter, the church at San Rafael had a roof of burned clay roof tiles, which was an innovation in construction techniques. As Schmid also noted, the roofing material had previously been thatch. The interior and exterior walls were plastered with a lime-base plaster, which also provided a surface for murals and design elements that were painted by native artists on the dry plaster.[7]

The freestanding bell towers were built of adobe brick or, as in the case of San José and San Juan Bautista, of stone. The only surviving adobe bell tower is at San Miguel mission. Its construction used the same technique already described, with the planting of six wooden columns in the ground and the filling in of the space between the columns with adobe brick protected by porticos. The construction of the freestanding bell tower at San Rafael followed a different technique that did not employ wooden columns as at San Miguel. Rather, it was built using alternating layers of adobe and burned brick, also protected from the rains.[8]

The Construction of the Sierra Gorda Missions

The Franciscans provided few details regarding the urban plan and development of the building complexes of the Sierra Gorda missions they administered. The Augustinians had directed the construction of a church at Xalpa, which José de Escandón described as a jacal (of wattle and daub), but they also left sections of the convent unfinished. These were later incorporated into the Franciscan complex. The Augustinians had also begun construction of a church and convent at Tilaco, although the act of possession also noted that jacal-like structures had been built to serve as a temporary church and residence for the Franciscans.[9]

The reports on the Sierra Gorda missions provide information on the construction of new churches at the five missions (see figures 11–15). The churches had been completed or were nearing completion as of 1758. The construction of the church at Concá lasted from 1754 to 1758. The church measured 37 by 8 varas, or 31 by 6.7 meters. Three of the churches reportedly had vaulted roofs, and the 1761 report noted that vaulted roofs were being added to the other two. They are known for the elaborate baroque iconography on the facades made of plaster with different food plants.[10]

Fig. 11. Santiago Xalpa (Jalpan, Querétaro).

Fig. 12. San Miguel de Fuenclara (Concá, Querétaro).

Fig. 13. Agua de Landa (Landa de Matamoros, Querétaro).

The five missions incorporated architectural elements also found in sixteenth-century central Mexican doctrinas. The complexes at Tancoyol and Tilaco conserve the most elements. They include walled atriums, atrial crosses aligned on the axis of the main church entrance, open chapels, cloisters, and capillas posa at Tancoyol and Tilaco used in processions. Capillas posa may have been built at the other three missions, but if so they no longer exist. Architectural diagrams prepared in connection with the application to place the five missions on the UNESCO World Heritage Site list document the details and configuration of the fully developed mission complexes as they exist today, with the architectural elements mentioned above.

The extant reports, however, do not provide information regarding housing for the Pames congregated on the missions. It is likely that they continued to live in traditional forms of housing clustered around the mission complexes. The same group of Franciscans later staffed the Baja California missions following the Jesuit expulsion in 1767–68, and they later established missions

Fig. 14. Tancoyol (Tancoyol, Querétaro).

Fig. 15. N.S.P. San Francisco del Valle de Tilaco (Tilaco, Querétaro).

in California. During their short tenure in Baja California (1768–73), the Franciscans directed the construction of churches and other structures, as at San Francisco de Borja mission (established 1762). A detailed 1773 inventory described the buildings at the mission but did not mention neophyte housing.[11] The Franciscans opened the California mission frontier in 1769 and administered this group of missions for more than sixty years. A Crown requirement for more detailed reporting on the progress of the missions resulted in a more complete record of the development of the mission building complexes. This development evolved in stages but included the construction of European-style housing for the neophytes.[12] A 1791 drawing of San Carlos mission (established 1770) shows the complex of adobe structures with thatch or burned tile roofs and neophyte housing that consisted primarily of some small adobe houses as well as traditional conical thatch houses. European-style adobe housing later replaced traditional housing for the entire neophyte population.[13]

In the 1850s, the Catholic bishop of California petitioned to the United States government for the return of the mission sites to Church control. As a part of the patenting process, the Church had plat maps prepared in 1854 that showed the surviving mission buildings at that time. The maps for Santa Barbara mission (established 1786) and San Miguel mission (established 1797) documented two forms and configurations of neophyte housing. In the first instance, there were rows of buildings that each contained five small apartments for neophyte families, similar to the housing at San José de Chiquitos mission. The San Miguel mission, on the other hand, had a U-shaped arrangement consisting of three long building wings containing apartments.[14]

The Franciscans staffed the California missions for a much longer period of time than they did the Sierra Gorda missions. Moreover, Crown policy changed by the time the Franciscans arrived in California, with a greater emphasis being placed on the acculturation and integration of the natives residing on the missions and more accountability on the part of the missionaries, hence the requirement for more reports. This is not to say that the reorganization of the Sierra Gorda missions in the 1740s was a consequence of the earlier missionary failure to modify the Pames's way of life. It is conceivable that the Franciscans would have had European-style housing built for the Pames had they remained in the Sierra Gorda longer, as they later did on the California mission frontier.

Evangelization

This section discusses the difficult question of religious conversion, or the extent to which indigenous peoples embraced Catholicism. Before I discuss the Chiquitos and Sierra Gorda missions, I provide a context for the methods and outcomes of the evangelization through an examination of the so-called "spiritual conquest" in sixteenth-century central Mexico. Although there were variations on a common theme, the argument here is that the methods and outcomes of evangelization were similar. The most significant difference was the political and social organization of the mission communities and not the ways in which the missionaries attempted to convert the natives to Catholicism. The missionaries placed considerable importance on compliance with the sacraments, and they believed that the ritual of baptism marked acceptance of Catholicism on the terms imposed by the missionaries. They quantified the number of sacraments administered and presented these numbers as evidence of conversion.

The missionaries used visual aids and translated doctrinal guides and other texts into indigenous languages. Catechism was an important part of the conversion program, but the natives mostly learned to repeat statements of belief and prayers through rote memorization. The missionaries taught the same basic doctrinal points on issues such as sin and the final judgment. They also measured the extent of conversion by the ability to repeat prayers learned in catechism classes. However, there is evidence that many natives did not fully embrace the new faith as the missionaries thought they should.

Sixteenth Century Evangelization Methods in Central Mexico

In the 1530s, the first bishop of Mexico, the Franciscan Juan de Zumárraga, O.F.M., orchestrated an inquisition campaign against what the missionaries defined as idolatry. The campaign culminated in the public execution in 1539 of Don Carlos Ometochtzin, a member of the ruling lineage of Tetzcoco (Estado de México) and the grandson of Nezahualcoyotl. Don Carlos had been an ally and protégé of the Franciscans, and his execution epitomized the failure of the Franciscan conversion strategy of the 1520s and early 1530s that was characterized by mass baptisms with minimal or no instruction in Catholic doctrine. The Franciscans erroneously assumed that through the sacramental ritual of baptism, the natives had abandoned their traditional beliefs and exclusively embraced Catholicism. Dominicans and Augustinians criticized the Franciscan methods, and a 1537 Papal Bull ruled that baptisms must be administered individually and not in an abbreviated form.[15]

Two years following the execution of Don Carlos, an incident reportedly occurred at the Dominican doctrina Tepetlaoxtoc (Estado de México), located close to Tetzcoco. According to a Dominican chronicle, a high-status native who perhaps was the *tlatoani* ("ruler" or "chief speaker" in Náhuat) died without receiving the sacrament of extreme unction. The Dominican missionary was away visiting another community, but upon his return he prayed to the Virgin of the Rosary. The native revived long enough to receive extreme unction, and then died. A mural at the Dominican doctrina Tetela del Volcán (Morelos) depicted the incident. It shows demons taking the soul of the deceased native and the subsequent salvation of his soul through the intervention of the Virgin of the Rosary. The story was a critique of the Franciscans and their methods. Their protégé Don Carlos was a backslider, and he was executed for his rejection of the true faith. The noble of Tepetlaoxtoc, on the other hand, complied with the sacramental imperative, and the Dominican missionary assured the salvation of his soul.[16]

These two stories get to the heart of what I have called the "culture war" in sixteenth-century central Mexico. On one side were the missionaries, with their efforts to evangelize the native populations, and on the other were the natives, who in different ways reacted to the new religion and incorporated it into their own religious system on their own terms. The early euphoria of the initial missionary impulse soon collided with growing evidence of the continued practice of pre-Hispanic beliefs, which the missionaries defined as idolatry, and a straying from the Catholic Church that in the missionaries' eyes amounted to apostasy. In the early stages of the evangelization campaign, the Franciscans used repression in an effort to suppress the practice of pre-Hispanic religion. The "lienzo de Tlaxcala," for example, a visual record created around 1580, depicted examples of executions of natives for idolatry. Lamina 14 illustrates a mass execution for idolatry in Tlaxcala orchestrated by Martín de Valencia, O.F.M., including the execution of the tlatoani of Tepeyanco, an important community located close to Tlaxcala City.[17] The Dominican triumphalism evidenced in the Tepetlaoxtoc story soon proved to be illusory in the face of an inquisition investigation in the doctrinas of the Sierra Mixteca of Oaxaca in 1544. The investigation included allegations of the continued practice of pre-Hispanic religion, including child sacrifices and the organization of a "war council" to plan a strategy to resist the imposition of Catholicism.[18]

Following Lockhart, David Tavárez proposed a chronology to conceptualize the approach the missionaries took in the evangelization of central Mexico. In the first stage (1530s to 1540s) the missionaries attempted to present doctrinal elements using roughly parallel native religious concepts.[19] Pedro de Gante, O.F.M., one of the first Franciscans to arrive in Mexico in 1523, pioneered a linguistic and visual approach.[20] Louise Burkhart documented examples of this approach. The missionaries, for example, presented Jesus as a solar deity.[21] In her seminal study *The Slippery Earth,* Burkhart presented other examples of this, such as the effort to translate the concept of sin into terms the Náhuas would understand.[22] However, this proved to be difficult, since the linguistic and cultural terms and concepts of the Náhuas were very different from Judeo-Christian terms and concepts. Pedro de Gante, O.F.M., also translated doctrinal guides into Náhuatl.[23] However, the same problem of translating culturally embedded religious concepts remained.

Language and embedded religious cultural concepts were important in the early phase of evangelization, as were visual aids. In the 1520s, the Franciscans employed pictures to help explain doctrinal points in catechism.[24] Later examples of the so-called "Testerian" (named for Jacobo de Tastera, O.F.M.) picture catechisms survive, although there is some controversy regarding the chronology of the use of Testerian catechisms. In a recent article, Burkhart argued that the use of Testerian catechisms with commentaries in different indigenous languages was a later innovation.[25] However, it is likely that—once the missionaries first translated doctrinal guides into indigenous languages—the early picture catechisms first employed in the 1520s and 1530s by missionaries such as Pedro de Gante and Jacobo de Tastera later evolved into the catechism guides with indigenous language commentaries that Burkhart analyzed.

In the second period (1540s to 1640s), the missionaries increasingly used Spanish loan words to try to teach doctrinal points.[26] At the same time the missionaries introduced another type of visual catechism aid. As the missionaries directed the construction of convent complexes, they used the walls of buildings to create murals that graphically presented the doctrinal points the missionaries emphasized. Examples of murals survive at a number of doctrina complexes. One example is the mural program in the *capilla de indios* ("open chapel") at the Augustinian doctrina San Nicolás Tolentino Actopan (Hidalgo) and the visita chapel of Santa María Xoxoteco (Hidalgo). The murals present in heavy-handed graphic terms the concept of original sin, the final judgment, and the torment of sinners in hell. The murals attacked the ritual consumption of *pulque*, a practice that the missionaries attempted to suppress. Finally, the murals also presented the prevailing belief among the missionaries that Satan inspired pre-Hispanic religious traditions, and that the missionaries were in a war with Satan, who sent his demonic minions to try to undermine the evangelization campaign.[27] A second example is the mural program in the capilla de indios at Tizatlán in Tlaxcala. The mural program depicts scenes from the life of Jesus and the final judgment. One panel shows Jesus rescuing sinners from the maws of hell, which emphasized the viewpoints that salvation came through the intervention of the Church and that the alternative was an eternity of suffering in hell.[28] Mural programs at other doctrinas depicted Jesus rescuing sinners from hell. One example is from the Dominican doctrina at Tepetlaoxtoc (Estado de México). One final example comes from the Franciscan doctrina Atlihuetzián (Tlaxcala). An exemplum mural in the church with text in Náhuatl told the story of the Spanish nobleman Valentín de la Roca, who was consigned to hell for sins that included giving false confession to a priest and in general a pattern of violating Church rules. The message was clear: even Spaniards who sinned ended up in hell.[29]

In the third stage (1640 to the present), Spanish syntax, grammar, and semantics increasingly modified Náhuatl. Other indigenous languages have not been studied to the same extent.[30] The question remains in my own mind if the natives really incorporated the European understanding and meaning or crafted their own. Beyond the Chichimeca frontier and in lowland South America, the missionaries encountered native groups that spoke different languages, which complicated the task of evangelization. As in the case of the Chichimeca mission San Felipe discussed in the previous chapter, the missionaries relied on interpreters, which potentially created more problems of misunderstanding of key doctrinal concepts.

The missionaries produced grammars and dictionaries of native languages and translated doctrinal guides, sermons, passion plays, and other related documents into indigenous languages,[31] but the problem of the translation of key religious Judeo-Christian religious concepts remained. Acts of public theater, such as plays and processions, were important elements of religious life[32] but also paralleled similar pre-Hispanic practices. The missionaries or catechists gathered the natives for catechism, where they learned the credo, prayers, and other statements of faith through rote memorization and repetition, which did not mean understanding and acceptance. Catechism classes generally were divided by age and gender.[33] However, in the mindset of the sacramental imperative, the repetition of prayers and statements of faith learned through rote memorization was evidence of conversion.

Rethinking the "Spiritual Conquest"

Robert Ricard's strictly Eurocentric interpretation of the so-called spiritual conquest has given way in recent decades to new interpretations—based on documents written in indigenous languages—of native culture, social life, and religion under colonial rule.[34] Scholars have also offered new interpretations of Spanish documents, such as records of investigations of native religious practices that did not conform to Catholic orthodoxy. There were the early high-profile cases in the first decades following the Spanish conquest of Mexico, such as the trial and execution of Don Carlos, or the Yanhuitlán-Coatlán inquisition investigation in the Sierra Mixteca of Oaxaca. However, violations of Catholic orthodoxy continued throughout the colonial period and included cases of "idolatry," such as making sacrifices to pre-Hispanic deities such as Tláloc or Zahui, sorcery, or practicing traditional rites for initiating the agricultural cycle or the birth of a child.[35] The Crown cooperated with and supported the activities of extirpators and the repression of practices that did not conform to orthodoxy. In 1686, for example, the Crown appropriated 3,000 *pesos de oro* for the construction of a prison in Antequera (Oaxaca City) to house idolaters. Construction of the prison concluded in 1692.[36]

How did "idolatry" appear to the missionaries? A 1540 case at the Augustinian doctrina of Ocuila (Ocuilan, Estado de México) gives a sense of what the missionaries categorized as "idolatry." The Augustinian missionary Antonio de Aguilar, O.S.A., discovered evidence of baptized and unbaptized natives making sacrifices, including blood sacrifices, in a cave close to the convent. The missionary discovered idols in the cave and other idols and paraphernalia associated with traditional religious practices in the homes of several natives. The Augustinian staged an auto-da-fé that included the burning of the idols and the flogging of the natives implicated.[37] What did it mean to natives being pressured to embrace a new faith? During one early inquisition trial in the mid-1530s, the defendant Mixcoatl asserted that the missionaries did not provide for the physical needs of the natives because "they do not know us and we do not know them [the missionaries]. Did our grandfathers and our fathers perhaps know these Fathers? Did they perhaps see what they preach, and what is that God they mention? This is not so, for they lie. We eat what the gods give us; they sustain you, and bring you up."[38]

Mixcoatl's statement echoed the assertion of a group of Mexica priests in one of their first confrontations with Franciscan missionaries around 1524, as reported by Bernardino de Sahagún, O.F.M., years later. "Truly it is through the deities that one lives . . . truly they themselves give us our supper, our breakfast, and everything that is drunk, that is eaten, our sustenance; maize, beans, amaranth, chia. It is they that we ask for water, for rain, with which [everything] is made on earth."[39] The missionaries and their deity could not automatically replace pre-Hispanic deities that had provided rain and harvests to Mesoamerican society for centuries. Inquisition and Crown officials relied on the threat of punishment in the face of the failure to win the meaningful conversion of the native populations, because they could not automatically replace the old gods in the hearts and minds of the people. One can imagine the response of many natives to the missionaries who belittled and demonized the elements of their religion and worldview and tried to impose a new set of gods. The Mesoamerican religious tradition had room for the incorporation of new gods, but not to the exclusion of the old ones.

Pre-Hispanic Iconography in Christian Space: Evidence of the Persistence of Pre-Hispanic Religious Beliefs

There is ample documentary evidence of the persistence of pre-Hispanic religious practices and worldviews in central Mexico following the initiation of the evangelization campaign. There is also iconographic evidence incorporated into churches, convents, and civil structures built during the sixteenth century. Several previous studies have examined the evidence.[40] This section summarizes representative examples related to different deities, including Táloc, Xipe Tótec, and Tezcatlipoca.

The first example comes from the *tecpan* or municipal palace of the indigenous government of Metztitlán (Hidalgo), a civil structure built in the mid-sixteenth century. There is a mural that depicts an eagle grasping a scorpion, which was a symbol of a pre-Hispanic pulque deity. The tecpan in Tlayacapan (Morelos), which was also built about the same time as the structure in Metztitlán, contains iconography associated with Táloc and Xipe Tótec, deities that brought rain and guaranteed the fertility of the soil. Pre-Hispanic stones of flowers associated with the fertility of the soil are embedded along the upper façade of the tecpan, and *chalchihuitl*, symbolizing

Fig. 16. A mural in the Metztitlán tecpan depicting an eagle grasping a scorpion. This was a symbol of a pre-Hispanic pulque deity.

Fig. 17. Detail of the upper façade of the tecpan in Tlayacapan (Tlayacapan, Morelos) showing embedded pre-Hispanic stones associated with the deities Táloc and Xipe Tótec.

Fig. 18. The pre-Hispanic deity Tezcatlipoca depicted as a Tepeyollotl, or jaguar, from the Codex Rios.

water and associated with Táloc, can be seen (see figures 16 and 17).[41] In the logic of an agrarian-based society, the most important deities were the ones that brought rain and sustained the fertility of the soil, and the new religion the Spaniards brought did not provide sustenance.

Indigenous civil structures that were not under the control or close scrutiny of the missionaries provided space for depictions of the iconography of their traditional beliefs, and it is not hard to imagine that this space would be used in this way. However, indigenous artists also incorporated pre-Hispanic iconography into what ostensibly was Christian iconography in the doctrina churches and convents that served as the base of operations for the evangelization campaign. There are examples of iconography associated with Tezcatlipoca. The jaguar, a solitary night hunter, was one iconographic manifestation of the deity and was known as the *Tepeyollotl* when shown as a jaguar as in the Codex Rios (see figure 18). Examples of the jaguar iconography are found, for example, in the church at San Miguel Arcángel Ixmiquilpan (Hidalgo),

Fig. 19. Detail of the mural program in the convent church San Miguel Ixmiquilpan (Ixmiquilpan, Hidalgo) depicting an eagle and two Tepeyollotl.

Fig. 20. Detail of a mural in the portería of the Franciscan doctrina San Gabriel Cholula (Cholula, Puebla) depicting a jaguar.

Fig. 21. Detail of a mural in the lower cloister of the Franciscan doctrina San Juan Bautista Cuauhtinchán (Cuauhtinchán, Puebla) depicting an eagle and a jaguar.

San Gabriel Cholula (Puebla), and Cuauhtinchán (Puebla) (see figures 19, 20, and 21). A segment of the Ixmiquilpan church mural program depicts two jaguars (*Tepeyollotl*) flanking an eagle, and they are next to the site glyph of Ixmiquilpan. Speech glyphs indicate that the two jaguars are talking. The mural is a representation of the iconography of the night and day and the associated deities. This juxtaposition forms a key element of the pre-Hispanic iconography in the church mural program. Eagles appear in different parts of the church. Moreover, there are representations of jaguar warriors engaged in battle with Chichimeca warriors. The native artists used the walls of the church built in the second half of the sixteenth century to do homage to the deities of the day and night, and the warriors who did battle in their name.

There are other somewhat more subtle representations of the iconography of Tezcatlipoca in other convents built in the sixteenth century. One is in the *portería* of the Franciscan doctrina San Gabriel Cholula (Cholula, Puebla). The mural program probably dates to the mid-sixteenth century, based on the construction chronology of the convent complex. Antonio de Ciudad Real, O.F.M., visited San Gabriel Cholula in October of 1585 and reported that construction of the church and convent had been completed.[42] This places the construction of the church and convent between about 1540 and 1580. The mural program is a fragment of what most likely was a depiction of an earthly paradise with representations of animals, birds, and plants, and it was also juxtaposed with a depiction of the king of death. However, the inclusion of the jaguar in an area of the convent that was public space changed the symbolism of the mural program.

A second example comes from the lower cloister of the Franciscan doctrina San Juan Bautista Cuauhtinchán (Cuauhtinchán, Puebla) that depicts a jaguar and an eagle flanking a clearly Christian iconographic theme. The Cuauhtinchán mural is similar to that of Ixmiquilpan in that it is a representation of the duality of the day and night, and the associated deities. The position of the jaguar and eagle suggest that the intent of the native artists was to frame Christian iconography with that of their own deities. The Cuauhtinchán mural also dates to the same period as those at Ixmiquilpan and Cholula. Ciudad Real visited Cuauhtinchán in September of 1585 and reported that the cloister had been completed.[43] The incorporation of pre-Hispanic iconography in the cloister is also interesting because of the earlier resistance to the first evangelization by the leaders of the community. Two of the so-called child martyrs of Tlaxcala destroyed idols in Cuauhtinchán and Tecali, which resulted in the two being beaten to death. The Spanish executed the tlatoani of Cuauhtinchán and several of his associates for the murder of the two boys.[44]

Natives incorporated pre-Hispanic iconography in other forms that ostensibly were Christian. An example is the atrial cross at the Franciscan doctrina San José Taximaroa (Ciudad Hidalgo, Michoacán) (see figure 22). An obsidian disk surrounded by the crown of thorns is in the middle of the cross. Tezcatlipoca translates as the "smoking mirror" as represented by an obsidian disk. The inclusion of the obsidian disk in the atrial cross invoked the manifestations of the deity as *Tloque Nahuaque,* or "Lord of Everywhere," *Ipalnemoani* "He through Whom We Live," and *Titlacahuan* "We Are His Servants." The missionaries attempted to associate the Christian God with Tezcatlipoca, and the inclusion of obsidian disks in atrial crosses as at Taximaroa was a part of this effort.[45] However, the inclusion of iconography associated with the deity in what ostensibly was Christian sacred space suggests that this was not entirely successful.

The last example analyzed here regards the so-called "Garden Paradise" murals in the lower cloister of the Augustinian doctrina Divino Salvador Malinalco (Estado de México). Different scholars have offered interpretations

Fig. 22. Detail of the atrial cross at San José Taximaroa (Ciudad Hidalgo, Michoacán) showing the obsidian disk in the center of the cross.

of the meaning of the mural program.[46] The native artists who painted the mural program included local plants, including many varieties used for medicinal purposes. Within the side wall and ceiling vault sections of the mural program the native artists incorporated pre-Hispanic speech and song glyphs (see figure 23) that converted the mural program into a flowery song with ritual significance.[47] Moreover, the mural program originally extended to the church, as evidenced by a fragment located above the main entrance to the church. In this case and the others discussed above natives converted what ostensibly were Christian sacred structures into temples with dual meaning in the flexible Mesoamerican religious tradition that allowed space for the inclusion of new gods.

The native artists who incorporated pre-Hispanic iconography in Christian buildings did so under the watchful eyes of the missionaries. This suggests the possibility that the rank and file missionaries were not familiar with the meaning of jaguars, song glyphs, or embedded stones. A handful of missionaries, such as Bernardino de Sahagún, O.F.M., and Diego Durán, O.P.,

Fig. 23. Detail from the vault mural program in the lower cloister of the Augustinian doctrina Divino Salvador Malinalco (Malinalco, Estado de México) depicting a pre-Hispanic song glyph.

collected and described information about native culture and religious beliefs. However, it appears that this information did not filter down to most of the missionaries working in the field.

Evangelization in the Chiquitos Missions

The Jesuit reports, both for individual missions as well as the general cartas anuas, contain some details regarding the evangelization methods used on the Chiquitos missions. The Jesuits recorded compliance with the sacraments such as communions (see table 2.1) as the litmus test of progress in the conversion of the natives. The 1735–42 carta anua, for example, reported that in 1734 Miguel Bernardino de la Fuente y Rojas, the bishop of Santa Cruz de la Sierra, confirmed some 7,000 natives on the Chiquitos missions during an Episcopal visitation.[48] Individual mission reports recorded the number of confirmations: 1,286 at San Rafael; 888 at Concepción; 1,016 at San Juan Bautista; and 1,137 at San José.[49]

As did the other missionaries, the Jesuits conceptualized the process of evangelization as a struggle against Satan and his demonic minions. Lucas

TABLE 2.1

Communions recorded on the Chiquitos missions, selected years

Year	S. F. Xavier	San Rafael	San Jose	S. J. Bautista	Concepcion	San Miguel	San Ignacio	Santiago	Santa Ana	Santa Corzon
1738	—	3052	—	—	—	4909	—	—	—	—
1739	3976	3032	3894	3512	2224	4132	294	—	—	—
1742	5544	3041	4046	2426	2233	3661	238	—	—	—
1743	3525	3015	3347	2378	1887	3653	474	—	—	—
1744	3923	2454	3486	1892	1942	2948	390	—	—	—
1745	3492	2465	3391	1873	1824	4174	—	—	—	—
1746	3569	2432	3711	1563	1940	5329	—	—	—	—
1747	1856	1235	4501	2059	2761	5000	—	—	—	—
1748	2526	2948	4071	2250	1993	2450	1845	—	—	—
1749	3142	2834	4044	1492	1847	2206	1790	—	—	—
1750	2486	2450	4490	2024	1781	2275	2332	—	—	—
1755	2265	2154	4049	2101	1949	4266	3050	697	130	—
1756	2095	2256	3756	2319	2085	4404	4040	880	1233	—
1757	2415	2278	4244	2894	2144	5269	3507	1120	1221	—
1758	2204	3030	4548	2272	2092	5234	3428	2623	1263	—
1760	2284	3054	4089	2459	2952	4006	3793	1857	1412	—
1761	3014	2710	2332	3210	3195	2014	3733	1769	1509	1654
1764	2731	2865	3151	2796	3418	1922	3447	2415	1967	3200
1765	2928	2843	3227	2792	3483	1944	4590	2212	2182	3855
1766	2883	2910	3688	2244	3413	1614	3980	2441	1807	3012

Source: General mission censuses titled "Catologo de la numeracion annual de las misiones de Chiquitos," Biblioteca Nacional, Archivo General de la Nacion, Buenos Aires, 6127-14, 6467-101.

Caballero, S.J., for example, described an incident during a 1707 *excursión* sent to recruit new converts. The Jesuits attempted to baptize pagan children in the villages they visited. However, Caballero found that the children at a Tesus village had apparently been sent away. The Jesuit noted, "I wanted to baptize the young children [*párvulos*], but I found that the demon had warned the [native] priests before I arrived to the said Tesus [village], and had ordered them to send the young children [*criaturas*], boys and girls, to other villages so I could not baptize them."[50]

The Jesuits employed tactics similar to those used by other missionaries in other places and at different times. They targeted leaders for baptism in the expectation that they would bring their subjects into the fold. When the Jesuits established a new mission or brought non-Christians to an existing establishment, they initially baptized the younger children. They baptized older children and adults only when they could repeat statements of faith based on the doctrine taught in catechism classes and could recite prayers learned through rote memorization.[51] The Jesuits assumed that the neophytes understood the basic elements of doctrine, and in particular the culturally embedded religious concepts; more important, they believed the neophytes accepted the doctrinal concepts as the Jesuits expected.

The Jesuits also employed visual aids—both murals and paintings—as tools in the evangelization of the natives congregated on the Chiquitos missions. Murals survived in the church at San Rafael that present different themes from the life, crucifixion, and resurrection of Jesus. Examples include Jesus's resurrection and appearance to his disciples before his ascent to heaven, and the angel that appeared to Mary.[52] A second theme taught using visual aids was the final judgment and the threat of an eternity of suffering in hell. Graphic images of the final judgment and in particular the torments in hell apparently influenced and caused an impression on the natives, as seen from a Jesuit account that reported a dream sequence attributed to one Lucas Xarupá. How did natives who viewed these images respond to them? Natives placed a great deal of importance on dreams as manifestations of their spirituality. One Jesuit missionary described the dream of Xarupá, who described his descent to hell and his ascent to heaven:

> [Xarupá saw] a corps of very ugly demons with terrible appearance and grotesque movements of body; some had a head of a tiger, others of a dragon and crocodile; still others had appearances of such monstrous

and terrible forms that anyone would be discouraged from looking at them. All were emitting terrifying black flames from their mouths and from other parts of their bodies. They were yelling and moving around from one side to the other, imitating the dances of the Indians until they laid hands on the poor new Christian who was trembling believing that the festival was for him, and made a big fuss, yelling, "It's him, him, Xarupá, our friend, who used to be our devotee and used the malicious witchcraft we had taught his grandparents."[53]

The dream description filtered through the lens of the Jesuit missionary demonstrates a consistent conceptualization by the missionaries of pre-Hispanic religion as having been inspired by Satan. The account has demons in hell greeting the native as a former adherent to the old beliefs that the demons had taught the natives. Moreover, the demons mimicked the dances that were important elements in native spirituality and religious practices prior to the arrival of the missionaries. Either Xarupá had fully embraced the Jesuit belief linking the old religion to Satan, or more likely the missionary used the dream description to emphasize a point in an account written for European audiences. However, what is also clear is that Xarupá had seen or had been taught a vision of hell populated by demons waiting to torment sinners.

Public theater was also an important element of conversion and religious life on the Chiquitos missions, and the Jesuits provided some details regarding processions organized during the week of Easter, as well as at times of societal crisis such as epidemics. In reports prepared beginning in the 1730s, the Jesuits described examples of what they believed to be native religiosity, but they described this through the colored lens of Jesuit perceptions and bias. The 1735–42 carta anua noted the organization of penitential processions with the use of *disciplinas* during epidemics at San Miguel (1735) and San Francisco Xavier (1737).[54] God sent epidemics as a punishment for sin, and the faithful had to mortify the flesh to eliminate sin and show repentance. The 1738 report for Concepción also recorded the organization of penitential processions with the use of disciplinas during the week of Easter, most likely on Good Friday.[55] The report did not provide more detail about the procession, but they most likely were penitential *santo entierro* processions. The santo entierro recreated the lowering of Jesus's body from the cross and its being taken to the tomb. Penitents flagellated their bodies with disciplinas to atone for Jesus's crucifixion. Several murals in sixteenth-century central Mexican doctrinas depict penitential processions. One is in the church of San Miguel Arcángel Huejotzingo (Puebla). Black-and-white robed penitents, some engaging in self-flagellation, carry the santo entierro.[56] Confraternities (*cofradias*) generally organized the processions in Mexico.

The Jesuits were steeped in Marianism. They included chapels dedicated to the Virgin of Loreto in the mission urban plan and organized processions to the chapels. A second example of Jesuit Marianism was the organization of congregations dedicated to the Virgin Mary. Jean Leunis, S.J., organized the first Congregation Mariana at the Colegio Romano in 1563. The Jesuit General Aquaviva approved rules for the congregation in 1578.[57] The Jesuits stationed on the Chiquitos missions organized congregations beginning in the 1730s, and they most likely were similar to the Mexican cofradias. A 1739 report for San Francisco Xavier mission noted that the congregations had captains and sergeants; the sergeants went through the streets of the neophyte village to make sure that all attended mass.[58] The missionaries at San José reported that neophytes asked to have the church opened an hour earlier to recite prayers to the Rosary.[59] This again reflected the general belief among the missionaries that the learning of prayers through rote memorization and repetition signified conversion and acceptance of the new faith on the terms of the missionaries. The 1743–50 carta anua further elaborated this by adding the members of the congregations who attended mass and complied with the sacraments.[60] Reports for San Francisco Xavier (1739) and San Miguel (1742) attributed the organization of penitential processions staged during the week of Easter to members of the congregations. The congregants at San Miguel reportedly used disciplinas tipped with nails, glass, or thorns in acts of self-flagellation.[61]

The 1734 report for San José mission described the funeral of a congregant. The leaders of the congregation attended to the dying member, and other congregants participated in the funeral procession the leaders organized. The missionaries participated in the funeral only marginally. The description also suggests that the congregation provided cover for the continuation of traditional burial practices and the reciprocity of social relations in the clans.[62] The congregations may have also been organized along clan lines.

The number of Jesuit missionaries available to staff the Chiquitos missions was limited, and, as already seen in the previous chapter, there were periods of retrenchment in the mission program as a consequence of shortages of missionary personnel. There normally were two missionaries assigned to each mission, and the missionaries had spiritual as well as temporal respon-

TABLE 2.2
The population of the Chiquitos missions, 1713

Mission	Previously baptized natives		Receiving religious instruction	
	Population	Families	Population	Families
San Francisco Xavier	1,677	424	119	29
San Rafael	1,124	292	16	—
San Jose	1,393	306	428	163
Concepcion	950	227	263	—

Source: Individual anuas for the four missions in Biblioteca Nacional, Archivo General de la Nacion, Buenos Aires, 6127–14.

sibilities on the missions and could not always directly oversee all details of religious instruction of recently congregated non-Christians (see table 2.2). The missionaries commonly employed catechists, but this again raises the issue of the difficulty of translating culturally embedded religious concepts and the filtering of these concepts by native catechists. Furthermore, with the frequent resettlement of non-Christians, the missions generally had mixed populations with varying levels of religious indoctrination. In functional terms and with the housing arrangements on the missions, baptized natives lived alongside and coexisted with pagans still adherent to the precepts of traditional religious practices. While the Jesuits reported the devotion of the neophyte to Catholicism, the realities, and in particular the dynamic of having pagans residing in the native village, in effect served to reintroduce traditional religious practices.

Evangelization in the Sierra Gorda Missions

The evangelization of the Sierra Gorda stared in the 1530s and 1540s, continuing until the end of the colonial period in the early nineteenth century. Despite efforts to change their way of life, the Pames and Jonaces frequently resisted or at best settled on missions only for short periods of time. The Augustinian responses to the report written by Escandón and his critique of the Augustinian mission program provide a clear picture of the status of evangelization efforts at the point of the transfer of the Augustinian missions to the Franciscans. In a letter directed to Escandón, Lucas Cabeza de Vaca,

O.S.A., the last Augustinian stationed on the mission at Xalpa, identified the pattern of Pames resistance to evangelization. He noted that many Pames did not come to catechism or mass, and that non-attendance was particularly a problem at the visitas of Pisquintla and Amatlán. Moreover, Pames continued to stage ritual dances at which they consumed wine and *tepache* (a fermented alcoholic beverage). Cabeza de Vaca suggested that two or three soldiers be stationed at Xalpa to help force the Pames to congregate on the mission.[63]

José Francisco de Landa wrote the Augustinian response to Escandón's 1743 report. His document echoed the frustration of the Augustinian and the conflicts between the missionaries and Spanish settlers, in particular the hacienda owners. José Francisco de Landa highlighted problems with two hacienda owners. The first was Cayetano de la Barreda, who also held the title of protector de indios. The Augustinians claimed that Barreda had not supported their mission, and they also noted that he had some three-hundred mules pastured on mission land at Pacula. The report further claimed that the Jonaces who lived at Pacula returned to the mountains because Spaniards had usurped their lands.[64] Moreover, José Francisco de Landa complained that Barreda provided soldiers to help the Franciscans force Jonaces to settle on Vizarrón but did not provide the same assistance to the Augustinians.[65] The second hacienda owner was Gaspar Fernández de la Rama, who owned the *trapiche* (sugar mill) and hacienda at Concá, close to the visita of Xalpa mission. Rama reportedly employed Pames and provided his workers with alcohol. His report also alleged that Rama forced natives to work on his mill and hacienda.[66]

The report also challenged Escandón's contention that the Augustinians had failed to teach the Pames and Jonaces Catholic doctrine. The report charged that the Jonaces living on the Dominican missions of San Miguelito and Soriano, the Franciscan missions San José de Vizarrón, San Pedro Tolimán, San Juan Bautista Xichú de Indios, and the Jesuit mission San Luis de la Paz also did not know doctrine.[67] As the report emphasized, "the Indians that don't know the doctrine are the mecos that are dispersed throughout the mountains."[68] However, the defensive tone of José Francisco de Landa's report and the finger pointing masked the reality that the Pames and Jonaces resisted the mission program of directed social change and evangelization regardless of the order that supplied missionaries, and preferred to live on small settlements in the mountains. Escandón sent soldiers to try to convince the Pames and Jonaces to settle on the missions, but many reportedly did not want to and did not want to learn doctrine nor have their children catechized.[69] However, once the Franciscans established the five missions, they resettled thousands of Pames, often by force. Local officials sent soldiers to the mountains to burn the residences of the Pames to pressure them to relocate to the mission communities.

A 1752 incident reported by Junípero Serra, O.F.M., namely, the discovery and destruction of the temple dedicated to *Cachum,* points to another form of Pames' resistance to the imposition of a new religion and worldview, and this some two-hundred years following the first visits by missionaries to the region and eight years following the establishment of the five Franciscan missions. Francisco Palou, O.F.M., described the discovery and destruction of the site. The Pames had incorporated Spanish elements into the rites associated with the deity as seen in the practice of making offerings in the form of paper.

> The name which they gave to this idol in the native tongue was Cachum, that is Mother of the Sun, who was venerated as a god. An old Indian took care of it and exercised the office of minister to the demon, and there the people would come in order to ask the Mother of the Sun for any remedy for which they were in need, such as rain for their crops, or health in times of sickness, or good luck in their journeys, or success in war, or the obtaining of a wife. In order to obtain these things they would come to the old man with a piece of white paper in their hand on which nothing was written, as they did not know either how to read or write, but which served as a means of communication. As soon as the false priest received this the parties were considered as thereby married. Whole basketfuls of these papers were found, together with a great many small idols, and these were all burned up with the exception of the principal idol. The later was regarded by the old man who took care of it as very sacred, and he kept it covered up and hidden away and allowed only a few people to see it, and then only to such of the pagans as came in pilgrimages from long distances to worship and to bring their votive offerings and to ask for help in their necessities.[70]

Pames who had been baptized gave Serra a statue of Cachum that the Franciscan in turn took to the apostolic college of San Fernando as a trophy of the evangelization campaign.[71] However, the act of taking the statue to Mexico City did not eradicate the fertility religion. Rather, the practice of the fertility religion among the Pames persists today, albeit in modified form. Archaeologists have documented a complex located on the Cerro de Sapo near Tilaco and used in ritual dances associated with the fertility religion.[72] José Guadalupe Soriano, O.F.M., stationed on Tilaco in the early 1760s noted,

> They also perform their dances that are called *mitotes* in Castillan.... These dances they perform when they plant, when the [corn] in the field is ripening [*en elote*], and when they harvest the corn, which is called *monsegui*, which mean "maiden field" [*milpa doncella*], and they dance this mitote to the music of a small round drum and pipes and with pauses they begin to play sad and melancholic songs [*sones*]; in the middle the shaman [*hechicero*] or *cajoo* sits with a small drum in his hands, and making a thousand grimaces, he fixes his gaze on the [dancers], and with a lot of space they stand and after dancing for many hours they sit on a bench, and with a spine he pierces his calf [*pantorrilla*] and sprinkles that blood on the field as a blessing.[73]

A modified form of the ritual fertility dance persists to this day at Tilaco and is staged to coincide with the harvest. While essentially pre-Hispanic, the dance is cloaked in Catholic trappings. For example, the dancers confess and take communion before dancing. However, the dance remains indigenous and essentially non-Catholic.[74] At about the same time (mid-eighteenth century), a native named Francisco Andrés led rituals at San Juan Bautista Xichú de Indios that was based on the fertility deity but that also paralleled Catholic mass. The parallel rituals included the use of peyote— also known as Rosa María—and corn tortillas instead of the host. Francisco Andrés also declared himself to be the *Cristo Viejo* ("Old Christ"). Francisco Andrés was involved in this parallel religion from the 1730s to the 1760s.[75]

In 1752, the Franciscans also reported what they identified as the "horrible crimes of sorcery, witchcraft, devil worship, and they have pacts with the devil and others" by settlers and some natives. Serra specifically named two women, Melchora de los Reyes Acosta and Cayetana. Serra described the activities of

> a large group of *gente de razón* at the mission [Xalpa], that is to say non-Indians, engaged in these activities (although some Indians also are involved). These gente de razón fly through the air at night and are in the habit of meeting in a cave in a hill near a rancho named El Saucillo. This rancho, which is at the core of these missions, is where they worship and offer sacrifices to the demons, who appear in the form of *chivatos* and other things of that sort.[76]

The persistence of traditional practices alongside Catholicism was common in Mesoamerica and beyond the Chichimeca frontier. As discussed above, it included the incorporation of pre-Hispanic religious iconography related to fertility and other similar themes in ostensibly Catholic and other colonial structures. One example comes from Sonora in the eighteenth century. The design element on the façade of the church of the Jesuit mission at Opodepe includes representations of the pre-Hispanic fertility deity known as the Flute Player.[77] The mostly Spanish-born Franciscan missionaries faced the challenge of popular beliefs that did not conform to Catholic orthodoxy. It was this reality that the Franciscans attempted to eliminate in the Sierra Gorda with mixed results.

What evangelization methods did the Franciscans from the apostolic college of San Fernando employ on the Sierra Gorda missions? Escandón's critique of the Augustinians called for a new approach to evangelization that implied greater social control of the Pames and Jonaces. The handful of existing reports on the missions provide clues to the methods used, methods that the same group of Franciscans later employed when they assumed responsibility for the former Jesuit missions in Baja California in 1768 and on the California missions established after 1769. The Franciscans placed greater emphasis on promoting the economic dependence of the Pames and Jonaces, which was also seen as the key to keeping the natives congregated on the missions. The Franciscans attempted to transform the natives into sedentary agriculturalists. The missionaries required them to work on communal projects that included agriculture, tending livestock, and building projects. Moreover, the Franciscans assigned the individual heads of household individual subsistence plots where they reportedly grew corn and frijol for their own subsistence.[78] The Franciscans had communal crops stored in a granary under their control, and they distributed a daily food ration.[79] The purpose of the food ration was to prevent the Pames from leaving in search of food, and to enhance economic dependence on the missions.

The Franciscans concentrated their evangelization efforts on children, which was a common mission strategy. It was easier to indoctrinate children. Moreover, the persistence of pre-Hispanic religious beliefs and the pattern of resistance to evangelization demonstrate that it was difficult to convince adults to abandon their belief system. In the daily routine on the missions, the Franciscans had the adults brought to the church before sunrise for catechism. Here they learned basic points of doctrine and prayers and statements of faith through rote memorization and repetition. Following catechism, the adults went to work. Children above the age of four attended catechism twice daily, in the morning and afternoon.[80]

What the reports did not describe are the resources used in attempting to teach the natives basic Catholic doctrine. However, the Franciscan most likely employed the same techniques pioneered by missionaries from the sixteenth century forward. It was common to study native languages and prepare grammar studies and vocabulary lists in order to translate doctrinal guides into native languages. However, key Christian concepts could not easily be translated and commonly were introduced in Spanish or Latin.[81] These key culturally embedded concepts were perhaps the most difficult doctrinal elements to teach. Some missionaries learned native languages, but those that did not relied on translators, which posed other problems. Neophytes may not have learned the doctrinal points as the missionaries intended, or worse interpreted religious concepts in line with their own established belief system.

Missionaries employed visual guides in the process of indoctrination. In the sixteenth century, visual aids commonly took two forms: pictorial catechisms translated into native languages such as Náhuatl, and murals painted in the public spaces of convents such as in open chapels. One example is a sixteen-century pictorial catechism written in Náhuatl that explains the trinity and the humanity of Jesus, as well as the Immaculate Conception and virginal birth of Jesus to Mary. The document presents these concepts in simple terminology for a general audience.[82] Another example of a visual aid is the mural program in the open chapel at the Augustinian doctrina at Actopan (Hidalgo) discussed above. The missionaries introduced rituals that were in effect a form of public theater to replace similar pre-Hispanic rituals. Processions were important prior to the conquest, and the missionaries introduced several types of processions. One example in the central Mexican doctrinas was the santo entierro procession staged during the week of Easter (usually on Good Friday) to reenact the lowering of Jesus's body from the cross and its being carried to the tomb. *Cofradias* (confraternities-lay brotherhoods) often organized the processions. Another form was the penitential procession in which penitents engaged in self-flagellation to scourge their bodies of sin. Penitential processions were often staged at moments of crisis, such as during epidemics, and some santo entierro processions also included self-flagellation.[83]

The Franciscan reports do not specifically mention the organization of processions in the Sierra Gorda missions, but there is indirect evidence of

Fig. 24. Capillas posa at Tilaco mission.

the practice. The central Mexican convent complexes included small chapels usually located at the four corners of the atrium that were known as capillas posa. Processions generally started in the church before exiting and moving counter-clockwise around the atrium. The procession stopped at each of the capillas, where the missionary presented prayers or a mini-sermon on a doctrinal point. Modern-day processions follow the same practice. The five Franciscan mission building complexes have experienced change over more than two centuries. However, capillas posa still exist at Tilaco and Tancoyol missions, and they most likely existed at the other three missions (see figure 24).

Imperial politics resulted in the secularization of the five Sierra Gorda mission in 1770. Three years earlier the Crown ordered the expulsion of the Jesuits from Spanish territories. Franciscans from the apostolic college of San Fernando replaced the Jesuits in the Baja California missions. Secular priests assumed responsibility for the five missions. However, despite the claims of the Franciscans, the Pames and Jonaces had acquired only a very thin veneer of Christianity during their twenty-six-year tenure. Groups of Jonaces and

Pames continued to live in dispersed settlement patterns, or they abandoned the missions. This latter occurred with a group of Jonaces that fled from Vizarrón in 1748. The process of evangelization was incomplete.

The Franciscans established several missions in the late eighteenth and early nineteenth centuries in an attempt to congregate groups of Jonaces and Pames. In 1776, José Guadalupe Soriano, O.F.M., who already had experience at Tilaco, established La Purísima Concepción de Bucareli mission at a site near the former Dominican mission at Ranas. Soriano was a veteran missionary who had previously been stationed on Jiliapa mission administered by the apostolic college of Pachuca. He attempted to congregate Jonaces and Pames. Soriano later relocated the mission to a site known as Plátano not far from the former Dominican mission at Pinol de Amoles. In 1793, the mission had a population of 291, mostly Jonaces and other Chichimecas. The church reportedly was a structure of stone and adobe.[84] A second example was La Purísima Concepción de Arnedó, established by the Franciscans in the first years of the nineteenth century at a site between San Luis de la Paz and Xichú de Indios (construction of the church began around 1808). The Franciscans attempted to congregate Pames on the new mission.[85]

Evidence does not exist to measure the degree of success of the Franciscans' effort to impose a new religion and worldview on the Pames in the Sierra Gorda, other than their own assertions that the neophytes knew prayer and doctrine learned through rote memorization and repetition. José Guadalupe Soriano, O.F.M., rejected the claim of conversion and instead documented the persistence of pre-Hispanic beliefs. In 1767, he wrote that "most of them are inclined to idolatry, they still have many abuses, and most of them still believe in shaman (*hechiceros*) and charlatans (*embusteros*)."[86] The Franciscans had failed to achieve the objective of profound conversion.

Mission Economics

The different native groups brought to live on the Chiquitos missions were sedentary agriculturalists, practicing seasonal shifting swidden (slash-and-burn) agriculture. The region where the Jesuits established the missions was characterized by a well-defined dry and wet season. Julian Knogler, S.J., described agricultural practices in the Chiquitos missions, which was also divided between communal production under the direction of the Jesuits and production by individual native families on their own subsistence plots.

Knogler identified the growing season as being between October and April, followed by a dry season from May to September or October during which there generally was no rainfall. Toward the end of the dry season in August and September, the natives burned the vegetation from the fields in preparation for planting. Moreover, the smoke produced by the fires fended off insect pests. The staple crop was corn, but the natives also collected wild plant foods including palm dates and other fruit.[87] Knogler also noted that although the Jesuits attempted to introduce Old World cereals and other plants, non-native plants did not thrive in the Chiquitos environment. One problem limiting production was the nutrient-depleted soil, leached by heavy rains during the wet season.[88]

The Jesuits developed a dual economy on the missions, since the natives already practiced swidden agriculture. Each head of household was assigned and exploited *chacras* (small parcels of land) for their own subsistence. In general, they cultivated corn, manioc, and banana, as well as cotton, which they traded for goods from the communal warehouse. The Jesuits controlled and sold communal production to defray the costs of running the missions and the hospital. The natives provided labor for communal production, and the crops produced included corn, rice, sugar cane, peanuts, cacao, and cotton. The Jesuits also defined forest products and livestock as communal production. For example, the natives collected beeswax, but the Jesuits marketed the wax as well as cotton and cotton textiles. The Jesuits marketed communal production in urban markets in Bolivia and Peru, such as Potosi, but they also illegally marketed communal production to Portuguese Brazil.[89]

The Jesuits maintained offices in colonial cities such as Potosi to handle all commercial transactions, such as the procurement of supplies for the missions and the sale of communal production. The Jesuits also traded with merchants from Santa Cruz de la Sierra, but they did not want the merchants to have direct contact with the mission communities. In 1727, the Crown issued a decree at the request of the Jesuits that prohibited the residents of Santa Cruz de la Sierra from entering the missions. Moreover, the Jesuits limited trade to the estancia of San Javier de Pinocas, located some twenty-five miles from the closest mission. The Santa Cruz merchants traded goods, mules, and horses in exchange for wax, cloth, and tropical fruit.[90] Mission livestock was also communal property, and the Jesuits had animals slaughtered to provide meat to the neophytes. However, the Jesuits also sold hides, leather products, and fat to benefit communal funds.[91]

TABLE 2.3

Income and expenses of the Chiquitos missions in pesos and reales, selected years

Years	Income	Expenses	Net balance
1689–1711	20,099p	20,829p	–730p
1736–1740	104,777p 2r	79,934p 4r	24,842p 6r
1745–ca. 1750	78,818p	60,335p	18,483p

Source: Estado del deber y Haber de las misiones de Chiquitos (1711), Archivo General de la Nacion, Buenos Aires, Sala 9-10-6-10; Robert H. Jackson, *Demographic Change and Ethnic Survival among the Sedentary Populations on the Jesuit Mission Frontiers of South America: The Formation and Persistence of Mission Communities in a Comparative Context* (Leiden: Brill, 2015), 31.

Communal production on the Chiquitos missions did not produce a wide range of products for sale in regional markets. The Jesuits exported beeswax and crude cotton textiles to the market in the Potosi mining center. The Jesuits shipped and imported goods to and from the Chiquitos missions primarily by land. Accounting figures for the Chiquitos missions indicate that the Jesuits carefully managed income and expenses and in most years covered expenses, which also included tribute payments for the mission residents. In the first years of their operation, the missions ran deficits, but as the Jesuits developed the communal economy, the mission accounts either showed a positive balance or at least broke even (see table 2.3). The communal property of the Chiquitos missions included the estancias and livestock slaughtered to provide meat to supplement the diet of the mission residents. Records regarding the estancias did not document the size of the mission properties. Land was abundant, and the missions did not face competition for land from settlers. Inventories prepared at the time of the Jesuit expulsion recorded a total of twenty-seven estancias belonging to the ten missions. The same inventories recorded the number of livestock. The ten missions owned 45,710 head of cattle and 5,749 horses and mules (see table 2.4).[92]

Following the expulsion, secular clergy replaced the Jesuits. The secular clergy maintained the dual economic system. The neophytes cultivated the land set aside to support the clergy and to provide goods for the churches. The post-expulsion Chiquitos economy was less prosperous than that of the Moxos mission. One royal official attributed this to the lack of capital to invest, for example, in looms. Another limiting factor was market, and the

TABLE 2.4

Livestock reported on the Chiquitos missions, selected years

Year	Number of missions	Number of estancias	Cattle	Horses, mules, asses
1740	7	18	14,917	6,041
1745	6	—	26,900	6,508
1767	10	27	42,098	5,018
1768	10	27	45,710	5,749
1791	10	—	44,645	3,363
1819	10	—	13,907	1,285

Source: Robert H. Jackson, *Demographic Change and Ethnic Survival among the Sedentary Populations on the Jesuit Mission Frontiers of South America: The Formation and Persistence of Mission Communities in a Comparative Context* (Leiden: Brill, 2015), 32–33; Alcides Parejas-Moreno, "Chiquitos, Historia de una utopia," in Pedro Querejazu (Ed.), *Las misiones jesuiticas de Chiquitos* (La Paz: Fundacion BHN, 1995), 300.

Chiquitos missions sent most products overland to Santa Cruz de la Sierra and Charcas. Under civil and secular administration, the mission livestock also declined, in particular in the early nineteenth century, because of indiscriminate slaughter.[93] In exchange for providing labor, native workers periodically received iron or steel, knives, needles, combs, imported cloth, and rosaries.[94]

The Economy of the Sierra Gorda Missions

The organization of the mission economy on the Sierra Gorda missions was one of the differences between the approaches of the Jesuits and Franciscans. The natives living on the Chiquitos missions retained economic independence and provided their own sustenance. On the other hand, the Franciscans in the Sierra Gorda attempted to enhance the economic dependence of the Pames on the missions as a strategy of social control and evangelization. The Franciscans wanted the Pames to remain living on the missions and to not return to their traditional way of life.

The existing reports on the Sierra Gorda missions provide few details regarding the mission economies. However, we can construct a general picture of a dual economy that functioned in a manner similar to the economy of the Chiquitos missions. When the Franciscans established the missions in

1744, the act of foundation included the recognition of a grant of land that the missionaries were to administer on behalf of the neophytes. Francisco Romero, for example, confirmed the grant of land at the establishment of Tilaco mission on May 2, 1744. The grant included a spring and a lake in Tilaco Valley, and lands that measured one league (2.6 miles) in each direction (north, south, east, and west). The land grant provided abundant irrigated and unirrigated lands.[95]

The neophytes provided labor for communal production, which included agriculture, tending the mission livestock, and construction projects. The main crops grown on communal lands were corn and frijol (pinto beans), and the missions had granaries for the storage of communal crops. As already discussed above, the missionaries provided food rations to the needy and when crop production was sufficient to feed the general population. The missions also had small numbers of livestock that were also communal property. A report on Concá, for example, noted that the mission owned 80 yoke of oxen for tilling the fields, and some 300 head of cattle.[96] The inventory prepared in 1770 at the secularization of Tilaco missions recorded a total of 665 cattle and oxen, 44 mules, 101 horses, 2 donkeys, and 703 sheep and goats.[97]

The individual neophyte heads of household received plots of land known as *solares* for the construction of their homes and for agricultural production on their own account. They reportedly produced corn, frijol, chile, cotton, sugar cane, and bananas. The Pames disposed of their crops as they wanted, and many sold surpluses in local markets. Individual families also owned small numbers of livestock, including fowl, cattle, goats and sheep, and swine. The Pames also produced artisanal handicrafts for sale locally, such as baskets made from palm fronds. Both men and women produced handicrafts, but the mission reports noted that women marketed their products while the men tended the crops.[98]

The Sierra Gorda was still a sparsely populated frontier region, and land was abundant. The parcels the neophyte heads of household received from the mission lands were large enough for their houses and for growing crops and keeping livestock. The officials who oversaw the secularization of the missions confirmed the lands to the heads of household. The size of the parcels varied from mission to mission and depended on the topography (flat or hilly), quality, and characteristics of the lands (irrigated or unirrigated, rocky) at each site. For example, Tilaco and Tancoyol are located in valleys with level land, whereas Xalpa is located in a narrower valley. The heads of household at Tilaco received parcels that measured 858 square varas (602.9 square meters), and the land there most likely was of higher quality than the larger parcels granted at other missions, such as at Xalpa. At Tancoyol the parcels measured 1,400 square varas (984 square meters), at Landa 1,200 square varas (842.2 square meters), at Concá the parcels measured 1,250 square varas (877.8 square meters), and at Xalpa 2,400 square varas (1,685 square meters).[99]

Conclusions

The goal of the Jesuit and Franciscan mission program was to create stable communities of Christians and loyal subjects of the king. The missionaries directed the construction of building complexes with the church at the geographic center of nucleated communities. In the case of the Chiquitos missions, the missionaries had European-style housing built for native families, whereas the Pames living on the Sierra Gorda missions continued to live in traditional housing made from poles and thatch. At the point of the secularization of the missions, the Franciscans had not had European-style housing built. The mission economies in general provided for the needs of mission administration, and the individual families produced for their own consumption or sold surpluses. On the Sierra Gorda missions, the Franciscans provided food rations as a strategy to keep the Pames on the missions, whereas the Jesuits afforded the natives living on the Chiquitos missions greater autonomy. This is one element that differentiated the approaches of the Franciscans in the Sierra Gorda and the Jesuits in lowland South America. Because of the long history of the Jonaces' and Pames' noncooperation with the missionaries and because of the government mandate to congregate the natives and keep them on the missions, the Franciscans attempted to enhance economic dependence as a means of achieving their goal.

The extent of the evangelization of the native populations is one aspect of the creation of utopia that was problematic. It is difficult to measure the beliefs of the natives and whether or not they embraced the new faith. The missionaries measured conversion by compliance with sacraments, generalizations about the fervor of the converts, their attendance at mass, and the recitation of prayers and statements of faith learned through rote memorization. In the Sierra Gorda missions, there is ample evidence that the Pames did not embrace Catholicism in the ways that the missionaries intended and believed, and they continued to practice their traditional religion nearly two-hundred years after the first missionaries entered the region. The creation of communities from whole cloth was also a part of the overall strategy to change their way of life.

Demographic patterns were a factor that determined the evolution of stable communities. In the next chapter, I analyze the demography of the Paraguay, Chiquitos, and Sierra Gorda missions. In particular, I examine what effect epidemics and different modes of family organization had both on the sedentary natives congregated on the Chiquitos missions and on the nonsedentary Pames. The discussion of demographic patterns on the Paraguay missions is included for context.

CHAPTER THREE

BIRTH, FAMILY FORMATION, AND DEATH

Indigenous Demographic Patterns

This chapter documents demographic patterns on the Paraguay, Chiquitos, and Sierra Gorda missions. The Paraguay missions are discussed to provide context for patterns on the Chiquitos establishments and are another example of demographic patterns among sedentary populations. Moreover, the inclusion of the Paraguay missions interjects two factors that frame demographic patterns and were absent on many other mission frontiers, including the Chiquitos and the Sierra Gorda. One was the effect of war and the organization for war on the Paraguay missions, in particular the ways in which the movement of mission militia facilitated the spread of contagion; and the second was the connection to a larger region by navigable rivers that facilitated commerce but also the rapid transmission of highly contagious "crowd" diseases such as smallpox. These factors, which were absent on the Chiquitos and Sierra Gorda frontiers, caused instances of epidemic mortality that reached levels not documented for missions on other frontiers. The discussion here also highlights differences in demographic patterns between sedentary and nonsedentary natives.

This chapter begins with case studies of epidemics in the Paraguay and Chiquitos missions. The first is a 1718–19 smallpox outbreak, and the second is the mortality crises of the 1730s. The populations of the Paraguay missions in general suffered higher epidemic mortality than did the Chiquitos mission populations, as is shown in the discussion of these two mortality crises. Contagion rapidly spread to the Paraguay missions along the rivers, whereas communication with the Chiquitos missions was overland, and as noted in the previous chapter, the Jesuits attempted to limit direct contact between the mission populations and the settlers in Santa Cruz de la Sierra. This presentation is followed by case studies of demographic patterns on individual missions. They are Santa Rosa (established in 1698) in Paraguay, Candelaria (established in 1626) in Argentina, Los Santos Mártires (established in 1632) also located in Argentina, and San Francisco Xavier (established in 1691) in Chiquitania. Finally, this chapter discusses demographic patterns on the Sierra Gorda missions in relation to patterns documented for the Paraguay and Chiquitos missions.

The 1718–1719 Smallpox Outbreak

The Jesuits did not standardize the type of census information they reported until the 1720s. However, earlier censuses provide information that can be used to calculate the range of crude birth and death rates and population shifts caused by epidemic mortality. Moreover, there are references to global mortality rates. An example is a 1705 report that noted that in 1695, "16,000 died in them [the missions] from measles."[1] The documentation for the 1718 smallpox outbreak is limited. It occurred twenty-three years after the 1695 measles epidemic, during a period of rapid population growth. What is documented, however, is a population transfer between missions in the aftermath of the outbreak. The analysis of the effects of epidemic outbreaks must take into account different factors that include the age and gender structure of a population, as well as the number of potentially susceptible hosts, generally those born since the previous outbreak. On average an epidemic spread through the Paraguay missions about once a generation, or about every twenty years. However, a given outbreak did not necessarily affect all of the missions, and mortality varied between different mission communities.

As was the case with other outbreaks, the 1718 smallpox epidemic began in Buenos Aires, Asunción, and Santa Fe, and then it spread to the missions. Some 5,000 reportedly died in Buenos Aires.[2] The epidemic spread to the missions most likely via river traffic. Yapeyú, which was the southernmost mission, appears to have been one of the first where the epidemic broke out. In 1718, Pedro Fajardo, the bishop of Buenos Aires, visited the missions and confirmed thousands of Guaraní. He was at Yapeyú from June 18–22 and reported that the epidemic had already spread to the mission. Fajardo also reported that smallpox had broken out at nearby San Tomé, San José (which he visited in mid-September), Santos Cosme y Damián (which he also visited in mid-September), Trinidad, and Ytapúa. Fajardo specifically noted that Santa Ana and San Luis Gonzaga were free of the contagion.[3] Fajardo concluded his visitation in early October of 1718, and smallpox had not spread to most of the missions at that point. The contagion later spread to other missions, as evidenced by the decline reported in the mission censuses, and the epidemic most likely continued into 1719.

The total population of the thirty Paraguay missions was 121,168 at the end of 1717. It dropped to 104,074 in 1719, a decline of some 14 percent. The populations of individual missions experienced higher rates of decline. The percentage difference between the populations in 1717 and 1720 showed examples of heavy mortality, and twelve missions experienced a decline of 19 percent or more. Of these, Fajardo noted that smallpox had already broken out at three. The greatest declines were at Guazú and Santiago, at 51 percent. The population of Guazú dropped from 5,651 in 1717 to 2,738 in 1720, and the population of Santiago fell from 4,387 in 1717 to 2,135 in 1720. La Cruz and San Tomé experienced declines of 44 percent. The numbers at La Cruz dropped from 5,481 in 1717 to 3,069 in 1720, and of San Tomé from 4,768 to 2,659 (see appendix A.1).

There is an example of the transfer of populations between missions in the wake of the epidemic. Smallpox reduced the population of Yapeyú, and the Jesuits shifted 500 families and some 2,200 people from San Francisco Xavier to Yapeyú around 1723 or 1724.[4] The population of San Francisco Xavier was 5,280 in 1720, and it still was one of the most populous of the Guaraní missions. Moreover, San Francisco Xavier was one of a group of five missions located west of the Uruguay River with large populations located in close proximity to each other. The five missions were San Francisco Xavier, Apóstoles, Concepción, Santa María la Mayor, and Los Santos Mártires del Japón. The Jesuits tapped the population of this group of five missions to shift Guaraní to less populous communities. Following the relocation, Yapeyú had a population of 4,360, while that of San Francisco Xavier dropped to 3,409 and 775 families (down from 1,244 families reported in 1720). The families from San Francisco Xavier were organized politically and socially into cacicazgos (the clan-based social-political unit) distinct from those of the original population of Yapeyú.[5]

A second case involved the merger of the populations of two missions, San Francisco de Borja and Jesús María de los Guenoas. The Guenoas were a clan of Charrúa, an ethnic group that lived in Tape (Rio Grande do Sul, Brazil). The Jesuits established Jesús María around 1682 at a site on the east bank of the Uruguay River close to San Francisco de Borja.[6] The first recorded population count was in 1690, and the Jesuits continued to list Jesús María as an independent mission up to 1717. The highest recorded population was 357 in 1714, and in 1717 the Black Robes enumerated 283. The 1720 census showed the populations of San Francisco de Borja and Jesús María together, and the 1724 census recorded only San Francisco de Borja.[7]

The Mortality Crises of the 1730s

Between 1733 and 1740, famine and a series of epidemics reduced the size of the populations of the Jesuit missions from a recorded high of 141,182 in 1732 to 73,910 at the end of 1740. A combination of factors contributed to the mortality crises and the heavy population losses. One was the mobilization of Guaraní militiamen for service in Buenos Aires, the *Banda Oriental* (Uruguay), and on the Río Tebicuary to confront the ongoing political crisis in Asunción known as the Comunero Rebellion.[8] The second was the high population densities of the mission communities and the large number of children and young adults born since the last major epidemic in 1718 who had not been exposed to contagion, making them highly susceptible to smallpox. The third was drought and famine conditions that contributed to large-scale flight from the missions as people left in search of food and to escape disease. Flight also exacerbated the crisis by spreading disease.

People in movement spread disease. This can be seen in two ways during the crisis of the 1730s. The first was the posting of Spanish troops and mission militia on the Río Tebicuary for months. Military encampments were notoriously unsanitary, and the evidence shows that the heaviest mortality during the lethal 1733 epidemic was in the missions located closest to the encampment. The Jesuits reported a total of 18,773 burials in 1733 and a net loss in population of some 13,000. Deaths at San Ignacio Guazú totaled 1,192 (crude death rate of 509.0 per thousand population), 2,618 at Nuestra Señora la Fe (crude death rate of 307.4 per thousand population), and 2,263 at Santa Rosa (crude death rate of 414.6 per thousand population). The population of these three missions dropped from 15,803 in 1731 to 8,292 at the end of 1733. Mortality was lighter at the other missions located further away from the military encampment. At Ytapúa, located on the Paraná River, for example, the Jesuits reportedly buried 811 (crude death rate of 115.9 per thousand population).[9]

The crises, which occurred during a period of drought and famine conditions, resulted in the flight of Guaraní from the Paraguay missions. The Jesuits reported in 1735 that 8,022 Guaraní had fled the missions, including a group that created a community on the edge of mission territory that was politically, socially, and spatially organized along the lines of the mission communities they had abandoned.[10] The cartas anuas contain graphic details of the scope of the crises, which began with a drought starting at the end of 1733 and lasting until March of the following year and exacerbated by an epidemic outbreak.[11] The same document reported a continuation of the crisis in 1735 and 1736. It noted,

> In 1735, year in which there was more hunger than the previous and considerable flight by [male] Indians and [female] Indians to the jungle and distant fields. They went with the unreduced [uncongregated-non-Christian] Indians and with the [C]harrúas dedicated to the carnal trade and to increase the number of women [they] killed their husbands. The more knowledgeable retreated to Iberá Lake where they were reduced [congregated] by those who were more capable, they performed some ceremonies and took the post of parish [priest] and married others with their license. To support themselves they made hostile raids on the city of Corrientes and the Spanish cattle ranches [estancias]. In this year there were 8,022 people who had disappeared that constitute 1,354 families not counting the deaths of 2,637 adults and 3,407 children [párvulos]. Many of those dispersed [fugitives] died on the roads or in fights among themselves or for other reasons.[12]
>
> [In 1736] Troops of 80 to 100 Indians not counting the children [párvulos] and the women that followed them, vagabonded in the ranches [estancias] attacking the cattle guards. Entire troops of thieves flooded the public roads running over travelers [and] robbing them of everything they had and in cases of resistance finishing them off. The cultivator had to fight true battles against them to defend their plantings, cattle, and very lives, and [had to] put themselves under arms, being able to defeat the assaulters with death. Others were defeated by the tigers [jaguars], the rest from pure hunger. . . . Others that retreated to the mountains perished from smallpox as did others who sought refuge in Santa Fe and Corrientes and Asunción. Outside of the villages [pueblos] true bands of refugees were found in the farms, in the missions, and in the nearby fields the dead [who died] of hunger and the cold and [were] halfway eaten by dogs. . . . Every day some of the reductions [missions] sent out workers to search around the village [pueblo] and in the month of August

they returned with cadavers or a lucky one still alive, naked from the loss of speech and they seemed to be not aware of anything. Others hid in the jungles or went with the pagans [*infieles*].[13]

Deaths in 1734 reached 16,222 but reflected a distinct pattern caused by famine conditions. Some 10,132 adults and 6,090 párvulos or young children under the age of ten died. Deaths in 1735 totaled 6,044, and more young children died than did adults. The Jesuits reportedly baptized 4,520, and the total population of the missions dropped by 1,524. In 1736, the Jesuits recorded 5,004 baptisms as against 7,787 deaths and a net decline in numbers of 2,723.[14] Mortality was particularly high at Loreto in 1736, where a total of 1,321 died (a crude death rate of 308.1 per thousand population). The Jesuits prepared general censuses but also more detailed tribute censuses that were required to enumerate the number of tributaries and the amount of tribute that was to be paid to the Crown. The crisis of 1733 and 1734 forced the Jesuits to prepare a new tribute count that was completed in 1735. The tribute censuses recorded the population by cacicazgo and family, but also tribute categories such as *reservado,* or individuals who did not have to pay tribute. The tribute categories need to be carefully separated from the strictly demographic information. The censuses reported the absence of 2,620 male tributaries (see table 3.1), but because of the narrow scope of the enumerations they did not record the absence of women and children. The individual censuses contain summaries, but it is more useful to also extract more complete data from the complete texts of the counts. The tribute census for Los Santos Mártires mission reported the absence of seven tributaries in the Spanish settlements (*"tierras de Españoles"*). The census for Santos Cosme y Damián summarized the time that fugitives had been absent. One tributary had been absent for four years, nine for three years, nine for two years, twenty-one for one year, and eight fled the mission in 1735. In other words, there were instances of flight from the mission community prior to the crisis.[15] The largest number of fugitives was from two groups of missions. The first were from the missions located east of the Uruguay River, and from Santa María la Mayor located close to the west bank of the river. A total of 160 tributaries reportedly were absent from Santa María, 327 from San Nicolás, 166 from San Luis Gonzaga, 262 from San Lorenzo, and 153 from Santo Ángel Custodio. The second was the group of missions located in what today is southeastern Paraguay. These missions were closest to the zone where the mobilized mission militia was posted and also to the fugitive community on Iberá Lake. It is possible that some of the fugitives were militiamen who

TABLE 3.1
Fugitive tributaries recorded in the 1735 tribute censuses

Mission	Population	Fugitives	Mission	Population	Fugitives
Candelaria	2,970	29	Apóstoles	3,884	41
Stos Cosme	2,143	54	Concepción	5,920	6
Sta Ana	4,083	3	Sta María	2,908	160
Loreto	5,523	20	San Xavier	3,494	47
San Ignacio	3,010	1	Mártires	3,416	7
Corpus C.	2,790	67	San Nicolás	6,986	327
Jesús	2,256	20	San Luis	5,305	166
Trinidad	1,829	141	San Lorenzo	5,177	262
Ytapúa	4,381	120	San Miguel	4,019	11
Santiago	3,237	27	San Juan	4,621	1
Nra Sra de Fé	2,465	291	Sto Angel	4,501	153
Sta Rosa	1,780	31	Sto Tomé	3,262	29
Guazú	2,691	333	S.F. Borja	3,562	41
San José	3,473	52	La Cruz	4,377	99
San Carlos	2,400	36	Yapeyú	5,106	92

Source: Individual tribute censuses, Archivo General de la Nación, Buenos Aires, Sala 9-17-3-6, 9-9-1-8, 9-18-8-2.

had been mobilized. The largest number of fugitives was 333 from San Ignacio Guazú, 291 from Nuestra Señora de Fe, 141 from Trinidad, and 120 from Ytapúa. Lesser numbers of tributaries fled the other missions (see table 3.1). The Franciscans stationed on the Sierra Gorda missions reported instances of flight from the missions, but they did not specifically record examples of Pames fleeing the missions during epidemic outbreaks.

Smallpox spread to the missions in 1738 from Buenos Aires and other urban centers in the region. In three years the Jesuits reportedly buried 35,104 people, and the population experienced a net decline of 22,575. This was perhaps the most lethal epidemic in the history of the missions, and mortality reached catastrophic levels at selected missions. In 1738, the Jesuits recorded 1,528 burials at Candelaria, which was about half of the population, 1,874 at San José, 2,262 at Apóstoles, and 2,168 at Concepción. In 1739, the contagion spread east of the Uruguay River and to the south along the river. Smallpox claimed the lives of 1,279 at Santa María la Mayor (a crude death rate of 565.4 per thousand population), 1,708 at San Nicolás (a crude death rate of 336.8 per thousand population), 2,445 at San Luis Gonzaga (a crude death rate of 565.1 per thousand population), 2,681 at San Lorenzo (a crude death rate of 557.0 per thousand population), and 1,605 at La Cruz (a crude death rate of 417.0 per thousand population). In 1740, 2,400 died at San Juan Bautista (a crude death rate of 481.1 per thousand population).[16]

The multiple crises between 1733 and 1740 were the most serious in the history of the missions. Altogether, some 86,000 Guaraní died, and heavy mortality accounted for the decline in the population. Following the crises, however, the mission populations rebounded or recovered. There were increased numbers of marriages immediately following the crises, as new families were formed and growth through robust birth rates occurred until the next severe crisis, which was a smallpox epidemic in the years 1763 to 1765. There was a relatively mild measles epidemic in 1748–49, but this only slowed recovery. These patterns of mortality crisis and postcrisis recovery stand in marked contrast to those of the nonsedentary populations of the Sierra Gorda missions that did not recover following epidemics.

Smallpox was the most lethal disease that spread through the Jesuit missions during the eighteenth century. However, epidemics of other maladies including measles killed large numbers of people. Measles is a highly contagious viral infection that is an airborne disease. It readily spread in the mission communities where people lived in close proximity to each other. After smallpox, measles most likely caused the highest number of deaths in the missions. In 1695, as already noted above, a measles epidemic reportedly killed 16,000 Guaraní.[17] As was also the case with smallpox, measles outbreaks occurred when there were a sufficient number of susceptible hosts to maintain the chain of infection, generally children born since the previous outbreak or adults not previously exposed to the contagion. Measles broke out at a number of the Paraguay missions in 1748 and 1749, but it was not a generalized epidemic as had been the series of devastating outbreaks in the 1730s. Moreover, mortality did not reach the same levels as in the previous decade, and in particular there were no instances of mortality in excess of 50 percent as occurred at some missions during the 1738–40 smallpox outbreak. The largest number of deaths in the Paraguay missions was at Santiago, where 1,003 people died in 1749. The crude death rate per thousand population was 216.5, or nearly 22 percent of the population at Santiago (see appendix A.2).

There was an outbreak at several of the Chiquitos missions in the same years, and this most likely was also measles. However, although there was elevated mortality at three of the missions (San Francisco Xavier, San Juan Bautista, and San José), mortality did not reach the same levels as in the Paraguay establishments. The highest death rate was at San Juan Bautista, where 222 people died in 1749, a crude death rate of 118.1 per thousand population. Death rates were higher than birth rates at San Francisco Xavier and San José, but in comparative terms the epidemic was mild. The crude death rate was 52.1 at the first named mission and 50.7 at the second. Documented epidemic mortality in the Chiquitos missions tended to be lower than on the Paraguay missions. One factor in the difference was the relative geographic isolation of the Chiquitos missions when compared to the Paraguay missions, which were connected to other communities in the larger Rio de la Plata region by river highways. Communications with and between the Chiquitos missions was by land, which buffered these missions somewhat from the spread of contagion, and as already noted the Jesuits attempted to limit contact with Santa Cruz de la Sierra.

This is not to say that there were documented instances of high epidemic mortality on the Chiquitos missions. The carta anua or narrative report on the Jesuit missions in the Province of Paraguay for the period 1735 to 1743, for example, reported heavy smallpox mortality at San Ignacio de Zamucos mission in 1736. More than 400 people died out of a population reported in the previous year to be 847. This indicates a crude death rate in the range of 472.3 per thousand population.[18] Several individual anuas for the Chiquitos missions reported other epidemics, such as of dysentery. Dysentery is an intestinal inflammation caused by bacteria, viruses, or protozoa. It causes diarrhea mixed with blood, hence the description of the malady as "bloody flux" (*flux de sangre*). Dysentery spreads through the oral consumption of contaminated food or water, and it most likely spread through the Chiquitos mission communities through contaminated water, in particular during the dry season. Dysentery reportedly killed 79 adults and 130 children (a crude death rate of 89.2) at San Francisco Xavier in 1739.[19] The malady killed 200 people (a crude death rate of 108.7 per thousand population) in forty days at San José mission at the end of 1743.[20]

Epidemics were one of the factors that shaped demographic patterns on the Paraguay and Chiquitos missions, but as already mentioned there were significant differences in patterns on the two groups of missions. How did natives respond to epidemics? The following section discusses native responses to epidemics. It is followed by summaries of demographic trends at selected missions. These case studies provide the basis for characterizing the differences in demographic patterns.

Native Responses to Epidemics

The missionaries who left written records generally did not record native responses to epidemic outbreaks, although there are several exceptions that provide indications of the horrors that contagion produced and what we can call the human side of demographics. We can judge native responses on the basis of observed behavior, such as flight in the face of epidemic outbreaks. One of the earliest mentions of flight in the Paraguay missions was in a 1618 report on Ytapúa mission that noted that an epidemic broke out in conjunction with a famine. Many Guaraní left in search of food and to escape contagion. But in their flight from the missions, the Guaraní also facilitated the spread of contagion. Moreover, non-Christians, in particular traditional religious leaders, used the outbreaks of epidemics to challenge the Jesuit missionaries. The Jesuits generally baptized those on the point of death. The rite of baptism became identified with causing death, and the traditional religious leaders who saw their status and authority challenged by the Jesuits used this identification as potent propaganda.[21] This occurred on mission frontiers from Canada to South America.

Disease treatment was rudimentary, and in the case of the Paraguay missions the Jesuits quarantined the sick and those that had been exposed to contagion. One can only imagine what the Guaraní thought of the plague hospitals, which, in many instances, became a place only to die. One detailed report of a 1786 smallpox outbreak at San José and Apóstoles missions described the creation of temporary plague hospitals and the measures taken to isolate the sick.[22] At Apóstoles the civil administrator and the doctor assigned to combat the smallpox outbreak selected a site outside of the mission for the temporary hospital. It was built in four days and consisted of two structures: the first one for the sick, and the second for those recovering from the malady. The site had water and was close to the cemetery. The doctor had 178 people transferred to the hospital, including one individual who reportedly was seriously ill. The report also noted that the family members of two individuals "had them hidden in the [mission] Village."[23]

The report recorded conditions in the temporary plague hospital in rather graphic terms. It was low and narrow. Coupled with the horror caused by the malady, the conditions in the hospital described by one official present make it easy to understand why family members hid the sick. The walls were described as being "of cane [*caña*], in it there are three rows of beds and in most two sick [people] in each one, that with the heat and sweating of so many smallpox [ridden] bodies it is insupportable on entering there."[24]

Given the rudimentary medical treatment and conditions described in the hospital, it is a wonder that so few died during the outbreak. It is difficult today to imagine the horror and dread of the outbreak of such highly contagious and lethal, painful, and disfiguring diseases as smallpox and measles, which in relatively short periods of time killed large percentages of the populations of communities. Moreover, individuals who survived saw loved ones, spouses, children, parents, and siblings die. Survivors had to pick up the pieces and in many instances form new families or, in the case of children, find adults to care for them. Today in the modern world we have no comparative point of reference to understand the horrors of catastrophic epidemics and their effects on people. The most recent Ebola outbreak in Africa received considerable attention in the world press, but mortality rates were small when compared to smallpox and measles mortality on the missions. The same can be said of the Zika virus, which is now receiving considerable attention.

How can we explain the resilience of the natives living on the Paraguay missions in the face of what at times was very high mortality caused by frightening and disfiguring diseases? By way of a hypothesis I would like to suggest that one key may have been the nature of social and political organization on the Paraguay missions, which was different from the missions administered by the Franciscans from the apostolic college of San Fernando, who later also administered the Baja California (1768–73) and California (1769–1834) missions. As noted above, the Jesuits and royal officials left the clan system fairly intact on the Paraguay and Chiquitos missions, and they instituted a system of shared governance. The clan chiefs retained status on the missions. Moreover, the natives living on the missions developed a sense of collective identity as residents of the missions, an identity that was reinforced in the case of the Paraguay missions by the military organization and the hierarchy of political and military positions. This can be seen, for example, in the native responses to the Treaty of Madrid (1750), which contained a provision to transfer the seven Paraguay missions located east of the Uruguay River to the jurisdiction of the Portuguese in an exchange of territory. The indigenous leaders resisted the transfer of the missions in rhetoric that showed their identity with the communities that they had developed over several generations. The Jesuit mission program was less disruptive of the social-political organization of the clan-based societies of lowland South America.[25]

The Franciscan approach, on the other hand, was different, and it marked one significant variation between the three groups of missions. The Franciscans had received a mandate from royal officials to congregate the Pames and Jonaces and to keep them on the missions. In other words, they were to finish the job that earlier missionaries had failed to accomplish in nearly two hundred years. The Franciscans received military support, and soldiers went to the extent of burning houses to force the natives to relocate. The extant reports do not shed much light on the measures of social control on the missions, but there is ample evidence from missions that the same group of Franciscans administered later, and in particular the California missions founded after 1769. The natives brought to live on the California missions were subject to stricter social controls that showed little regard for high-status individuals, and the Franciscans attempted to impose social norms and a moral code that were alien to indigenous culture. They used different forms of corporal punishment to maintain discipline, and in particular to the discipline of the labor force. With the beginning of civil war in central Mexico in 1810, the Franciscan missionaries assumed the responsibility of supplying the military in California and increased agricultural production, which also implied more labor discipline. The control measures that disrupted social relations and the labor demands on the California missions were conducive to high mortality and demographic collapse. The housing arrangements on the California missions, and in particular the dormitories for single women, also contributed to the spread of contagion. Junípero Serra, O.F.M., who was also stationed at Xalpa in the Sierra Gorda, was the architect of the California mission system. He based its structure, in part, on his previous experience in the Sierra Gorda.[26]

The Population of Santa Rosa de Lima Mission, Paraguay

Detailed demographic studies of early modern populations rely on several sources that include registers of baptisms, marriages, and burials, as well as censuses prepared with varying levels of detail. Only small fragments of sacramental registers survive for the Paraguay missions, but there is a short run of baptisms for Santa Rosa in the 1750s and 1760s. As discussed in the introduction, the Jesuits prepared narrative accounts on the missions known as *Littre Annuae,* detailed tribute censuses, as well as annual censuses that reported different categories of information. The *Annua Enumeratio Reductionum* divided the mission populations into age and gender categories as well as civil status. The *Católogo de la numeración annual de las Doctrinas,* on the other hand, also summarized the number of baptisms, marriages, and burials for each mission. Since the Paraguay missions had closed populations, which means that the Black Robes congregated few non-Christians on the mission communities, the figures on the number of baptisms corresponds to the number of births. The Jesuits, who prepared both types of censuses, did not standardize the census format until the 1720s. Not all survive, but there is a large enough sample to reconstruct vital rates and demographic patterns.[27]

Santa Rosa was one of the last missions in Paraguay established in 1698 at a site close to San Ignacio Guazú in what today is southern Paraguay, with natives originally from the Itatín region northeast of Asunción who resided at Nuestra Señora la Fe mission.[28] The population of Santa Rosa grew robustly in the first three decades of the eighteenth century owing to high birth rates, and the vital rates were typical of the Paraguay missions that were high-fertility and high-mortality populations. Death rates were high, but in non-epidemic years birth rates were higher. The crude birth rate for Santa Rosa was 82.1 per thousand population in 1702, and 74.1 in 1724. In 1702, four years following the establishment of the mission, 2,879 natives lived at Santa Rosa, and this number increased to 6,093 in 1731, making Santa Rosa one of the most populous of the Paraguay missions (see appendix A.3).

The 1718–19 smallpox epidemic interrupted the growth of the population of Santa Rosa.[29] In examining the effects of epidemic mortality, it is necessary to take into consideration mortality patterns in previous outbreaks. Epidemics generally culled the population of those born since the previous outbreak, which would be children defined in the mission censuses as párvulos (under the age of ten) and young adults (age ten to 20). Any difference can be explained, in part, as being related to what occurred during previous outbreaks. There are no figures on births or deaths, but the scale of the decline can be measured as the percentage change in the population between 1717 and 1720, the two years for which censuses exist. In 1717, the population of Santa Rosa was 5,389, and dropped to 4,230 in 1720, which was a decline of 21.6 percent, or a crude death rate of about 210 per thousand. As I noted above, Bishop Pedro

Fajardo of Buenos Aires visited the missions in 1718 and confirmed thousands of Guaraní. However, he did not report that the contagion had reached Santa Rosa at the time of his visit.[30]

The epidemics that spread through the missions in 1733, 1735–36, and again in 1738–40, killed many on the missions. The crude death rate at Santa Rosa was about 414.6 per thousand population in 1733 during the first of the three outbreaks, and 44.9 per thousand population in 1736 during the second. Deaths in 1733 were distributed between 900 adults and 1,363 párvulos. The mission population declined by 76 percent between 1731 and 1736, and it was 1,671 at the end of 1736 (see appendix A.3). The 1738 to 1740 smallpox epidemic appears to have killed few people at Santa Rosa. The previous two outbreaks culled the population, and the numbers began to slowly grow again. Between 1736 and 1738, the population increased from 1,671 to 1,828, or a growth in numbers of 9 percent. The minimal effect of smallpox on the population of Santa Rosa was an important factor in the high mortality from smallpox in 1764. There was nearly thirty years between catastrophic epidemics. The measles outbreak in 1748 killed a smaller number of people: a total of 249 died on the year, or a crude death rate of 195.8. The population of Santa Rosa recovered and grew following the epidemics of the 1730s. The crude birth rate in 1736 was 189.3 per thousand population, which was the highest birth rate recorded in the mission and may have included baptisms of non-Christians congregated there. In 1746, the population was 2,288. It reached 3,056 in 1756 and 3,196 in 1760. A fragment of a baptismal register survived for the years 1754 to 1763.[31] In ten years the Jesuits baptized 1,809 children, or an average of 181 per year. In this period the population experienced robust growth.

The situation was similar at Loreto, the other mission that suffered catastrophic mortality during the 1763–65 smallpox epidemic. The crude death rate at Loreto was 145.0 in 1733 and 308.4 in 1736. The total decline in the population was 68 percent. Following the 1736 epidemic, the population of Loreto recovered and grew. For example, it increased by 15 percent between 1736 and 1738. One of the mechanisms for population growth was the formation of new families following the earlier epidemics, as well as higher birth rates. This can be seen in increased numbers of marriages. Marriages at Loreto totaled 14 in 1724 and 59 in 1728 (see appendix A.5). This increased to 263 in 1733. Guaraní women also married at a young age—soon after puberty at about 13 or 14 years of age—and had large numbers of children.[32]

In 1750, the kings of Spain and Portugal signed the Treaty of Madrid to define the boundaries of Portuguese Brazil and the Spanish territories in South America. Under the terms of the treaty, Spain ceded the territory of the seven Jesuit missions located east of the Uruguay River to Portugal in exchange for Colonia do Sacramento, located in modern Uruguay. One clause in the treaty called for joint Spanish-Portuguese military action should the Guaraní residents of the missions resist the transfer of jurisdiction. The Spanish government gave the Guaraní residents of the seven missions the option to relocate to Spanish territory or remain under Portuguese rule. The Guaraní clan leaders of the seven missions chose to resist the transfer of jurisdiction. In 1755, the Guaraní militia from the seven missions forced a Spanish military force to withdraw from mission territory, but a larger joint Spanish-Portuguese force routed the Guaraní militia in the following year at the battle of Caibaté.

In 1762, a new Spanish king unilaterally annulled the Treaty of Madrid and ordered the reoccupation of the mission territory east of the Uruguay River. Another decade of declared and undeclared war ensued as Spain and Portugal disputed the borderland region of Rio Grande do Sul. In 1777, the two countries signed the Treaty of San Ildefonso, which defined the boundaries of Brazil and Spanish territory in South America until the early nineteenth century. The mission territory east of the Uruguay River remained under Spanish control until 1801.[33]

Paraguay mission censuses between 1756 and 1766 documented the Guaraní diaspora from the seven eastern missions and the reoccupation of the eastern missions after 1762. The largest number of refugees went to those missions immediately west of the Uruguay River and closest to the territory transferred to the Portuguese. The year 1759 found 9,133 of the refugees living at seven missions in this area (Concepción, San Francisco Xavier, San Carlos, San José, Apóstoles, Los Santos Mártires, and Santa María la Mayor). At the time of the relocation, royal officials believed that the transfer of population would be permanent. Where possible, the Jesuits moved the Guaraní from the eastern missions to missions to which there were historical, social, or family ties so as to make the influx of new population as least disruptive as possible. The Jesuits had transferred Guaraní from this district to establish several of the eastern missions at the end of the seventeenth century, and social and familial links still existed.

Smaller numbers of refugees were relocated to other Jesuit missions. A total of 5,133 lived on missions located in what today is southeastern Paraguay

(Trinidad, Santos Cosme y Damián, Jesús de Tavarangue, Ytapúa, Santa Rosa, Santiago, and Nuestra Señora la Fe). Several missions of this group had relatively small populations and could easily absorb the influx. In 1759, for example, Santos Cosme y Damián had a population of 1,672. At that time the mission occupied a site near the west bank of the Paraná River, close to several other missions (Santiago, Nuestra Señora la Fe, Santa Rosa, and San Ignacio Guazú). The influx of refugees from the eastern missions may have been the deciding factor in the decision to relocate Santos Cosme y Damián in 1760 to a new site in the same area, west of the Paraná River but further away from other missions so as to avoid any potential conflicts over land with nearby missions.[34] In 1753, the population of the four neighboring missions totaled 13,495.[35] In 1765, following the formal conclusion of the war, 2,207 refugees still resided on three missions, and in the following year, when the majority of the refugees had already returned to the eastern mission sites, 2,072 refugees still remained.

Two missions located in modern Corrientes on the west bank of the Uruguay River hosted 3,782 refugees in 1759. The majority (3,721) resided on Santo Tomé, located across the river from San Francisco de Borja, one of the eastern missions. The Guaraní residents of San Francisco de Borja had historical, social, and perhaps familial links to the residents of Santo Tomé, and unlike the establishments in other parts of the Paraguay mission territory, Santo Tomé was located at some distance from neighboring missions. Thus there was no potential for conflicts over land. In 1759, the population of Santo Tomé was 3,277, and in that year there were 3,721 Guaraní from San Francisco de Borja at the mission that Spanish officials had relocated the short distance across the Uruguay River. Some Guaraní remained in the territory now claimed by Portugal under the terms of the treaty. In 1759, there were 3,836 Guaraní refugees living on estancias in the former mission territory now under Portuguese jurisdiction. These refugees apparently relocated later to the missions west of the Uruguay River.

Following the Spanish abrogation of the Treaty of Madrid, the Guaraní population of the seven eastern missions returned to their communities. However, the reoccupation of the eastern missions was a graduated process taking several years, with the population of the missions located closest to Portuguese settlements (San Juan Bautista, Santo Ángel Custodio, San Luis Gonzaga) recovering at a slower rate. Following the cessation of hostilities during the Seven Years War, Spain and Portugal fought an undeclared war for control of Rio Grande do Sul that lasted a decade. In 1766, there were 3,187

BIRTH, FAMILY FORMATION, AND DEATH   113

refugees from these two missions still residing at other missions, and they were there when smallpox spread through the missions.

In 1763, a Spanish army used the Paraguay missions as a base of operations for an invasion of Portuguese settlements in Rio Grande do Sul. The soldiers carried smallpox into the mission district. A severe epidemic spread through the missions at the end of 1763, killing at least 12,029 Guaraní in the last two years of the outbreak, as reported in the 1764 and 1765 censuses that summarized smallpox deaths. The contagion first broke out at Santos Cosme y Damián mission, where the Jesuits recorded 331 burials in 1763, or a crude death rate of 215.6 per thousand population. The contagion had run its course by early 1764, as the number of deaths at the mission dropped to 144 in 1764 and 173 in the following year.[36] Contagion next broke out at Santa María la Mayor at the end of 1763, continuing into the next year. In 1763, the number of Guaraní who died there was 316; another 712 died in 1764. The crude death rate reached 123.7 in the first year and 354.8 in the second. From these two missions, smallpox spread to almost all of the Paraguay establishments.

Smallpox spread to Santa Rosa at the end of 1763 and turned particularly lethal in 1764. The crude death rate in 1763 reached 69.2 per thousand, which was more than the crude birth rate of 57.1 per thousand. Burials totaled 228, up from 177 recorded in 1762. In the following year, a total of 1,614 natives died, with 1,199 being adults and 415 being párvulos. The 1764 and 1765 general censuses also recorded the number of deaths attributed to smallpox, and the contagion claimed the lives of 1,596 at Santa Rosa, or 98.9 percent of all deaths on the year. The crude death rate reached 490.3, which was one of the highest recorded in the Paraguay missions. The population declined to 1,934 at the end of 1765. Smallpox spread to Loreto mission in 1765 and killed 1,833. Total burials at Loreto in 1765 reached 2,306, where 198 of those were adults and the remainder, or 2,108, were young children. This reflected a crude death rate of 464.6 per thousand population. The population of Loreto dropped from 4,937 in 1764 to 2,395 in 1765.[37] The populations of Santa Rosa and Loreto were particularly vulnerable to smallpox in the early 1760s as a consequence of the patterns of mortality during the epidemics in the 1730s. The first two epidemics culled the population of Santa Rosa and Loreto, but few died from smallpox during the 1738–40 outbreak. The number of potentially susceptible hosts was high at both missions in the early 1760s.

The population of Santa Rosa recovered slowly following the devastating smallpox epidemic, and it continued to grow in the years immediately following the Jesuit expulsion and their replacement by Franciscans. Two factors were important in the recovery of the mission population. First, despite the heavy mortality, women of child-bearing age still constituted a large percentage of the total mission population. The percentage of females as a percentage of the total population of Santa Rosa dropped following the epidemic, but not to the point of causing a gender imbalance in the population. The same occurred at Loreto. The percentage of the female population dropped from 53.6 in 1764 to 49.2 in 1765. The second factor that contributed to the recovery of the mission's population was an increase in family formation following the epidemic, as shown in an increase in the number of marriages (see appendix A.5). The Jesuits stationed at both Santa Rosa and Loreto performed 70 marriages prior to the epidemic. This number increased to 238 at Santa Rosa and 303 at Loreto. This also led to increased birth rates. In 1767, the population of Santa Rosa was 2,243, and it increased slightly to 2,265 in 1772.

The Jesuit expulsion from the Paraguay missions in 1767 resulted in a sea-change in demographic patterns on Santa Rosa. Franciscans replaced the Jesuits there, and royal officials created a civil administration to replace the Jesuit administrative system.[38] In the 1780s and 1790s, the population of Santa Rosa declined as a consequence of outmigration and epidemics. In 1785, there were a total of 1,264 inhabitants; there were 1,261 in 1801 and 1,193 in 1802. The 1799 census documented outmigration. In that year 1,228 natives lived on the mission, and another 286 were absent. Royal officials classified them as "fugitives" since they were supposedly legally tied to the missions.[39] Of those absent, 218 or 76.2 percent were men and boys of working age. Only 55 women (19.2 percent) were absent. Many left the mission to find work in the expanding regional economy.

A second fragmentary baptismal register survives for Santa Rosa for the years 1806 to 1828, and it documents important changes in the population of Santa Rosa. It documents continuity in the social and political role of the cacicazgo. Following the Jesuit expulsion, the priests continued to record the cacicazgo that the parents belonged to at the time of the baptism of their children.[40] The caciques retained social and political authority, even when some no longer had subjects or only a greatly reduced number of subjects. At about the same time, non-natives settled on Santa Rosa. Between 1806 and 1827, the priests at Santa Rosa baptized 483 non-native children. They also baptized 461 children of native couples in the years 1822 to 1828, or an average of 66 per year. By the end of the 1820s, Santa Rosa was becoming an ethnically mixed community.

The Population of Candelaria Mission (Argentina)

The Jesuits established Candelaria mission in 1626 at a site east of the Uruguay River in what today is Rio Grande do Sul, Brazil. The mission operated at this site until 1637, when the Jesuits evacuated the mission residents to a new site in the face of bandeirante raids. They refounded the mission at a site on the east bank of the Paraná River, which was also the definitive site of the mission community. In the aftermath of the bandeirante raids of the 1620s and 1630s, the Jesuits relocated the bulk of the missions to the same region between the Paraná and Uruguay Rivers. In 1643, there were ten missions located on and close to the Paraná River in the Paraná District, having a total population of 16,011. They were Candelaria, Santos Cosme y Damián, San Ignacio Guazú, Ytapúa, Santa Ana, Loreto, San Ignacio Yaveviry (Miní), San Carlos, San José, and Corpus Christi. In the same year, there were ten missions located along the western bank of the Uruguay River in the Uruguay District. These tens missions had a population of 19,982. They were Concepción, San Miguel, Santa María la Mayor, Apóstoles, Los Santos Mártires, San Nicolás, San Francisco Xavier, La Asunción (La Cruz), Santo Tomé, and Yapeyú. Two additional missions, Santiago and Nuestra Señora la Fe, had a combined population of 3,500 in 1643. This populations had been relocated from the Itatín missions located in northern Paraguay. The Jesuits relocated Santos Cosme in 1638 to a site very close to Candelaria, and from the 1660s until 1720 they administered it as a part of Candelaria, although they enumerated the populations of the two separately. The same was done with San Nicolás, which was also merged with Apóstoles in the 1660s until it was relocated to a site east of the Uruguay River in the 1680s.[41]

The population of Candelaria mission grew slowly during the last decades of the seventeenth century. Its growth was interrupted periodically by epidemics and subsistence crises. One such crisis occurred in the 1640s, and the population of Candelaria experienced a net decline of 413 between 1643 and 1647. The population of Santos Cosme saw in the same period a decline of 1,025. In 1657, Candelaria counted a population of 1,471 divided among twenty *cacicazgos*. This number increased to 2,596 in 1702 and 3,275 in 1717, the year before a lethal smallpox outbreak. The mission experienced a net decline in population from the 1717 figure to 2,641 in 1719. Santos Cosme did not experience such a large net decline. The population was 2,033 in 1717 and 1,851 in 1719.[42] In 1720, the Jesuits relocated Santos Cosme to a new site about five kilometers from Candelaria and administratively separated the two missions.

In the 1720s and early 1730s, Candelaria experienced robust population growth. One factor was the large percentage of women in relation to the total population. This percentage was as high as 57 percent in 1736. The population grew from 2,506 in 1720 to 3,317 in 1731, on the eve of the mortality crises of the 1730s. The 1733 outbreak caused only light mortality at Candelaria, with a crude death rate of 61.6 and a net decline in population of 50 (see appendix A.6). The heaviest mortality at Candelaria was in 1738, with a total of 1,628 deaths recorded (1,163 adults and 365 párvulos). This was a significant increase in the numbers of deaths from the 124 reported in the previous year. In contrast, deaths at Santos Cosme totaled only 318 (220 adults and 98 párvulos) in 1738.[43] The population of Candelaria dropped from 3,049 reported at the end of 1736 to 1,511 at the end of 1738, suggesting mortality in the range of 50 percent.

With the formation of new families and robust birth rates following the crises, the population of Candelaria recovered slowly. The population grew to 2,266 in 1754; by 1764 it had reached 2,817, and on the eve of the Jesuit expulsion from the missions in 1767 it had reached 3,064 (see appendix A.6). Mortality at Candelaria was relatively low during the lethal 1763–65 smallpox outbreak. The Jesuits recorded only one smallpox death at the mission in 1765.[44]

The population of Candelaria dropped in the decades following the Jesuit expulsion as a consequence of outmigration and epidemics. The population was 3,077 in the first postexpulsion census prepared in 1772; it was 1,513 in 1783 and 1,565 in 1799; by 1803 it fell to 1,400, and in 1807 it was counted at 1,240.[45] The largest part of the population decline resulted from outmigration. A smallpox epidemic in 1798 claimed the lives of 100 Guaraní at Candelaria (a moderate crude death rate of 68.0 per thousand population).[46] A detailed 1801 census of tributaries documented the scale of outmigration from Candelaria mission. The population of the mission was divided between twenty-nine cacicazgos, but the census also reported that six of the caciques themselves were fugitives. The census reported that 1,354 Guaraní still lived at the mission, but that 624 were absent.[47]

The Population of Los Santos Mártires Mission (Argentina)

In what today is Rio Grande do Sul, Brazil, the Jesuits in 1628 established the Los Santos Mártires mission in the Tape region east of the Uruguay River. They relocated the mission to a site west of the Uruguay River in the 1630s as a response to bandeirante raids. The population of the mission grew during the course of the seventeenth century following a second relocation of the community to yet another site west of the Uruguay River in the late 1630s. In 1643, there were 1,040 Guaraní living on the mission, and their numbers increased to 1,980 in 1682, to 2,371 in 1691, and to 2,124 in 1702, which was two years before the relocation of the missions to its final site in 1704. In 1731, the population totaled 3,874, but this was just prior to the first of three epidemic outbreaks during the decade that spread through the missions. The numbers declined to 2,777 in 1739. A tribute census prepared in August of 1735 provides a detailed look at the population of the mission at one point in time, and in particular it showed the effects of epidemics on the mission population. There are several indications of heavy mortality from two epidemics that struck the mission population in 1733 and 1735. There was a large number of orphans—a total of 129 boys and 131 girls. Moreover, an analysis of the actual family size shows that the majority of families consisted of a married couple only (35 percent), or a couple with one (28.3 percent) or two children (19.4 percent). If this structure had persisted over time, the population of the missions at best would have remained stable with minimal growth, or perhaps would have declined (see appendix A.7). Moreover, it suggests heavy mortality among young children during the epidemics in 1733 and 1735. Data from 1733 shows that the crude death rate was 124 per thousand population. Slightly more than 12 percent of the population died during the year. Deaths were higher among children than among adults. A total of 491 Guaraní died—154 adults and 337 párvulos. The net decline in the number of children was 135.

The census record divided the population into cacicazgos, as was the common practice for tribute censuses for the Paraguay missions. There were a total of thirty-five caciques who governed populations of different sizes. The largest was the Quaratimivi with a population of 252, and the smallest the Abatubi with only 17 people. Regardless of the size of the population, the caciques retained their status within the mission community. This status included exemption from the obligation of having to pay tribute. The epidemics claimed the lives of caciques, and there were five under the age of ten who most likely replaced a parent who succumbed to the contagion.

The population of Los Santos Mártires mission experienced a net decline of 1,097 between 1731 and 1739, but it then recovered through the 1740s and early 1750s. Crude birth rates exceeded death rates, and the number of Guaraní living at the mission increased from 2,777 in 1739 to 3,176 in 1751 and 2,981 in 1753. In 1756, the death rate reached 101.7 and was the highest recorded in all of the missions. In 1759 and again in the years 1762 and 1763, death rates were slightly higher than birth rates, and the numbers fluctuated. The population was 3,328 in 1760 and 3,099 in 1763. Smallpox spread through the missions in 1764 and 1765, killing hundreds of Guaraní at Los Santos Mártires. At the time of the epidemic, 381 refugees still living there. They had been evacuated from the missions east of the Uruguay River to the missions west of the river following an uprising in the mid-1750s. In 1764, 808 Guaraní native to Los Santos Mártires died of smallpox, as did another 149 fugitives from Santo Ángel Custodio. Another 421 residents of the mission died from smallpox in 1765.

The number of refugees from Santo Ángel Custodio still numbered 330 in 1765, but the report on smallpox mortality at Mártires in 1765 did not specify how many of the refugees died in that year. However, smallpox claimed the lives of 560 of the refugees at different missions. At the end of 1765, there were only 1,688 Guaraní native to the mission still living at Los Santos Mártires, and 1,662 two years later in 1767, on the eve of the expulsion of the Jesuits. The last report on the status of refugees from the eastern missions prepared in 1766 showed that 300 Guaraní from Santo Ángel Custodio still resided at Los Santos Mártires mission. A total of 853 from Santo Ángel Custodio were at five missions located west of the Uruguay River, and 1,509 reportedly had returned to the mission. Not all Guaraní had returned to San Luis Gonzaga and San Juan Bautista mission as of 1766. In the case of the first named 2,194 had returned to the mission, and 961 still lived on four other missions. In the case of San Juan Bautista 2,562 had returned to the mission, and 1,229 lived on four other missions, including 6 who were at Los Santos Mártires.[48]

Following the expulsion of the Jesuits, their replacement by Dominicans, and the appointment of civil administrators to manage the mission, the population of Los Santos Mártires declined owing to epidemics as well as outmigration. Postexpulsion censuses reported residents of the mission who were absent and considered fugitives, and it showed evidence of epidemic mortality. In 1772, the population of the mission totaled 1,724, which was up from the number reported in 1767. But it then dropped in subsequent years: 1,321 in 1785; 892 in 1793; 609 in 1803; and 548 in 1808. Outmigration was the more important factor in the decline of the mission population following the Jesuit expulsion. A 1776 count, for example, reported the absence of 352 Guaraní who, since they had not been legally emancipated, were classified as fugitives. Others were also absent but not classified as fugitives because they were working in the mission estancias (67 individuals) or were in the "service to the King" (32 individuals).

Later enumerations documented years of mortality rates higher than birth rates, as well as continued outmigration. In the years 1797–99, there were 127 deaths as against 104 baptisms/births, indicating a net decline in numbers of 23. In 1797, the number of fugitives reached 41. In the following year, there were 38 fugitives including 17 adult men, but 15 reportedly were returned. There were 18 fugitives and 15 returned in 1799. Altogether, the record shows 97 new fugitives and 30 individuals returned, or a net loss to the population of 67. Data from 1801 for Los Santos Mártires del Japón shows gender imbalances in specific age cohorts. This is consistent with information abstracted above from the 1799 counts, which showed the absence of men. The age pyramid constructed for Los Santos Mártires del Japón showed an excess of females in the age groups 5–9 and 25–29, which would be the ages at which boys and men would be expected to leave. Moreover, the numbers in the age groups 20–24 and 25–29 were considerably smaller than would be expected. The shortfall in numbers in this age group may have reflected, in part, mortality during a smallpox epidemic in 1777 but also the absence of young adults in their prime who would be more likely to leave the mission to find work.[49]

How did demographic patterns on the Chiquitos missions compare to the Paraguay missions? The following section examines the population of San Francisco Xavier, the first of the Chiquitos missions.

Demographic Patterns on
San Francisco Xavier Mission (Chiquitania)

The available evidence shows that in most years the number of births and baptisms of non-Christians was greater than the number of deaths, and the Chiquitos mission populations grew at slow to moderate rates. Periodic epidemics, which were not as severe as in the Paraguay missions, slowed but did not stop population growth. The population of San Francisco Xavier grew from 1,690 reported in 1718 to 2,342 in 1739, and to 3,302 in 1765. In the years 1738 to 1767, for which there is a complete record, the Jesuits baptized 4,433 natives. In the years with both baptisms and burrials, the Jesuits baptized 3,497 natives and recorded 2,764 burials, or a net population increase of 733.

Graph 3.1
The population of San Francisco Xavier mission, 1710–1733

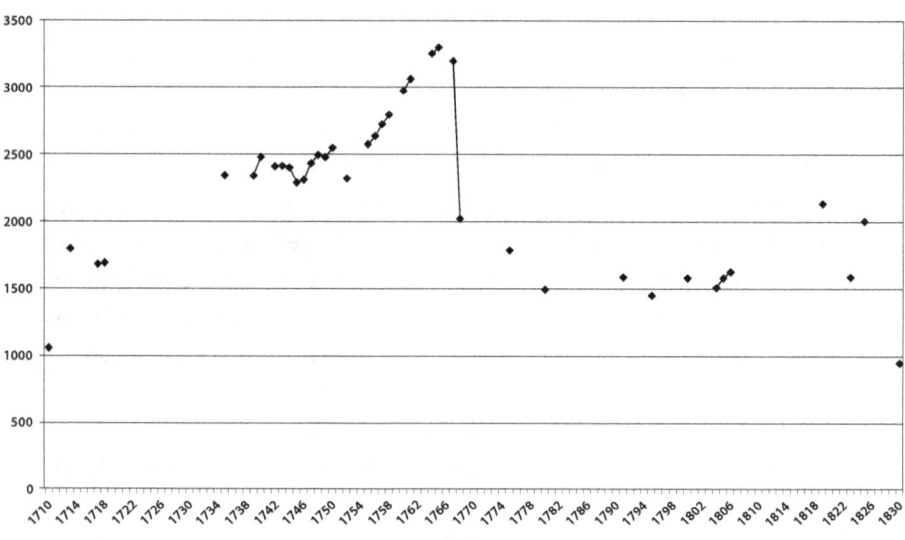

Similarly, the population of Concepción increased from 1,087 in 1718 to 1,858 in 1739, and to 3,287 in 1765. The Jesuits baptized 2,980 natives and registered 1,891 burials, a net increase in population of 1,089 (see appendix A.8).

The Chiquitos mission can be characterized as having been high-fertility and high-mortality populations, meaning that although death rates were high, in most years birth rates were higher. Moreover, the Jesuits periodically resettled non-Christians on the missions. In 1717, for example, the Jesuits congregated 24 non-Christians on San Francisco Xavier. In 1731, it was 142, and in 1738 it was 24. Another 100 were congregated in 1760, 322 in 1762, and 45 in 1763 (see appendix A.8 and graphs 3.1 and 3.2).[50]

This is not to say that there were no epidemics. There were early outbreaks on the Chiquitos missions in 1697, 1702, 1705–7, and 1722. However, there is no information on mortality during these outbreaks.[51] The years 1738–39, 1743–45, and 1747 evidenced higher mortality rates. However, these were not major mortality crises on the scale documented for individual Paraguay missions, such as the crude death rate of 557 per thousand population recorded at San Lorenzo Mártir in 1739. In 1738 and 1739, the Jesuits at San Francisco Xavier recorded 380 burials as against 267 baptisms, or a net decline of 113. The crude

GRAPH 3.2

Baptisms and burials registered at San Francisco Xavier mission, 1712–1768

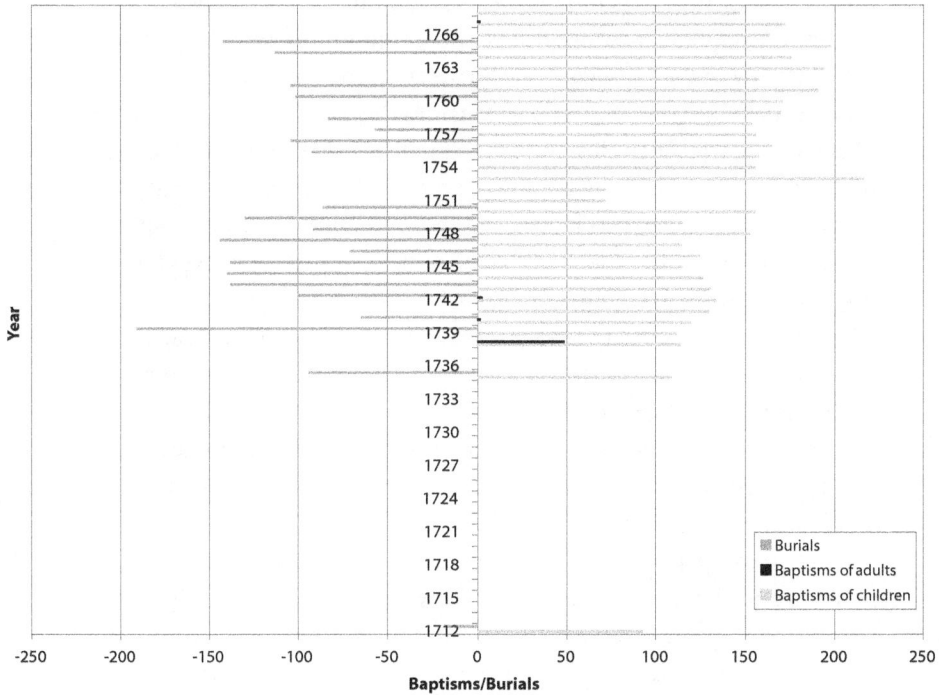

death rate reached an estimated 79.1 per thousand in 1738 and 81.6 in 1739. In contrast, at San Lorenzo 2,681 died in 1739, and the population experienced a net decline of 2,521. The population of San Lorenzo was 4,814 at the end of 1738, and the number dropped to 974 at the end of the following year. Similarly, 416 reportedly died at San Francisco Xavier in the years 1743 to 1745 as against 373 baptisms, resulting in a net decline in population of 43. The crude death rate reached 58.0 per thousand in 1743 and again in 1744, and 57.4 in 1745.

Many contemporary populations, including those of the Paraguay missions, evidenced a slight gender imbalance with more females (girls and women) than males. The evidence for San Francisco Xavier and the other Chiquitos missions shows the opposite, with slightly more males (boys and men) in most years. In 1742 and again in 1744, females represented a small majority, constituting 50.1 percent of the population in both years. In other years for which there is a record, on the other hand, there were more males. The lowest figure was of females constituting 44.4 percent of the population in 1713.[52]

What effect did this gender imbalance have on demographic patterns on San Francisco Xavier mission, and on the Chiquitos missions in general? The Jesuits usually did not disaggregate births from the baptism of new convents in the extant baptismal register and censuses that registered the total number of baptisms and burials. However, they did differentiate between baptisms of children and adults. The calculation of crude birth rates is slightly inflated by the inclusion of converts, as in 1738–42 and 1767 when there were baptisms of adults, but not by much. Men may have had difficulty finding sexual partners, and marriage rates were lower when compared to the Paraguay missions that did not experience similar gender imbalances. The crude marriage rate per thousand population at San Francisco Xavier ranged from 9.1 to a high in non-crisis years of 18.6. The highest rates were 30.1 in 1746 and 35.4 in 1747. These higher rates followed three years of increased mortality from 1743 to 1745. They represented both the formation of new families and the remarriages of widows and widowers.[53]

A useful comparison can be made with marriage patterns on the Paraguay missions and those on San Francisco Xavier mission, located in Misiones Province in Argentina. One difference in the patterns on the two missions was the periodic registration of larger numbers of marriages at the Paraguay establishment. The Jesuits performed large numbers of marriages at the same time, perhaps when a cohort of girls came of age. In 1739, for example, the Jesuits recorded 153 marriages, the largest number of marriages performed in a single year. This large number of marriages came at the end of the cycle of three epidemics that spread through the Paraguay missions between 1733 and 1740. The heaviest mortality at San Francisco Xavier during the decade was caused by smallpox in the years 1738–40. The population of the mission dropped from 2,873 at the end of 1736 to 1,876 at the end of 1738, and to 1,710 in 1739. The net decline in population in 1738 and 1739 was 1,163. The evidence shows that the Black Robes performed few marriages during the epidemics, and none in 1736. The Jesuits opted to postpone marriages and remarriages until the epidemics had burned themselves out. There were also other years with a similar pattern of unusually large numbers of marriages, as in 1741 with 73, 1750 with 72, and 1762 with 62.

Patterns on the two missions were distinct. The mean crude marriage rate was lower on the Chiquitos mission at 16.4 per thousand population, as against

19.9 per thousand for the Paraguay establishment. There were larger numbers of marriages on the Paraguay mission even following population decline and in the same period that the population of the Chiquitos missions was expanding. The Jesuits in both regions performed more marriages following epidemics, but there were no examples in the Chiquitos missions of what appears to have been large cohort marriages in non-crisis years. The year 1762, for example, evidenced significantly higher numbers of marriages at several Paraguay missions, including Santa Ana, Loreto, Corpus Christi, Concepción, San Juan Bautista, and San Francisco Xavier.

The gender imbalance did not contribute to an imbalance in the age structure of the population of San Francisco Xavier mission. In other words, children under about the age of fourteen or fifteen (the age at which children were generally considered to be adults and girls married following puberty) constituted a large percentage of the population. The Jesuits categorized children in this age group as párvulos and muchachos. The evidence shows that the population grew robustly, and that it was a young population with children constituting a large percentage of the total, in certain years more than half. However, periodic epidemics killed a disproportionately larger number of children. This can be seen, for example, with the epidemic in the mid-1740s already discussed above. The percentage of children in relation to the total population dropped from 52.9 percent in 1742 to 47.9 percent in 1747 after the epidemic had run its course (see appendix A.9).

The population of San Francisco Xavier grew during most years prior to the Jesuit expulsion in 1767. From the 1,690 reported in 1718, the numbers nearly doubled by 1765, in which year the population was 3,302. What factors contributed to this growth? Birth rates were one factor, but so too was the resettlement of non-Christians, in particular in the 1760s. The Jesuits congregated 467 new converts on San Francisco Xavier in 1760, 1762, and 1763, and the population jumped from 2,799 in 1758 to 3,256 in 1764 and 3,302 in the following year.[54] The number of children also increased from 1,422 in 1758 to 1,813 in 1764, suggesting that many of the non-Christians congregated on the mission were children. In the years 1760 to 1765, the Jesuits baptized 1,088 children, but no adults.[55] The percentage of the population that were children also increased from 52.2 percent in 1758 to 55.7 percent in 1764 (see appendix A.9).

The expansion of the mission population ended with an epidemic in 1766 (most likely smallpox) that killed 265 (for a crude death rate of 80.3 per thousand population) and the Jesuit expulsion in 1767. The population dropped to 2,019 in 1768 and continued to decline over the following decades. The population was 1,586 in 1797, 1,758 in 1800, 1,625 in 1806, and 1,576 in 1823 on the eve of Bolivian independence. Some mission residents, perhaps the most recently congregated or those brought to live on the mission from longer distances, elected to leave following the Jesuit expulsion. However, despite the exodus, the nucleus of a stable community continued to exist at San Francisco Xavier in the last years of the colonial period.

Demographic Patterns on the Sierra Gorda Missions

For nearly two centuries, Augustinian, Franciscan, Dominican, and Jesuit missionaries attempted to evangelize the nomadic natives living in the Sierra Gorda region. Small colonies of sedentary natives coexisted with bands of nomadic natives collectively known by the Spanish by the derogatory term *Mecos Barbaros*. They lived in small bands scattered across the mountainous region, and the missionaries failed to convince them to abandon their way of life and settle on permanent mission communities. In the 1740s, the Crown named José de Escandón to colonize the region known as Nueva Santander and to finalize the evangelization of the Sierra Gorda.

In 1743, Escandón conducted a survey of the Sierra Gorda region. Lucas Cabeza de Vaca, O.S.A., administered the Augustinian mission at Xalpa. The mission district consisted of Xalpa, the settlements of San Juan Pisquintla, San Juan Sagav, Atamcama, Santiago de Tongo, Santo Tomás de Sollapilca, San Agustín Tancoyol, San Nicolás Malitlaand, San Antonio Amatlán, and San Nicolás Concá, which was also an hacienda that belonged to one Gaspar Fernández del Pilar de Rama. There were thirteen small settlements described as *rancherías*. The Augustinian churches were described as jacales, or structures made of wattle and daub. Escandón described and enumerated the missions in the region staffed by Dominicans, Franciscans, and the Augustinians. The Augustinians administered several larger Pames settlements classified as *rancherías* that they visited periodically from the missions at Xilitlán, Pacula, and Xalpa.

José Ortés de Velasco, O.F.M., from the apostolic college of San Fernando, visited the Sierra Gorda in 1739, and in the following year he convinced seventy-three Jonaces to settle on the reestablished mission at San José de Vizarrón (previously San José del Llano). The Franciscans from San Fernando administered the mission at Vizarrón differently than did the Franciscans from Pachuca who staffed the Jonaces mission at Tolimán located close to Zimapán. The missionaries expected the Jonaces settled on Vizarrón to radically change their way of life in a short period of time, and in particular to become a disciplined labor force to work in communal agricultural production and ranching. The Jonaces did not respond well to this approach of directed social-cultural change, and the majority had abandoned the missions by 1748. In response, royal officials sent soldiers to recapture the fugitives, and they distributed the natives among *obrajes* (textile mills) in Querétaro as forced laborers.[56] In contrast, the Jonaces at Tolimán continued to collect wild foods and were not subject to the same pressures to change their way of life and become a disciplined labor force.[57] The Franciscans from San Fernando experienced a similar problem with the nomadic hunter-gatherer group known as the Guaycuros, who lived on Todos Santos mission in southern Baja California. The Fernandinos tried to convert the Guaycuros into a disciplined labor force after they replaced the Jesuits in Baja California in 1768, but the Guaycuros also resisted the forced and rapid change in lifestyle. The Franciscans ended up having to hire non-native laborers to work the Todos Santos mission lands.[58]

Escandón gave the Fernandinos jurisdiction over the Augustinian mission at Xalpa and the visitas at Tancoyol and Concá, and he ordered the establishment of new missions at Landa and Tilaco. The Franciscans congregated thousands of Pames on the new and reorganized missions. A census prepared in 1744 enumerated 3,767 Pames congregated on the five missions, with the largest number settled on Xalpa.[59] Periodic epidemics decimated the mission populations, and flight was one common response to the outbreak of contagion.

There were two severe epidemic outbreaks in the Sierra Gorda missions during the first two decades of the Franciscan administration. A report drafted about 1748 noted that in four years 1,422 Pames had died at four of the missions (there is no data for Tancoyol because a fire destroyed the burial register).[60] Martín de Heredia, O.F.M., Juan de Urinate, O.F.M., and Lucas Ladrón de Guevara, O.F.M., all died during the 1746–47 outbreak.[61] A smallpox epidemic in 1762 killed hundreds of Pames, as well as three Franciscan missionaries. Some 200 Pames died from smallpox in 1762 at Tilaco.[62] The Franciscans attempted to maintain the population levels of the missions through the congregation of small numbers of non-Christians, although the populations of the missions slowly declined (see appendix B.3). The fragility of the mission populations becomes evident on examining the net balance between baptisms and burials on the missions. Several reports summarize the total number of baptisms and burials recorded between 1744 and 1764 (see appendix B.4). Over two decades there were 1,782 more burials than baptisms. During roughly the same period, the population of Xalpa dropped from 1,445 in 1744 to 869 in 1762. The recruitment of non-Christians buffered to a certain extent the decline on the other missions. Flight from the missions, which reflected the unwillingness of many Pames to abandon their way of life, also continued to be a problem.[63]

Burial registers do not exist for the Sierra Gorda missions. However, the extant reports recorded the total number of burials in rough age groups: párvulos (under age six) and adults including children over age six. The data for Tancoyol is incomplete because a fire in April of 1747 destroyed the church and the baptismal and burial registers. Burials at Tancoyol between 1747 and 1758 totaled 292 adults and 239 párvulos.[64] The 1758 report for Landa recorded burials of 303 adults and 329 párvulos between 1744 and 1758.[65] The total reported for Tilaco was 286 burials of adults and 348 of párvulos in the same years.[66] Finally, burials at Xalpa totaled 601 adults and 721 párvulos.[67] The Sierra Gorda evidenced mortality patterns distinct from those documented for the Paraguay and Chiquitos missions. Prior to the concerted effort to congregate the natives on the five Franciscan missions, the Pames lived in a dispersed pattern in small and often isolated settlements in the valleys and mountains. This settlement pattern most likely limited the effects of epidemics. Once brought to live on larger nucleated communities, on the other hand, contagion more readily spread between and within mission communities, and mortality was higher among that part of the population, both adults and children, that had not been previously exposed to contagion and thus was particularly susceptible.

Two crude measures show a different dynamic than that documented on the Chiquitos missions, with smaller numbers of children in relation to the total population. The first is the calculation of the average family size (AFS), which gives a general idea of family size and shows a pattern of smaller families than on the Chiquitos missions and in most years an average of only one child per family. Families of this size were too small to guarantee the reproduction of the population. The calculation of children (under the age of fifteen) as a percentage of the total population provides a second useful comparison with the Chiquitos missions. Children constituted a smaller percentage than on the Chiquitos missions, in some instances less than a third of the total. Several factors perhaps explain this pattern. Infant and child mortality rates were likely high, and increases in the number of children resulted from birth rates but also the periodic baptism of small numbers of non-Christians. This last perhaps explains the increase in the percentage relationship of children to the total population at Concá and Landa in the 1760s (see appendix B.5). In the absence of more complete records, the explanation offered here for the causes of the patterns observed on the Sierra Gorda missions is more a hypothesis than a conclusion.

Comparisons can be made between the Sierra Gorda missions and other missions located on the northern frontier of New Spain with similar types of populations, in this case the Pimeria Alta, Baja California, and California. The natives congregated on the Pimeria Alta missions were sedentary agriculturalists who also practiced seasonal transhumance for the collection of wild plant foods and also for hunting. Periodic epidemics reduced the mission populations that also experienced high infant and child mortality rates. A family reconstitution of a sample of 123 children born on Guevavi-Tumacacori mission in the years 1773–1825 shows that 46 percent died within the first year and only 7 percent reached age ten.[68] The Jesuits, and later the Franciscans who replaced them following the expulsion, maintained mission population levels only by congregating non-Christians.

The natives living on the Baja California missions were nomadic hunters and gatherers, and they more closely resembled the Pames congregated on the Sierra Gorda missions. The populations experienced high epidemic-mortality rates and chronically high infant- and child-mortality rates, and rapid demographic collapse within several generations followed the establishment of missions. A series of reports prepared by the Jesuit missionaries in 1744 recorded the total number of baptisms at individual missions up to the point of the drafting of the reports, as well as the populations. Baptisms at eight missions reportedly totaled 14,830, and the population of the same missions was 4,220. This indicates a decline of 72 percent from the number of people the Jesuits had baptized.[69] A family reconstitution of Santa Rosalia de Mulege mission showed that of a sample of 142 children born to 75 women between 1771 and 1835, 50 percent died before reaching age one, and only 6 percent lived to age ten.[70] The native populations reached the point of near biological and cultural extinction within 100 to 150 years of the establishment of the first mission in the Peninsula.

The final example is the pattern of high mortality and particularly high infant and child mortality on five missions established in California among the group known today as the Chumash. The populations of the five missions increased only during periods of the resettlement of large numbers of non-Christians, and they rapidly declined once the number of new converts settling on the missions dropped. Most children born on the missions did not live to age ten, and the mission populations were not demographically viable. In other words, they did not grow through natural reproduction as did the populations on the Chiquitos missions. They more closely paralleled demographic patterns on the Sierra Gorda missions.[71]

The most complete record among the five Sierra Gorda missions exists for Tilaco and Tancoyol. This record includes the detailed censuses prepared in 1744 that enables the construction of a profile of the population when the Franciscans arrived, as well as baptismal registers. The 1744 censuses prepared when Escandón oversaw the establishment of the five Franciscan missions divided the population into family groups and also identified widowers, widows, and their children, as well as single adults (see appendices B.6 and B.7). The censuses also differentiated between those couples that were married by the Catholic Church and those that were not. The number of cases of relationships of couples not in Church-sanctioned marriages totaled 49 at Tancoyol, or 23 percent of the families enumerated. The figures at Tilaco were even higher. Of 184 families enumerated at Tilaco, El Lobo, and Laguna Grande, 121 or 66 percent were not in Church-sanctioned marriages. None of those congregated at Tilaco had been married by the Church, whereas the majority at El Lobo and Laguna Grande were. A substantial number of Pames had formed families along traditional lines, and in particular those that preserved their traditional way of life in small settlements in the mountains. The majority of the couples at Tancoyol, Soyapilca, El Lobo, and Laguna Grande, communities with a longer period of contact with missionaries and sedentary natives, had been married by the Church.[72]

The act of possession at Tilaco on May 1, 1744, provides more details regarding the family structure and the large numbers of couples in traditional relationships not sanctioned by Catholic marriage some 200 years following the first visits by missionaries to the region. The Augustinians stationed on the doctrina at Xilitlán had had jurisdiction over the sedentary natives at El Lobo and Laguna Grande. Luis de Trejo, O.S.A., who presided over the transfer of the Augustinian jurisdiction to the Franciscans, noted that he could not turn the original sacramental registers over to the Franciscans, since they also contained the baptisms, burials, and marriages of the Otomí and Náhuas, who remained under their jurisdiction. The Augustinian offered to have a copy made of the records for the Pames, who were now the Franciscans' responsibility. The same was the case with the church ornaments that the Augustinians retained for their Otomí and Náhuas congregants.[73] A 1571 report on the Augustinian doctrina at Xilitlán noted that the population of Tilaco was predominately Otomí, and it did not indicate that the Augustinians attempted to evangelize the Pame.[74] It is not clear if the natives enumerated at El Lobo and Laguna Grande were all Pames or were also Otomís and Náhuas. The Augustinians had not had jurisdiction over the valley where the Franciscans established Tancoyol, and they did not participate in the establishment of that mission.[75]

The censuses reveal subtle differences in the family structure of the communities enumerated. The majority of couples had no children, or only one or two. Appendices B6 and B7 summarize the information on the size of families. At Tancoyol and Soyapilca, 65 percent and 75 percent of the families, respectively, had two or fewer children. Similarly, 72 percent of the families at Tilaco had two or fewer children, 65 percent at El Lobo, and 60 percent at Laguna Grande. Two factors most likely explain this pattern. One was the small size of families in nomadic populations, coupled with high infant and child mortality. The Franciscans may have encouraged larger families but could not solve the problem of high mortality rates.

To maintain population levels, couples would have to have had two children survive to adulthood, and three or more for population growth. There were a number of larger families with three, four, or five children enumerated in the 1744 censuses. The populations of Tancoyol, Soyapilca, and Tilaco counted 28 percent, 25 percent, and 26 percent of families having three to five children. The populations of El Lobo and Laguna Grande evidenced a somewhat different dynamic with a larger number of families with three or more children; 35 percent and 40 percent, respectively. This may indicate a difference between the structures of the population of Otomí and Náhuas.

How did the structure of the populations of Tancoyol and Tilaco compare to the populations of the Jesuit missions of lowland South America? Detailed tribute censuses of the Paraguay and Chiquitos missions also divided the population into family groups. The most valid comparison can be made based on censuses prepared in years that did not evidence mortality crises. A comparison is made based on a 1759 count of the population of Corpus

Christi mission (Misiones, Argentina). Corpus Christi had a high-fertility and high-mortality population with high birth rates and robust growth. The numbers increased from 4,192 in 1750 to 4,753 in 1759, the year of the population count. Moreover, it was a young population. Children and adolescents under the age of nineteen constituted 58 percent of the population. The family size on the mission ranged from two to nine, and there were families larger than those documented for Tancoyol and Tilaco. Moreover, families with three to seven children constituted 47 percent of all families, a higher percentage than on the two Sierra Gorda missions.[76]

A second comparison can be made with the family structure of the populations of two of the Chiquitos missions based on a detailed 1745 tribute census. The two missions are San Francisco Xavier and Concepción. Both missions evidenced robust population growth, with families that ranged in size from two to ten. In the case of San Francisco Xavier, 65 percent of the families ranged in size from two to four, and 35 percent of families had from three to eight children. More important, however, families with three or more children (excluding widows and widowers and their children) made up 51 percent of the population enumerated in families. With this dynamic, the population of San Francisco Xavier grew through natural reproduction, as already discussed above. Similarly, 65 percent of the families living on Concepción mission lived in families of two to four members. However, there was a larger percentage of families with two or more children: 55 percent of those enumerated in families were in families that ranged in size from five to ten members. Although the ages recorded in the tribute censuses are not reliable, they do document an early age of marriage for women living on the Chiquitos missions, and as early as age thirteen or fourteen. Those women of child-bearing age that survived child birth and other health threats bore many children, since there were no economic restraints on family formation and family size. The census also shows that a sufficient number of children survived to adulthood to form new families and reproduce the population.[77] The sedentary populations of the two Chiquitos missions evidenced different patterns from the nomadic populations of Tancoyol and Tilaco.

Baptismal registers exist for the Tancoyol and Tilaco missions and provide additional information regarding demographic patterns on the missions. The register for Tancoyol records the first baptisms in 1747, but the Franciscans started recording complete information on those baptized only in 1754. In other words, they only then began to record information in the individual baptismal entries as to whether it was a newborn child or a non-Christian resettled on the mission. The Franciscans stationed on Tilaco began to record the complete information only in 1753. Therefore, the analysis of baptismal patterns is limited to these years.

Between 1754 and 1770, the year that the Franciscans turned the mission over to parish priests following the secularization of the five Sierra Gorda establishments, they baptized 383 children born on the mission and on several other *rancherías* administered from Tancoyol. That was an average of 23 births per year. The summary of the number of burials at Tancoyol indicates that on average the Franciscans buried 39 natives per year. The number of deaths was greater than the number of births. There were still a small number of unbaptized natives in the Tancoyol district. The Franciscans baptized 31 adults and 23 young children who were non-Christians. Between 1752 and 1765, the Franciscans stationed on Tilaco recorded 435 births, or an average of 31 per year. The crude birth rate can be calculated for several years. It was 39.1 per thousand population in 1759, 35.3 in 1762, and 45.5 in 1765, which were a bit lower than birth rates on the Chiquitos and Paraguay missions. The Franciscans recorded an average of 57 burials per year. From 1750 to 1765, the Franciscans baptized 56 adults who previously had not been baptized. Even with the influx of small numbers of non-Christians, the population of Tilaco constantly declined as the number of deaths was consistently greater than the number of births and baptisms of non-Christians.[78]

Conclusions

The comparison of demographic patterns shows the relative fragility of nomadic populations when brought to live on missions administered by missionaries who sought to radically change their way of life. The sedentary populations on the Paraguay and Chiquitos missions were high-fertility and high-mortality populations. Death rates were high, but birth rates were even higher in non-mortality crisis years. The populations of nonsedentary natives congregated on the Sierra Gorda missions, on the other hand, could not reproduce themselves in the face of mortality, which was consistently higher than their birth rates. Pames women bore children, but the evidence suggests that, unlike the populations of the Paraguay and Chiquitos missions, infant- and child-mortality rates among the Pames were high, and periodic epidemics culled the populations that did not rebound or recover following mortality crises.

The populations of the Paraguay missions were linked to regional markets by navigable rivers that facilitated the movement of goods and people, but also of contagion. Birth rates were high, and in non-crisis years birth rates were higher than death rates. There were no economic restraints on family formation and the size of families, and limited evidence suggests that Guaraní women generally married at a young age shortly after puberty. Epidemics spread through the missions about once every generation, when there were a sufficient number of potential hosts to maintain the chain of infection. The large size of the mission populations and the number of young children also contributed to catastrophic mortality during epidemics of highly contagious crowd diseases such as smallpox and measles. There are recorded instances of mortality in excess of 50 percent of the population of individual missions. However, despite heavy mortality, the Paraguay mission populations did not evidence a gender imbalance, and females generally constituted a slight majority. Moreover, there was an increase in family formation following epidemics, and high birth rates resulted in the rebound or recovery and growth in population levels.

The Chiquitos mission populations evidence somewhat different patterns. Birth rates were also higher than death rates, but epidemics generally did not reach the catastrophic levels documented for the Paraguay missions. The Chiquitos missions were located on an isolated frontier, and the movement of people and goods was over land and not by river, as was the case on the Paraguay missions. Moreover, the Jesuits attempted to limit direct contact with settlers from Santa Cruz de la Sierra, the closest Spanish settlement. Isolation somewhat buffered the effects of epidemics on the Chiquitos missions, and most epidemics did not reach the same levels as on the Paraguay missions. Moreover, the Chiquitos mission populations were open populations, meaning that the missionaries periodically sent out expeditions to recruit and congregate non-Christians on the missions. The Chiquitos missions experienced moderate rates of growth through natural reproduction and the resettlement of non-Christians.

The populations of Pames and Jonaces congregated on the Sierra Gorda missions, on the other hand, were not demographically viable. The evidence suggests that the families of nomadic indigenous groups tended to be smaller than those of sedentary natives, as shown through the comparative analysis of the family structure of the mission populations. Escandón criticized the Augustinians for having failed to congregate the Pames and Jonaces on the mission communities. However, it was this failure that contributed to the demographic and social-cultural survival of the small bands that lived scattered in the mountains. This dispersed settlement pattern provided some protection against the spread of contagion for some two hundred years. Once brought to live on the missions in large communities, however, the Jonaces and Pames experienced mortality rates higher than birth rates in the 1740s, 1750s, and 1760s. Had this pattern persisted, the populations would have faced virtual biological extinction within several generations, something that occurred, for example, on the Baja California missions populated by nomadic hunters and gatherers. The secularization of the Sierra Gorda missions in 1770, however, modified the demographic dynamic, although mortality among the Pames was higher than birth rates even after the Franciscans left the missions.[79]

Conclusion

In a demographic study of the indigenous populations on the missions of northwestern New Spain (northern Sonora, Baja California, and California), I made several concluding statements that proved to be controversial, particularly in light of the ongoing campaign by members of the Catholic Church to canonize Junípero Serra, O.F.M., the architect of the California mission system and a veteran of the Sierra Gorda missions. The native peoples congregated on the missions, and especially those in Baja California and California, experienced drastic demographic collapse. I concluded that "the demographic collapse and cultural and biological extinction of the Indian populations of Northwestern New Spain was not intended, but it was intentional."[1] In other words, "Colonial officials and the missionaries realized that the Indian populations were disappearing, but they made no adjustment in a program that in the short run fulfilled the objectives of the colonial state."[2] I concluded by writing that "it was on the basis of the sense of superiority of the Iberian culture, worldview, society, and economy that the missionaries and colonial bureaucrats pushed forward with the mission programs in northwestern New Spain regardless of the fact that they knew from past experience that Indian populations brought into the missions most likely would experience a drastic decline in numbers."[3] Over the past two decades I have expanded the scope of my inquiry to include missions in sixteenth-century central Mexico and the Jesuit Paraguay Province, and my interpretation has been refined but has not changed.

How did nonsedentary and sedentary indigenous populations fare when brought to live on mission communities? Although the record is incomplete, the evidence supports the hypotheses that there were differences in the demographic patterns of the nonsedentary and sedentary indigenous populations in the Sierra Gorda and Chiquitos mission frontiers. The same holds for other mission frontiers. Nonsedentary populations proved to be demographically fragile, which means that once brought on the missions, they failed to grow through natural reproduction and experienced demographic collapse. The Pames population in the Sierra Gorda had survived several centuries of contact with Spanish settlers and missionaries because they resisted attempts to be relocated to nucleated communities on the model of the pueblos de indios in central Mexico. The Pames lived in small hamlets scattered across the rugged mountainous region, and the missionaries who attempted to evangelize them complained that the Pames would not cooperate and come live on the mission communities. However, this pattern of resistance also accounts for their demographic survival, since the dispersed settlement pattern and geographic isolation buffered the population from epidemics. Once congregated, however, the Pames population declined after experiencing heavy epidemic mortality.

The comparison of the demographic profile of the Pames population and other nonsedentary indigenous peoples with that of the Guaraní and the natives congregated on the Chiquitos missions highlights the differences between the two types of populations. The residents of the Paraguay and Chiquitos missions experienced robust birth rates and growth in noncrisis years. This can be seen, for example, in larger family sizes and in elevated birth rates that remained greater than death rates in noncrisis years. Moreover, the sedentary populations proved resilient in the face of catastrophic mortality, and in particular in the face of smallpox mortality rates that, in the case of individual missions, reached 40 or even more than 50 percent of the population. Following epidemics resulting in catastrophic mortality, marriage rates increased, new families were formed, and higher birth rates led to population growth. The sedentary Paraguay and Chiquitos mission populations were viable, whereas the nonsedentary Pames population was not. The evidence for the Sierra Gorda missions shows that the Pames mission populations experienced catastrophic epidemic mortality and death rates that were higher than birth rates. The congregation of the Pames on the Franciscan missions accelerated the process of demographic collapse, and the same occurred among other nonsedentary indigenous populations.

The demographic patterns on the five Franciscan missions in the Sierra Gorda were not unique. There are many other examples of nonsedentary populations that experienced demographic collapse when brought to live on missions in the seventeenth and eighteenth centuries. Examples include the nonsedentary groups living in the Pampas and in the Chaco region, although the analysis of the equestrian Chaco groups such as the Abipones show a distinct pattern of resistance and engagement with the Jesuit missionaries. On the frontiers of Mexico there are numerous examples. The Chichimeca groups, including the Pames and Jonaces, disappeared over time. The populations of the Coahuila-Texas frontier, Baja California, and California experienced a similar fate.[4] At the same time sedentary mission populations, such as those documented in this study, survived despite catastrophic mortality. Examples include the Guaraní on the Paraguay missions, the populations of the Chiquitos and Tarima missions, and populations in parts of Sonora and Sinaloa in northern Mexico.

Can demographic patterns be correlated to the different organizational structures and policies of the Jesuits and Franciscans from the apostolic college of San Fernando? There is evidence of this. The Franciscans worked closely with reform-minded royal officials to bring their mission program in line with royal policy objectives. The first example was the collaboration with José de Escandón, who gave the Franciscans the mandate to congregate the Pames on the missions in the Sierra Gorda and to more fully integrate them into colonial society. The demographic consequence of this initiative was population decline.

A similar pattern occurred in the Baja California and California missions when the Franciscans, under the leadership of Junípero Serra, assumed responsibility for these missions and implemented the policy initiatives of José de Gálvez, an important architect of the so-called "Bourbon Reforms" at the end of the eighteenth century. The debacle of the policy to put to work the Guaycuros at Todos Santos in Baja California was a consequence of one of Gálvez's mandates to make the Peninsula missions self-sufficient. To exploit the well-watered lands at Todos Santos, he relocated the Guaycuros to work there, but the outcome was resistance and rapid depopulation as a consequence of epidemics. The Jesuits had made minimal changes in their way of life and, as was also the case on the Chiquitos missions, limited contacts with neighboring regions in northern Mexico. Gálvez suppressed the two Guaycuro missions Dolores del Sur and San Luis Gonzaga, and he relocated more than 800 people to Todos Santos mission. In 1771, a mere three years later, only 170 survived.[5]

Gálvez's policies and his scheme to colonize California resulted in increased contact between Baja California, Sinaloa, Sonora, and other areas on the mainland. The movement of soldiers and settlers through the Peninsula facilitated the spread of contagion. The case of San Francisco Xavier mission (established in 1699) illustrates both the demographic consequences of the policy changes and the Franciscan collaboration with Gálvez. After an initial demographic decline caused by epidemics and other factors in the first decades of the eighteenth century, the population of San Francisco Xavier experienced several decades of growth through natural reproduction. The numbers increased from 352 in 1744 to 482 in 1768, when the Franciscans arrived in the Peninsula. Gálvez had population from San Francisco Xavier shifted to San José del Cabo mission, and epidemics over the next decade decimated the population, which dropped to 169 in 1782 following a particularly lethal smallpox outbreak.[6]

The California missions provide even more compelling evidence of the demographic consequences of the Franciscan mission organization and in particular of their social policies. In Baja California, the Franciscans had been the handmaidens of the reform policies of Gálvez, but as had been the case also in the Sierra Gorda missions, they cooperated in the implementation of these policies. On the other hand, Serra designed both the organization of the California missions and the social policies implemented there. To the new California missions Serra and his cohorts applied the lessons learned and the methods used in the Sierra Gorda and Baja California missions. They imposed a system of strict social control enforced through the use of corporal punishment. This translated into a demographic catastrophe for the native peoples brought to live on the missions, where they experienced chronically high death rates and gender and age imbalances in the population. Santa Cruz mission (established in 1791) offers an extreme example of the gender and age imbalances that contributed to demographic collapse. In 1832, the population of the mission was 284, but women and girls constituted only 31 percent of the total. The Franciscans had baptized 1,133 women and girls from 1791 to 1832, but in 1832 only 87 females survived, which was only 8 percent of all females the Franciscans had baptized over a period of 41 years. The majority of women and girls had died. By the 1830s there were gender imbalances in the populations of the other missions that were in a period of decline.

As already noted above, infant and child mortality rates on the California missions were high, and children there constituted a percentage of the population that was even smaller than on the Chiquitos and Paraguay missions. In the case of Santa Cruz mission, in 1828 the population totaled 364. Of this only 14 percent were children under the age of ten.[7] The other California missions also evidenced age imbalances by the 1820s and 1830s, some fifty years following the implementation of the Franciscan mission program.

Jesuit policies and organization on the Chiquitos and Paraguay missions differed from those of the Franciscans from the apostolic college of San Fernando and reflected demographic patterns on these missions. The populations of the Paraguay missions experienced catastrophic mortality, but they also proved to be resilient and recovered following mortality crises. This difference in demographic patterns can be attributed to Jesuit policies that included shared governance with indigenous leaders, as well as the characteristics of sedentary versus nonsedentary populations. The Jesuits, for example, did not implement the same type of measures of social control as did the Franciscans, such as incarcerating girls and single women at night in unsanitary and crowded dormitories. The Jesuits pursued a similar approach on the Chiquitos missions, which as a consequence evolved as demographically stable communities. This was a consequence of the geographic isolation of the missions and the Jesuit approach to organization. Nonsedentary indigenous populations proved to be demographically fragile when they were congregated on missions and exposed to contagion. However, the social policies implemented on the Sierra Gorda, Baja California, and California missions by the Franciscans from the apostolic college of San Fernando accelerated the process of demographic collapse.

The second question posed in this study is if there were meaningful differences in the methods of evangelization and organization of mission communities employed by the orders that staffed the missions. The conclusion proffered here is that there was a significant difference in the organization of the mission communities, the social policies of the missionaries, and the role of the missions in the larger colonial system, but not in terms of the methods used to try to indoctrinate the native populations in the new faith.

The question of the outcome of evangelization is difficult to answer. The missionaries, clerics, and other Spaniards themselves created the existing written record, which often contains a tone of triumphalism that masked a quite different reality. Recent scholarship has challenged the markedly Eurocentric assumptions of Robert Ricard, who argued for a rapid and meaningful conversion to Iberian Catholicism of the indigenous peoples of central Mexico. At the same time, the documentary evidence shows the persistence of pre-Hispanic worldviews and religious beliefs that the missionaries classified as "idolatry" and "apostasy." Moreover, visual evidence of the persistence of pre-Hispanic beliefs can be seen in the incorporation of symbols of the old deities into what was ostensibly Christian iconography.

Evidence of conversion as opposed to the persistence of traditional religious beliefs on the frontier missions is tantalizing. The evidence from the Sierra Gorda is clear. Some two hundred years of missionary activity had done little to purge pre-Hispanic beliefs. In the late sixteenth century, during the course of the conflict known today as the Chichimeca War, most missionaries focused on the colonies of sedentary natives who had settled beyond the Chichimeca frontier. The Augustinian doctrinas at Chichicaxtla and San Felipe, Zimapán, and the Jesuit mission San Luis de la Paz established in the 1590s were exceptions. The discovery of the temple dedicated to Cachum, the writings of the last Augustinian missionary stationed on Xalpa, and other evidence make this clear. The Jesuits stationed on the Chiquitos missions did not leave similar written evidence, but there are fleeting clues to a different reality. In general there is a lack of iconographic evidence for the frontier missions, although one hypothesis suggests that indigenous peoples interpreted Christian iconography on their own terms. The bottom line, however, is that we will never know for sure what individual natives living on the missions really believed, or if they had embraced Catholicism.

In a recent study, I discussed and analyzed the design element on the façade of the Jesuit church at Opodepe in Sonora.[8] Native artists created the element by creating designs with small stones embedded in plaster, a technique also employed in central Mexico. The iconography incorporated into the design element more closely resembles elements commonly found in pre-Hispanic petroglyphs, including several representations of the fertility deity known as the flute player. Many structures on frontier missions have been altered over time or have fallen into ruin. One wonders if there were other instances of the incorporation of pre-Hispanic iconography in mission structures that have been covered over or completely lost. Scholars have described Guaraní iconography drawn in the wet clay of the floor of the church at Trinidad.[9] The meaning of these drawings, which include a bird, has been debated. However, the drawings may constitute evidence of the persistence of traditional religious beliefs similar to that found on the façade of the church at Opodepe.

The Jesuit missions in lowland South America more closely resembled the Franciscan, Dominican, and Augustinian missions in central Mexico in the sixteenth century and the early missions established beyond the Chichimeca frontier after about 1550. The Jesuits did not attempt to radically transform native society but rather retained the existing clan system and status of the clan chiefs. The leaders of the pueblos de indios in sixteenth-century central Mexico retained local autonomy, and the missionaries grafted their missions onto existing communities and had to establish a working relationship with the indigenous leaders. In the 1520s and 1530s, the first generation of Franciscan missionaries attempted to impose religious orthodoxy on indigenous leaders. This resulted in the executions of tlatoque in Tlaxcala orchestrated by Martín de Valencia, O.F.M., in 1527 and culminated with the 1539 execution in Tlatelolco of Don Carlos on the orders of Juan de Zumárraga, O.F.M., who was the first bishop of Mexico and also had inquisitorial authority. However, the hysteria of the early Franciscan morals campaign threatened the stability of the colonial order being created in central Mexico that relied on the cooperation of indigenous leaders, and the Crown had Zumárraga stripped of his inquisitorial authority and prohibited further executions. Three decades later Diego de Landa, O.F.M., who orchestrated the *auto-da-fé* at Maní in the Yucatán in 1562, could not impose the death penalty on the indigenous leaders he accused of idolatry.[10]

The Jesuits in the missions in lowland South America cogoverned with native clan chiefs and created an economic system that retained considerable autonomy for native families. The clan chiefs controlled lands that they distributed in usufruct to heads of household, who produced crops and kept livestock on their own account. The Jesuits did not interfere in the self-sufficiency of the mission residents. Rather, the Jesuits directed and managed a communal economy, and the clan chiefs mobilized labor for crop production, the tending of livestock, craft industrial production, and building projects. The tlatoque and community leaders in central Mexico similarly functioned as intermediaries in relations with the Spanish and the missionaries and were responsible for delivering tribute and labor. Clan chiefs were responsible for maintaining social norms and social control on the missions.

The approach of the Franciscans from the apostolic college of San Fernando was quite different and also reflected the changing demands of royal bureaucrats who wanted more results and greater accountability on the part of the missionaries. What did this imply? In his 1743 report on the Sierra Gorda missions, Escandón set the tone for what was to follow. It is ironic that Escandón empowered the Franciscans to take measures that the last Augustinian stationed at Xalpa complained he had been unable to do, namely, to force the Pames to congregate on the missions and abandon their traditional religious beliefs. The discovery of the shrine dedicated to Cachum in 1752 reflected the problem that Escandón's mandate to get the job done was designed to achieve. Escandón posted more soldiers in the Sierra Gorda to support the new mission program. Soldiers discovered the shrine by accident when they were burning Pames houses in the mountains, which was one method used to force the Pames to relocate to the missions. Once on the missions, the Franciscans imposed tighter measures of social control and labor exploitation, and they attempted to create dependence on the mission economy as a way to keep the Pames on the missions. In this way, the organization of the mission economy on the Sierra Gorda missions differed from that of the Jesuit missions in lowland South America.

The underlying failure of the earlier Sierra Gorda missions was rooted in the use of methods adapted from the earlier experience among the sedentary populations of central Mexico, methods that did not work beyond the Chichimeca frontier. The Augustinians, for example, concentrated their missionary activity on colonies of sedentary natives, Náhuas and Otomís, living beyond the frontier at places like Xilitlán and Tilaco.[11] They achieved little success among the nonsedentary Chichimecas, such as the Pames and Jonaces, and the nexus of this failure can be seen when the Franciscans assumed responsibility for the mission at Tilaco. The Augustinians retained responsibility for the sedentary natives who lived in the Tilaco Valley, and they proverbially washed their hands of the Pames. The efforts to evangelize the Jonaces proved equally difficult, and Franciscans, Augustinians, and Dominicans established what proved to be in most cases ephemeral missions that lasted for only short periods of time.

What was the outcome of the method Escandón and the Franciscans introduced in the Sierra Gorda missions? In the short run the Pames congregated on the missions, but the secularization of the five Franciscan missions in 1770 effectively ended the mission program after only twenty-seven years. There were still bands of Jonaces and Pames living outside of effective Spanish control, and Franciscans later established several missions in an effort to evangelize them. The experience of the Jonaces was quite different and reflected the contentious relationship between the natives and Spanish authority. The effort to use military force to congregate the Jonaces in the second decade of the eighteenth century backfired, as it resulted in the destruction of the Dominican mission La Nopalera and the dispersion of the Jonaces congregated on the mission. The Franciscan mission at Vizarrón had a similar fate. The Jonaces congregated there did not respond well to the methods of the Franciscans from the apostolic college of San Fernando, and in particular to the labor demands. In 1748, the Jonaces abandoned the mission as they had in the past, but in this instance Spanish soldiers tracked many of them down and consigned them to forced labor in the *obrajes* (textile mills) in Santiago de Querétaro. Some of the fugitive Jonaces resettled on the mission at Tolimán, which was administered by the Franciscans from the apostolic college of Pachuca, whose methods differed from those used by the Franciscans from San Fernando.

Junípero Serra, O.F.M., and the Franciscans from the apostolic college of San Fernando moved on to the ex-Jesuit mission in Baja California in 1768. A year later they participated in the colonization of California. Serra designed the mission program in both regions in conjunction with another royal official, Gálvez, who had the same philosophy as Escandón, namely, to get the job done. This meant to integrate the native populations into colonial society as quickly as possible, and to do so in a cost-effective fashion consistent with the Bourbon reform agenda that aimed to make the American territories economically self-sufficient. The outcome in Baja California was similar to the experience of the Jonaces at Vizarrón in the 1740s, as shown in the experiences of the Guaycuros in southern Baja California. During the Jesuit tenure, the nonsedentary Guaycuros continued to live as they had prior to the arrival of the missionaries, largely supporting themselves by hunting and collecting wild plant foods.

In 1769, Serra and the Franciscans opened a new mission frontier in California, and for sixty-nine years the Franciscans administered what would become twenty-one missions. Serra and his successors designed a mission program in California based on the methods they first developed in the Sierra Gorda missions. They also responded to the Bourbon mandate to incorporate the natives into colonial society in an accelerated program that was designed to put the natives to work to help defray the costs of colonization. Moreover, Serra and the Franciscans imposed their moral and social norms on California natives. They implemented harsh measures of social control, including corporal punishments such as flogging, and segregated segments of the population, in particular the girls and women, into unhealthy dormitories. The social norms and methods of social control were alien to pre-Hispanic California indigenous culture and contributed to demographic collapse.[12]

The geographic isolation of the California mission frontier buffered the missions from epidemics. This was also the case in the Chiquitos missions.

However, the California mission populations experienced demographic collapse as a result of high mortality rates that were brought about by particularly high rates of infant and child mortality, chronic ailments including syphilis, high mortality among girls and women, unhealthy living conditions that were a part of Franciscan methods of social control, and other factors.[13] As already discussed, the differences in demographic patterns on the Paraguay, Chiquitos, Sierra Gorda, and California missions can be directly attributed to the different methods of organizing the mission communities and the different social policies and methods of control adopted by the Jesuits and Franciscans from the apostolic college of San Fernando. The outcomes on the Sierra Gorda and later the California missions reflected the construction of a Franciscan vision imposed on the natives, which was quite different from that of the Jesuits in lowland South America.

Appendix A

*Demographic Indicators of the
Jesuit Missions of Lowland South America*

Appendix A.1
Population of the Paraguay missions and the 1718–1719 smallpox epidemic

Mission	1717 Population	1717 Families	1718– Fajardo Report Families	1718– Fajardo Report Smallpox	1720 Population	Percent change 1717–1720
Guazú	5651	1377	1500	No	2738	−51
La Fe	4404	1110	900	No	5557	+26
Santa Rosa de Lima	5389	1523	1000	No	4230	−21
Sr. Apóstol Santiago	4387	890	900	No	2135	−51
Ytapúa	5871	1287	1200*	Yes	5163	−12
Candelaria	3275	785	600	No	2596	−21
S. Cosme	2033	499	600*	Yes	1855	−9
S. Ana	3032	688	700	No	3117	+3
Loreto	5526	1402	1600	No	5617	+2
S. I. Miní	3040	649	NA	NA	2865	−6
Corpus	2816	678	700	No	3157	+12
Trinidad	2925	737	700*	Yes	2771	−5
Jesús	1527	326	350	No	1790	+17
S. Carlos	3596	744	844	No	2795	−22
S. José	3510	740	800*	Yes	2819	−20
Apóstoles	3996	1184	1200	No	3235	−19
Concepción	4186	996	900	No	3936	−6
Mártires	3265	787	700	No	3222	−1
La Mayor	3134	825	700	No	3249	+4
S. Javier	5600	1271	1400	No	5280	−6
S. Nicolás	6993	1584	1800	No	6072	−13
S. Luis	5326	1924	900	No	4324	−19
S. Lorenzo	4905	1109	1090	No	4967	+1
S. Miguel	2909	742	890	No	3598	+24
S. Juan	3472	873	800	No	3946	+14
Santo Ángel Custodio	3239	795	700	No	3592	+11
Santo Tomé	4768	1131	1020*	Yes	2659	−44
S. Borja	3757	843	800	No	2864	−24
La Cruz	5481	1229	1200	No	3069	−44
Yapeyú	2873	611	600	Yes	1886	−34

*Number of families before the smallpox epidemic.

Source: Annua Reductionum Anni 1717, Archivo General de la Nación, Buenos Aires, Sala 9-6-9-6; Annua Reductionum Anni 1720, Archivo General de la Nación, Buenos Aires, Sala 9-6-9-6; "Razon de la visita que hizo el ilustrisimo y reverendisimo Senor don Fray Pedro Fajardo, Obispo de Buenos Aires, el ano de 1718," in Pablo Pastells, *Historia de la Compañía de Jesús en la Provincia del Paraguay.* 9 vols. (Madrid: Self-published, 1912), 6:172–77.

Appendix A.2
Crude birth and death rates (1748–1749) on selected Paraguay and Chiquitos missions

Mission	1748		1749	
	Crude birth rate	Crude death rate	Crude birth rate	Crude death rate
Selected Paraguay				
Ytapúa	74.7	60.9	65.7	112.6
Santa Rosa	66.7	195.8	64.4	29.7
Jesús	77.7	39.7	59.0	84.7
Santiago	50.1	43.5	63.7	216.5
Trinidad	48.1	41.3	44.6	125.1
Candelaria	93.6	53.3	99.7	105.6
Santa Maria la Mayor	80.9	45.9	86.5	98.0
San Carlos	76.4	58.9	75.7	119.2
San Nicolás	97.5	39.6	82.7	101.3
San Miguel	51.0	32.8	62.5	95.2
Selected Chiquitos				
San Francisco Xavier	62.8	37.4	46.1	52.1
San Juan Bautista	47.4	40.2	26.6	118.1
San José	58.7	45.5	40.3	50.7

Source: Robert H. Jackson, *Demographic Change and Ethnic Survival among the Sedentary Populations on the Jesuit Mission Frontiers of South America: The Formation and Persistence of Mission Communities in a Comparative Context* (Leiden: Brill, 2015), appendix 4 and appendix 8.

APPENDIX A.3
The population and vital rates of Santa Rosa mission, selected years

Year	Population	Families	Baptisms	Burials	Crude birth rate	Crude death rate	Avg. family size
1702	2879	661	224	73	82.1*	26.8*	4.4
1724	4742	1076	345	257	74.1*	55.2*	4.4
1728	6064	1170	289	217	48.2*	18.2*	5.2
1733	2775	546	110	2263	20.2*	414.6*	5.1
1736	1671	389	99	80	53.3	44.9	4.3
1739	1916	460	126	82	68.9	44.9	4.2
1740	1973	486	146	94	76.2	49.1	4.1
1741	2031	506	184	117	93.3	59.3	4.0
1744	2170	550	192	110	92.7	53.2	4.0
1745	2245	565	183	90	84.3	41.5	3.9
1746	2288	575	182	113	82.2	54.6	4.0
1747	2354	578	201	177	87.9	52.9	4.1
1748	2455	578	157	249	66.7	195.8	4.3
1749	2524	579	158	73	64.4	29.7	4.5
1750	2601	582	174	106	68.9	42.0	4.5
1753	2838	608	175	110	63.0	40.0	4.7
1754	2921	621	179	103	63.1	36.3	4.7
1755	3051	644	153	—	52.4	—	—
1756	3056	674	180	113	59.0	37.0	4.5
1757	3121	694	185	—	60.5	—	—
1758	—	748	161	—	51.6	—	—
1759	3150	752	168	130	53.9*	41.8*	4.2
1760	3197	—	203	—	64.4	—	—
1761	3236	—	190	—	59.4	—	—
1762	3294	781	202	177	62.4	54.7	4.2
1763	3292	781	188	228	57.1	69.2	4.2
1764	2031	178	211	1614	64.1	490.3	11.4
1765	1934	414	59	211	29.0	40.9	4.7
1767	2243	497	126	59	57.5*	4.7*	4.5
1802	1193	—	131	82	103.9	65.0	—
1803	1578	373	107	82	89.7	68.7	4.2

*Estimated.

Source: Robert H. Jackson, *Demographic Change and Ethnic Survival among the Sedentary Populations on the Jesuit Mission Frontiers of South America: The Formation and Persistence of Mission Communities in a Comparative Context* (Leiden: Brill, 2015), 215.

Appendix A.4
Females as a percentage of total population of Santa Rosa, Candelaria, and Santos Mártires missions, selected years

Year	Santa Rosa	Candelaria	Santo Mártires
1724	51.0	55.1	45.0
1733	54.5	55.2	53.1
1736	55.8	57.5	52.5
1739	55.0	54.2	51.0
1740	54.7	53.0	51.2
1741	53.8	54.1	51.3
1744	54.3	55.2	51.4
1745	51.8	55.1	51.6
1746	49.7	55.1	51.2
1747	51.7	53.9	51.1
1753	51.4	54.8	49.6
1756	52.0	53.9	50.0
1759	51.9	53.1	48.6
1762	52.3	52.7	49.5
1763	51.9	52.7	50.5
1764	51.8	52.6	49.2
1765	50.4	53.1	47.8
1767	51.9	54.0	48.3
1772	51.7	51.4	46.8
1799 Present	50.6	—	—
1799 Absent	23.9	—	—

Source: Robert H. Jackson, *Demographic Change and Ethnic Survival among the Sedentary Populations on the Jesuit Mission Frontiers of South America: The Formation and Persistence of Mission Communities in a Comparative Context* (Leiden: Brill, 2015), 200–204.

Appendix A.5
Marriages recorded at Santa Rosa, Loreto, Candelaria, and Santos Mártires missions, 1733–1767

Year	Santa Rosa	Loreto	Candelaria	Santo Mártires
1691		32	36	69
1724	41	14	40	29
1728	50	59	21	39
1733	57	263	43	93
1736	36	45	36	46
1739	49	53	28	154
1740	88	51	43	40
1741	32	83	38	53
1744	96	44	18	70
1745	31	37	30	40
1746	22	27	26	47
1747	26	46	19	48
1753	23	34	14	45
1756	47	30	31	75
1759	52	46	25	59
1762	72	101	36	52
1763	31	142	43	55
1764	70	70	24	53
1765	238	303	30	193
1767	79	79	45	52

Source: Robert H. Jackson, *Demographic Change and Ethnic Survival among the Sedentary Populations on the Jesuit Mission Frontiers of South America: The Formation and Persistence of Mission Communities in a Comparative Context* (Leiden: Brill, 2015), 206–10; "Anua numeración de los Indios del Paraná y Uruguay que estan a cargo de la Com[pañí]a de IESVS hecho al fin del año de 1691," ARSI Paraguaria 12; for 1728 from "Catalogo de la Numeración de las Doctrinas ... Año de 1728," AGN, Sala 9-7-2-1.

Appendix A.6
The population and vital rates of Candelaria mission, selected years

Year	Population	Families	Baptisms	Burials	Crude birth rate	Crude death rate	Avg. family size
1691	2508	663	229**	125	87.7*	47.9*	3.8
1702	2596	622	199	114	79.3*	5.4*	4.2
1724	2863	626	213	143	76.3*	1.2*	4.6
1728	3294	651	205	118	63.9*	36.8*	5.1
1733	3134	702	196	246	61.6*	7.3*	4.5
1736	3049	611	136	150	43.8	48.3	5.0
1739	1503	352	146	79	96.6	52.3	4.3
1740	1441	382	65	80	43.3	53.2	3.8
1741	1639	410	71	98	49.3	68.0	4.0
1744	1764	482	91	97	54.1	57.6	3.7
1745	1814	503	153	95	86.7	53.9	3.6
1746	1881	523	198	129	109.2	71.1	3.6
1747	1933	528	178	111	94.6	59.0	3.7
1748	2017	549	181	103	93.6	53.3	3.7
1749	2031	529	201	213	99.7	105.6	3.8
1750	2083	539	181	84	89.1	41.4	3.9
1753	2253	541	200	94	90.8	42.7	4.2
1754	2266	560	173	86	76.8	38.2	4.1
1756	2409	595	128	101	54.8	43.2	4.1
1759	2585	613	155	144	60.2*	560.1*	4.2
1762	2724	647	174	126	64.8	46.9	4.2
1763	2723	661	156	138	57.3	50.7	4.1
1764	2817	668	174	147	63.9	54.0	4.2
1765	2879	682	215	121	76.3	43.0	4.3
1767	3064	754	222	130	74.7*	43.7*	4.1
1798	1433	339	62	100	42.2*	68.0*	4.1
1799	1365	331	64	76	44.7	53.0	4.1
1802	1334	—	78	65	58.1	48.4	
1803	1400	297	73	67	54.7	50.2	4.7

*Estimated.
**Plus seven baptisms of adults.

Source: Robert H. Jackson, *Demographic Change and Ethnic Survival among the Sedentary Populations on the Jesuit Mission Frontiers of South America: The Formation and Persistence of Mission Communities in a Comparative Context* (Leiden: Brill, 2015), 221; "Anua numeración de los Indios del Paraná y Uruguay que estan a cargo de la Com[pañí]a de IESVS hecho al fin del año de 1691," ARSI Paraguaria 12.

APPENDIX A.7

The population and vital rates of Los Santos Mártires mission, selected years

Year	Population	Families	Baptisms	Burials	Crude birth rate	Crude death rate	Avg. family size
1691	2317	537	113	77	49.5*	33.8*	4.3
1702	3536	897	289	259	82.4*	73.9*	3.9
1724	3343	795	190	155	57.4*	46.9*	4.2
1728	3637	866	216	143	60.6*	40.1*	4.2
1733	3665	901	202	491	51.1*	124.2*	4.1
1736	3396	861	188	199	55.0*	58.3*	3.9
1739	2777	723	132	545	40.9	184.2	3.8
1740	2829	682	170	95	61.2	34.2	4.2
1741	2833	701	192	160	67.9	56.6	4.0
1744	2834	699	184	201	64.7	70.7	4.1
1745	2847	710	170	141	60.0	49.8	4.0
1746	2930	723	220	134	77.3	47.4	4.1
1747	2074	734	214	143	73.0	34.1	4.1
1748	2981	735	180	171	60.5	57.5	4.1
1749	3075	737	210	166	64.9	51.3	4.2
1750	3112	789	201	164	65.4	53.3	3.9
1753	3235	812	188	144	59.0	45.2	4.0
1754	3282	792	235	181	72.6	56.0	4.1
1756	3217	737	205	341	61.0	101.4	4.4
1759	3218	763	187	198	57.9*	61.3*	4.2
1762	3225	760	169	182	51.8	59.2	4.3
1763	3099	729	167	185	51.8	59.2	4.3
1764	2220	324	173	1129	54.1	364.3	6.9
1765	1688	365	83	561	37.4	252.7	4.6
1767	1662	430	115	128	67.6*	75.3*	3.9
1797	751	185	44	58	57.5*	75.8*	4.1
1798	715	191	32	41	42.6	54.6	3.7
1799	681	173	28	28	39.2	39.2	3.9
1802	605	—	13	38	20.5*	59.9*	—
1803	609	155	14	32	23.1	52.9	3.9
1808	548	128	20	38	35.3*	67.1*	4.3

*Estimated.

Source: Robert H. Jackson, *Demographic Change and Ethnic Survival among the Sedentary Populations on the Jesuit Mission Frontiers of South America: The Formation and Persistence of Mission Communities in a Comparative Context* (Leiden: Brill, 2015), 221; for 1691, "Anua numeración de los Indios del Paraná y Uruguay que estan a cargo de la Com[pañí]a de IESVS hecho al fin del año de 1691," ARSI Paraguaria 12; for 1808, Jose Ignacio Ayala, "Los Santos Mártires, January 1, 1809, Annua Numeración de los Yndibiduos Existentes de Ambos Sexos en este Pueblo de la Real Corona nombrado los Santos Mártires del Japón oy dia 1 de Enero de 1809 Asaver," Archivo Nacional, Asunción, Paraguay.

Appendix A.8
The population and vital rates of San Francisco Xavier mission, selected years

Year	Families	Population	Baptisms Children	Baptisms Adults	Burials	Crude birth rate	Crude death rate	Avg. family size
1712	478	1955	93	—	19	49.4*	10.1*	4.0
1718	505	1688	75	—	22	44.6	13.1	3.3
1735	605	2345	109	—	94	46.8*	40.3*	3.9
1738	559	2342	138	7	189	57.8*	79.1*	4.2
1739	560	2364	111	1	191	47.4	81.6	4.2
1740	564	2481	120	2	65	50.8	27.5	4.4
1741	558	2378	130	3	75	52.4	30.2	4.3
1742	545	2413	135	3	110	56.8	46.3	4.4
1743	546	2416	131	—	138	55.1	58.0	4.4
1744	556	2403	127	—	140	52.6	58.0	4.3
1745	552	2293	115	—	138	47.9	57.4	4.2
1746	582	2314	125	—	71	54.5	31.0	4.0
1747	612	2435	115	—	144	49.7	62.2	4.0
1748	620	2497	153	—	91	62.8	37.4	4.0
1749	622	2480	115	—	130	46.1	52.1	4.0
1750	633	2550	156	—	86	62.9	34.7	4.0
1751	—	—	72	—	—	28.2	—	—
1752	568	2323	72	—	—	—	—	4.1
1753	—	—	216	—	—	—	—	—
1754	—	—	156	—	—	—	—	—
1755	606	2578	158	—	92	62.9*	36.6*	4.3
1756	615	2639	165	—	104	64.0	40.3	4.3
1757	631	2728	156	—	57	59.1	21.6	4.3
1758	642	2799	154	—	83	56.5	30.4	4.4
1759	—	—	170	—	—	—	—	—
1760	656	2978	171	—	101	58.8*	34.7*	4.5
1761	666	3065	191	—	104	64.1	34.9	4.6
1762	—	—	158	—	—	51.6	—	—
1763	—	—	194	—	—	—	—	—
1764	703	3256	176	—	113	55.1*	35.4*	4.6
1765	728	3302	198	—	142	60.8	43.6	4.5
1766	720	3201	164	—	265	49.7	80.3	4.5
1767	—	—	173	2	—	—	—	—
1768	—	2022	147	—	—	45.9	—	—

*Estimated.

Source: Robert H. Jackson, Demographic Change and Ethnic Survival among the Sedentary Populations on the Jesuit Mission Frontiers of South America: The Formation and Persistence of Mission Communities in a Comparative Context (Leiden: Brill, 2015), 260.

Appendix A.9
Children (under age 15) as percentage of the total population of San Francisco Xavier mission, selected years

Year	Population	Number of children	Percentage	Average family size
1712	1,796	614	34.2	4.0
1718	1,690	616	49.1	3.3
1738	2,342	1,152	49.1	4.2
1739	2,364	1,174	49.7	4.2
1740	2,421	1,235	51.0	4.4
1741	2,378	1,236	52.0	4.3
1742	2,413	1,276	52.9	4.4
1743	2,416	1,269	52.5	4.4
1744	2,403	1,258	52.4	4.3
1745	2,293	1,126	49.1	4.2
1746	2,314	1,119	48.4	4.0
1747	2,435	1,167	47.9	4.0
1748	2,497	1,203	48.2	4.0
1749	2,480	1,185	47.8	4.0
1750	2,550	1,245	48.8	4.0
1755	2,578	1,308	50.7	4.3
1756	2,639	1,347	51.0	4.3
1757	2,728	1,422	52.1	4.3
1758	2,799	1,462	52.2	4.4
1760	2,978	1,629	54.7	4.5
1761	3,065	1,700	55.5	4.6
1764	3,256	1,813	55.7	4.6
1765	3,302	1,790	54.0	4.5
1766	3,201	1,679	52.5	4.5

Source: General mission censuses titled "Catologo de la numeracion annual de las misiones de Chiquitos," Biblioteca Nacional, Archivo General de la Nacion, Buenos Aires, 6127–14, 6467–101; individual anuas for San Francisco Xavier mission 1738, 1740, and 1741.

APPENDIX A.10
The population of the Moxos missions, selected years

Mission	Founded	1691	1698	1713	1717	1732	1748	1768
Trinidad	1686	2254	2693	1700	—	2208	1720	700
Esposorio	1694	—	—	—	1576	1623	1199	—
Santa Rosa	1705	—	—	1600	666	624	388	—
Loreto	1682	3822	—	2000	1768	1255	1054	850
San Xavier	1691	2361	1863	2000	—	1717	1710	1200
San Pedro	1697	—	—	1900	2864	3223	3296	2100
Exaltación	1709	—	—	1400	1684	1851	1593	1900
San Ignacio	1689	3014	3202	1505	1981	974	621	1160
San José	1691	2036	—	2105	1008	923	686	—
San Miguel	1696	—	—	—	—	1298	3444	—
San Luis Gonzaga	1698	—	—	1630	1011	906	523	—
SF Borja	1693	—	—	1924	1256	1826	998	—
San Pablo	1703	—	—	1390	2048	2000	1324	—
Reyes	1710	—	—	1500	1641	2108	1782	1060
San Juan	1710	—	—	1304	581	—	—	—
Concep.	1708	—	—	—	2152	3157	2803	1295
San Joaquín	1708	—	—	1206	2310	2622	2112	680
Santa Ana	1709	—	—	200	—	1378	1394	1000
Magdalena	1720	—	—	—	—	2782	3112	4300
San Martín	1717	—	—	—	—	1557	1222	600
San Nicolás	1740	—	—	—	—	1514	1816	400
San Simón	1744	—	—	—	—	914	493	—

Source: "Catalogus redoctionum misionis Moxorum in Provincia Peruana Jesu Die 1 Aprilis 1732," Archivo Histórico de la Compañía de Jesús, Paraguay; Pablo Pastells, S.J., *Historia de la Compañía de Jesús en la Provincia del Paraguay*, 9 vols. (Madrid: Self-published, 1912), 6:157–58; 7:746–48; Pedro Querejazu, ed., *Las misiones jesuíticas de Chiquitos* (La Paz, 1995), 336.

Appendix B

Demographic Indicators of the Sierra Gorda Missions

Appendix B.1
The Dominican missions in the Sierra Gorda region, ca. 1700

Mission	Heads of household (vecinos) / families	Population
Nuestra Señora de los Dolores Zimapán	120	—
Nuestra Señora del Rosario de la Nopalera	50	—
Nuestro Padre Santo Domingo de Guzmán Soriano	—	600
San José del Llano	70	—
San Miguel de la Cruz Milagrosa de Palmas	100	—
Nuestra Señora de Guadalupe de Ahuacatlán	50	—
Puxinguia	130	—
Santa Rosa de las	Minas de Xichú	—	—
Total	—	3,220*

*Total population excluding Santa Rosa. The Dominicans reported the population in different categories, but then reported the total population in their missions as 3,200.

Source: Santiago Rodríguez López, O.P., "Los Dominicos en Querétaro: Tierra facunda de vocaciones religiosos," in *Los Dominicos y el Nuevo Mundo Siglos XIX–XX. Actas del quinto Congreso Internacional, Querétaro, Qro (Mexico) 4–8 Septiembre 1995* (Salamanca, Spain: Editorial San Esteban, 1997), 205–6.

Appendix B.2
The number of soldiers stationed in the Sierra Gorda in 1743

Location of garrison	Number of officers and soldiers
San Pedro Tolimán	63
Cadereyta	200
San José de Vizarrón	7
Zimapán	47
Pacula	40
Xalpa	30
Between Xalpa and Concá	42
San Juan Bautista de Xichú de Indios	10
Total	**439**

Source: José de Escandón, Querétaro, February 23, 1743, "Informe del Coronel José de Escandón acerca de su visita a la Sierra Gorda y proyecto de reorganización de sus misiones," in Lino Gómez Canedo, *Sierra Gorda: Un típico enclave misional en el centro de Mexico (siglos XVII–XVIII)* (Querétaro: Provincia Franciscana de Santiago, 2011), 197–98.

Appendix B.3
The population of the Sierra Gorda missions, selected years

Mission	1744	1746	1758	1761	1764
Xalpa	1,445	1,205	980	985	-
Concá	449	248	423	407	365
Landa	564	401	646	407	537
Tilaco	659	416	894	935	704
Tancoyol	574	207	547	515	253

Source: Robert H. Jackson, *Demographic Change and Ethnic Survival among the Sedentary Populations on the Jesuit Mission Frontiers of South America: The Formation and Persistence of Mission Communities in a Comparative Context* (Leiden: Brill, 2015), 139.

Appendix B.4
Baptisms and burials recorded in the Sierra Gorda missions, 1744–1764

Mission	Baptisms	Burials	Net +/−
Santiago de Xalpa	1,277	1,772	−495
San Miguel Concá	338	699	−361
Agua de Landa	780	952	−172
Tilaco	877	1,138	−306
Tancoyol*	336	784	−448
Total	**3,608**	**5,390**	**−1,782**

*1747–1764.

Source: Robert H. Jackson, *Demographic Change and Ethnic Survival among the Sedentary Populations on the Jesuit Mission Frontiers of South America: The Formation and Persistence of Mission Communities in a Comparative Context* (Leiden: Brill, 2015), 140.

Appendix B.5
Children as a percentage of the total population on the Sierra Gorda missions

Mission	1758	1761	1764
Xalpa	36	37	–
Concá	36	45	44
Landa	37	40	40
Tilaco	37	36	41
Tancoyol	29	33	38

Source: Lino Gómez Canedo, *Sierra Gorda: Un típico enclave misional en el centro de Mexico (siglos XVII–XVIII)* (Querétaro: Provincia Franciscana de Santiago, 2011), 221–42, 251–54.

Appendix B.6
Structure of the population of Tancoyol mission in 1744

TANCOYOL (total population: 364)						
Family size	Two	Three	Four	Five	Six	Seven
# Families	40	23	22	8	8	2
# People	80	69	88	40	48	14

		Their children
Widowers	5	8
Widows	1	1
Single	10	—

RANCHERIA DE SOYAPILA (total population: 210)						
Family size	Two	Three	Four	Five	Six	Seven
# Families	29	29	3	8	2	0
# People	58	87	12	40	12	0

		Their children
Widowers	0	0
Widows	0	0
Single	1	—

Source: Joaquin Meade y Sainz Tapaga, *La Huasteca Queretana* (México, D.F.: Imprenta Aldina, 1951), 425–31.

Appendix B.7
Structure of the population of Tilaco mission in 1744

TILACO (total population: 448)						
Family size	Two	Three	Four	Five	Six	Seven
# Families	22	35	43	18	3	1
# People	44	105	172	90	18	7

		Their children
Widowers	4	7
Widows	0	—
Single	0	—

RANCHO DE EL LOBO (total population: 149)						
Family size	Two	Three	Four	Five	Six	Seven
# Families	10	11	11	8	2	0
# People	20	33	44	40	12	0

		Their children
Widowers	0	—
Widows	0	—
Single	0	—

LAGUNA GRANDE (total population: 62)						
Family size	Two	Three	Four	Five	Six	Seven
# Families	5	1	6	5	0	0
# People	10	3	24	25	0	0

		Their children
Widowers	0	—
Widows	0	—
Single	0	—

EL HUMO		
Families: 20	Total Population: 90	Average family size: 4.5

Source: Joaquin Meade y Sainz Tapaga, *La Huasteca Queretana* (México, D.F.: Imprenta Aldina, 1951), 408–13.

Notes

Abbreviations

AC, BNB	Angelis Collection, Biblioteca Nacional do Brasil, Rio de Janeiro, Brasil
AGI	Archivo General de las Indias, Sevilla, Spain
AGN	Archivo General de la Nación, Buenos Aires
ANP	Archivo Nacional de Paraguay, Asunción, Paraguay
ARSI	Archivum Romanum Societatis Iesu, Vatin City
BNAGN	Biblioteca Nacional, Archivo General de la Nación, Buenos Aires
BNB	Biblioteca Nacional do Brasil, Rio de Janeiro, Brasil
LPA	Landa Parish Archive, Landa de Matamoros, Querétaro
SRPA	Santa Rosa Parish Archive, Santa Rosa, Paraguay

Introduction

1. Robert H. Jackson and Erick Langer, eds., *The New Latin American Mission History* (Lincoln: University of Nebraska Press, 1995).
2. See, for example, Susan Deeds, *Defiance and Deference in Mexico's Colonial North: Indians under Spanish Rule in Nueva Vizcaya* (Austin: University of Texas Press, 2010); Erick Langer, *Expecting Pears from an Elm Tree: Franciscan Missions on the Chiriguano Frontier in the Heart of South America, 1830–1949* (Durham: Duke University Press, 2009); James Saeger, *The Chaco Mission Frontier: The Guaycuruan Experience* (Tucson: University of Arizona Press, 2000); Guillermo Wilde, *Religión y poder en las misiones de guaraníes* (Buenos Aires: Editorial Sb, 2009); Rafael Carbonnell de Massy, S.J., *Estrategias de desarrollo rural en los pueblos guaraníes (1609–1767)* (Barcelona: Antoni Bosch Editor, 1992); Barbara Ganson, *The Guaraní under Spanish Rule in the Río de la Plata* (Stanford: Stanford University Press, 2003); Cynthia Redding de

Murrieta, *Wandering Peoples: Colonialism, Ethnic Spaces, and Ecological Frontiers in Northwestern Mexico, 1700–1850* (Durham: Duke University Press, 1997); Cynthia Radding de Murrieta, *Landscapes of Power and Identity: Comparative Histories in the Sonoran Desert and the Forests of Amazonia from Colony to Republic* (Durham: Duke University Press, 2005); Julia Sarreal, *The Guaraní and Their Missions: A Socioeconomic History* (Stanford: Stanford University Press, 2014); Robert H. Jackson, *Indian Demographic Decline: The Missions of Northwestern New Spain, 1687–1840* (Albuquerque: University of New Mexico Press, 1994); Robert H. Jackson and Edward Castillo, *Indians, Franciscans, and Spanish Colonization: The Impact of the Mission System on California Indians* (Albuquerque: University of New Mexico Press, 1995). Other scholars have documented native relations with colonists in lowland South America outside of missions, in particular in Portuguese Brazil. Recent studies include Heather Flynn Roller, "Colonial Collecting Expeditions and the Pursuit of Opportunities in the Amazonian Sertao, ca. 1750–1800," *The Americas* 66, no. 4 (2010): 435–67; Heather Flynn Roller, *Amazonian Routes: Indigenous Mobility and Colonial Communities in Northern Brazil* (Stanford: Stanford University Press, 2014); Hal Langfur, "The Return of the Bandeira: Economic Calamity, Historical Memory, and Armed Expeditions to the Sertao in Minas Gerais, 1750–1808," *The Americas* 61, no. 3 (2005): 429–61; and Hal Langfur, *The Forbidden Lands: Colonial Identity, Frontier Violence, and the Persistence of Brazil's Eastern Indians, 1750–1830* (Stanford: Stanford University Press, 2006).
3. See, for example, Maria de Fatima Wade, *Missions, Missionaries, and Native Americans: Long-Term Processes and Daily Practices* (Gainesville: University Press of Florida, 2008); Robert H. Jackson, *From Savages to Subjects: Missions in the History of the American Southwest* (Armonk: M.E. Sharpe, 2000); Robert H. Jackson, *Missions and the Frontiers of Spanish America: A Comparative Study of the Impact of Environmental, Economic, Political, and Socio-Cultural Variations on the Missions in the Rio de la Plata Region and on the Northern Frontier of New Spain* (Scottsdale: Pentacle Press, 2005).
4. Radding, *Wandering Peoples*; Radding, *Landscapes of Power and Identity*.
5. See Jackson, *Indian Population Decline*; Jackson and Castillo, *Indians, Franciscans, and Spanish Colonization*; Robert H. Jackson, "A Frustrated Evangelization: The Limitations to Social, Cultural and Religious Change among the 'Wandering Peoples' of the Missions of the Central Desert of Baja California and the Texas Gulf Coast," *Fronteras de la Historia* 6 (2001): 7–40; Robert H. Jackson, "Congregation and Depopulation: Demographic Patterns in the Texas Missions," *Journal of South Texas* 17, no. 2 (Fall, 2004): 6–38; Robert H. Jackson, "A Colonization Born of Frustration: Rosario Mission and the Karankawas," *Journal of South Texas* 17, no. 1 (Spring, 2004): 31–50.
6. See, for example, Robert H. Jackson, "Demographic Patterns on the Chiquitos Missions of Eastern Bolivia, 1691–1767," *Bolivian Studies Journal* 12 (2005): 220–48; Robert H. Jackson, "Demographic Patterns in the Jesuit Missions of the Rio de la Plata Region: The Case of Corpus Christi Mission, 1622–1802," *Colonial Latin American Historical*

Review 13, no. 4 (2004): 337–66; Robert H. Jackson, "The Population and Vital Rates of the Jesuit Missions of Paraguay 1700–1767," *Journal of Interdisciplinary History* 28, no. 3 (2008): 401–31; Robert H. Jackson, "The Post-Jesuit Expulsion Population of the Paraguay Missions, 1768–1803," *Revista de História Regional* 13, no. 2 (2008): 134–69; Robert H. Jackson, "Missions on the Frontiers of Spanish America," *Journal of Religious History* 33, no. 3 (September, 2009): 328–47; Robert H. Jackson, *Demographic Change and Ethnic Survival Among the Sedentary Populations on the Jesuit Mission Frontiers of Spanish South America, 1609–1803: The Formation and Persistence of Mission Communities in a Comparative Context* (Leiden: Brill Academic Publishers, 2015); Robert H. Jackson, "The Chichimeca Frontier and the Evangelization of the Sierra Gorda, 1550–1770," *Estudios de Historia Novohispana* 47 (Julio–Diciembre, 2012): 46–91; Robert H. Jackson, "The Virgin of the Rosary at Tetela del Volcán (Morelos), Conversion, the Baptismal Controversy, a Dominican Critique of the Franciscans, and the Culture Wars in Sixteenth Century Central Mexico," in Robert H. Jackson, ed., *Evangelization and Culture Conflict in Colonial Mexico* (Newcastle upon Tyne: Cambridge Scholars Publishing, 2014), 1–29; Robert H. Jackson, *Conflict and Conversion in Sixteenth Century Central Mexico: The Augustinian War on and Beyond the Chichimeca Frontier* (Leiden: Brill Academic Publishers, 2013); Robert H. Jackson, *Visualizing the Miraculous, Visualizing the Sacred: Evangelization and the "Cultural War" in Sixteenth Century Mexico* (Newcastle upon Tyne: Cambridge Scholars Publishing, 2014).

7. For a detailed discussion of the eighteenth-century reform impulse in late eighteenth-century Spain, see Richard Herr, *The Eighteenth-Century Revolution in Spain* (Princeton: Princeton University Press, 1958); Richard Herr, *Rural Change and Royal Finances in Spain at the End of the Old Regime* (Berkeley: University of California Press, 1989). For studies of liberalism in Latin America, see Charles Hale, *Mexican Liberalism in the Age of More, 1821–1853* (New Haven: Yale University Press, 1968); Jan Bazant, *The Alienation of Church Wealth in Mexico: Social and Economic Aspects of the Liberal Revolution, 1856–1875* (Cambridge: Cambridge University Press, 1971); Charles Berry, *The Reform in Oaxaca, 1856–76: A Microhistory of the Liberal Revolution* (Lincoln: University of Nebraska Press, 1981); Robert H. Jackson, *Regional Markets and Agrarian Transformation in Bolivia: Cochabamba, 1539–1960* (Albuquerque: University of New Mexico Press, 1994); Robert H. Jackson, ed., *Liberals, the Church, and Indian Peasants: Corporate Lands and the Challenge of Reform in Nineteenth-Century Spanish America* (Albuquerque: University of New Mexico Press, 1997), among others.

8. Jackson, *Demographic Change and Ethnic Survival*, 158.

9. Ibid., 128–33.

10. For a useful discussion of the "Neolithic Revolution," see Jacob Weisdorf, "From Foraging to Farming: Explaining the Neolithic Revolution," *Journal of Economic Surveys* 19, no. 4 (2005): 561–86.

11. See, for example, Renee Pennington, "Did Food Increase Fertility? An Evaluation of !Kung and Herero History," *Human Biology* 64, no. 4 (1992): 497–501.

12. Andrew P. Dobson and E. Robin Carper, "Infectious Diseases and Human Population History," *Bioscience* 46, no. 2 (February, 1996): 115–26.
13. Jackson, *Demographic Change and Ethnic Survival*, 61–62.
14. Ibid., 166–78.
15. French demographers such as Louis Henry pioneered the method in studies of French communities. See, for example, Etienne Gautier and Louis Henry, *La population de Crulai, paroisse normande: Étude historique* (Paris: Presses universitaires de France, 1958). In a study published in 1989, a research team used sacramental registers and other sources to reconstruct demographic patterns in early modern England. See Edward Wrigley and Roger S. Schofield, *The Population History of England 1541–1871* (Cambridge: Cambridge University Press, 1989). Michael Flinn summarized demographic studies to provide a profile of early modern European patterns. See Michael Flinn, *The European Demographic System 1500–1820* (Baltimore: Johns Hopkins University Press, 1981). One influential demographic study of mission frontiers is that of Daniel Reff, *Disease, Depopulation, and Culture Change in Northwestern New Spain, 1518–1764* (Salt Lake City: University of Utah Press, 1991). By examining the effects of epidemic disease on the native populations of Sonora and neighboring regions, Reff took on the challenge of documenting demographic change during the sixteenth century, which is a difficult proposition given the limitations of the sources. He analyzes the existing evidence and convincingly argues for the early introduction into the region of smallpox and other highly contagious "crowd" diseases along trade routes and through contact with the first Spaniards who ventured into the region. However, Reff's study also manifests some of the weaknesses of scholarship regarding sixteenth-century mortality crises and demographic change. I criticize these weaknesses in a recent study titled "Los efectos de las enfermedades del Viejo Mundo en los nativos americanos: La viruela en las Misiones Jesuíticas de Paraguay," *IHS Antiguos Jesuitas en Iberoamérica* 2, no. 2 (2014): 88–133. Evidence of demographic change in the sixteenth century is limited, and scholars examining this period often make assumptions not supported by the evidence. Moreover, there is little evidence of patterns following major mortality crises. In other words, was there a rebound effect or demographic recovery following an epidemic outbreak? Reff is more cautious than others who have attempted to document sixteenth-century demographic change, but the fundamental problem of underlying assumptions about the period and evidence remains. Moreover, a more substantial criticism can be made of Reff's study. Sacramental registers do not exist for the sixteenth century, but they do exist for the late seventeenth and the eighteenth centuries. Moreover, in the case of Sonora detailed censuses exist for the eighteenth century, which is the terminal point for Reff's study. However, the author did not make full use of these sources. The analysis of burial registers, for example, more fully documents mortality patterns during epidemics and demographic patterns following mortality crises.
16. Jackson, *Demographic Change and Ethnic Survival*, 140–43.
17. Ibid., 117–18.

18. Ibid., 107–9.
19. Tancoyol Baptismal Register, Landa de Matamoros Parish Archive, Landa de Matamoros, Querétaro.
20. Ibid., 42–44.
21. See, for example, Louise Burkhart, *The Slippery Earth: Nahua-Christian Moral Dialogue in Sixteenth-Century Mexico* (Tucson: University of Arizona Press, 1989); Louise Burkhart, "The Solar Christ in Nahuatl Doctrinal Texts of Early Colonial Mexico," *Ethnohistory* 35, no. 3 (1988): 234–56; Louise Burkhart, "The 'Little Doctrine' and Indigenous Catechesis in New Spain," *Hispanic American Historical Review* 94, no. 2 (2014): 167–206.
22. See David Tavárez, *The Invisible War: Indigenous Devotions, Discipline, and Dissent in Colonial Mexico* (Stanford: Stanford University Press, 2011); David Tavárez, "Idolatry as an Ontological Question: Native Consciousness and Juridical Proof in Colonial Mexico," *Journal of Early Modern History* 6, no. 2 (2002): 114–39; David Tavárez, "The Passion According to the Wooden Drum: The Christian Appropriation of a Zapotec Ritual Genre in New Spain," *The Americas* 62, no. 03 (2006): 413–44.
23. Eleanor Wake, *Framing the Sacred: The Indian Churches of Early Colonial Mexico* (Norman: University of Oklahoma Press, 2010).
24. Robert H. Jackson, *Visualizing the Miraculous, Visualizing the Sacred*.

Chapter 1

1. On the origins of the altépetl in central Mexico as related to the Culhua-Mexicas, see Federico Navarrete Linares, *Los orígenes de los pueblos indígenas del valle de México: Los altépetl y sus historias* (México, D.F.: UNAM, 2011). The classic studies of the construction of a colonial regime in central Mexico remain Charles Gibson, *The Aztecs under Spanish Rule: A History of the Indians of the Valley of Mexico 1519–1810* (Stanford: Stanford University Press, 1964), and James Lockhart, *The Náhuas after the Conquest: A Social and Cultural History of the Indians of Central Mexico, Sixteenth through Eighteenth Century* (Stanford: Stanford University Press, 1992).
2. Stephen Kowalewski et al., "La presencia azteca en Oaxaca: La provincia de Coixtlahuaca," *Anales de Antropología* 44 (2010): 77–103. The 1581 relación geográfica of Guaxilotitlan (Huitzo) noted that the Culhua-Mexica tribute collectors had their seat in three towns, namely, Oaxaca (Oaxaca City), Guaxilotitlan, and Cuestlauaca (Coixtlahuaca-Inguiteria. The original in the report noted that "y tenia para recoger este tribute tres principales que los llamaban 'calpizques.' El uno estava en Guaxaca, e el otro en este pueblo, y otro en Cuestlauaca, que es en la provincial de la Misteca, a donde el calpizque deste pueblo enviaba el maiz y mantas, y lo demas llevaban a Mexico al propio Motecsuma." See Francisco del Paso y Troncoso, ed., *Papeles de Nueva España publicados de orden y con fondos del gobierno mexicano. Segunda serie geográfica y estadística. Tomo IV: relaciones geograficas de la diócesis de Oaxaca* (Madrid: Tip. "Sucesores de Rivadenyra," 1905), 198.

3. Francisco del Paso y Troncoso, ed., *Papeles de Nueva España publicados de orden y con fondos del gobierno mexicano. Segunda serie geografía y estadística: Tomo I: Suma de visitas de pueblos por orden alfabético* (Madrid: Tip. "Sucesores de Rivadenyra, 1905), 131.
4. Ibid., 148.
5. Ibid., 282.
6. On the political structure of the Oaxtepec region, see Susana Gómez Serafín, *Altepetl de Huaxtepec: Modificaciones territoriales desde el siglo XVI* (México, DF: INAH, 2011), 39–44.
7. George Kubler, *La arquitectura mexicana del siglo XVI* (México, D.F.: Fondo de Cultura Económica, 1983), 553–54, 576, 577–78, 581.
8. Del Paso y Troncoso, *Papeles de Nueva España: Tomo I*, 206.
9. Francisco del Paso y Troncoso, ed., *Papeles de Nueva España publicados de orden y con fondos del gobierno mexicano. Segunda serie geografía y estadística: Tomo V: Relaciones geográficas de la Diócesis de Tlaxcala* (Madrid: Tip. "Sucesores de Rivadenyra," 1905), 19.
10. Ibid.
11. Kubler, *Arquitectura Mexicana*, 578, 581.
12. Ibid., 553–54.
13. Antonio De Ciudad Real, O.F.M., *Relación breve y verdadera de algunas cosas de las muchas que sucedieron al padre Fray Alonso Ponce en las provincias de la Nueva España*, 2 vols. (Madrid: Imprenta de la Viuda de Caero, 1875), 1:144.
14. Ibid.
15. The reports prepared around 1580 and known today as the *relaciones geográficas* testify to the effects of disease and in some instances make estimates of population loss. One example is the report for Tepoztlán, which describes the newly introduced diseases. See René Acuña, ed., *Relaciones geográficas del siglo XVI: México tomo primero* (México, D.F.: UNAM, 1984), 190–91.
16. Quoted in Jackson, *Conflict and Conversion*, 20.
17. In Francisco del Paso y Troncoso, *Papeles de Nueva España: Tomo I*, 110. The original quote reads, "Este pueblo de Teticpaque solía ser pueblo de muchos naturales e avía en el cómo dos mil indios, e a presente ay mil; la causa de aver al presente menos son las enfermedades y pestilencias que an tenido."
18. In René Acuña, ed., *Relaciones geográficas del siglo XVI: Antequera. Tomo Primero* (México. D.F.: UNAM, 1984), 151.
19. Ronald Spores, "Yucundáa: Su etnohistoria y consideraciones de relaciones arquitectónicas y patrones de urbanismo con españa," in Ronald Spores and Nelly M. Robles Garcia, eds., *Yucundáa: La ciudad mixteca y su transformación prehispánica-colonial*, 2 vols. (México, D.F.: INAH, 2014), 628.
20. Christina Gertrude Warinner, "Life and Death at Teposcolula Yucundáa: Mortuary, Archaeogenetic, and Isotopic Investigations of the Early Colonial Period in Mexico," unpublished Ph.D. dissertation, Harvard University, 2010, 194–96. There may be

as many as 2,000 burials in the great plaza, most likely dating to the 1540s. On the Dominican complex, see Elizabeth J. Galeana Cruz, "La iglesia vieja-casa religiosa dominica de Yucundáa y la casa de la cacica e iglesia y convento de San Pedro y San Pablo Teposcolula. Dos ejemplos de sincretismo arquitectónica en la primera mitad del siglo XVI: Mixtecos y dominicos," in Spores and Robles García, *Yucundáa*, 335–48.

21. On the early Dominican mission at Yucundáa and the resettlement of the community, see Ronald Spores et al., "Avances de investigación de los entierros humanos del sitio Pueblo Viejo de Teposcolula y su contexto arqueológico," *Estudios de Antropología Biológica* 13 (2007): 285–305; James B. Kiracofe, "Architectural Fusion and Indigenous Ideology in Early Colonial Teposcolula: The *Casa de la Cacica*: A Building at the Edge of Oblivion," *Anales del Instituto de Investigaciones Estéticas* 17, no. 66 (Spring, 1995): 45–84.
22. Kevin Terraciano, "The Colonial Mixtec Community," *Hispanic American Historical Review* 80, no. 1 (February 2000): 1–42; James B. Kiracofe, "Architectural Fusion."
23. Del Paso y Troncoso, *Papeles de Nueva España: Tomo I*, 30.
24. Ibid., 43–44. The original quote reads: "ya esta como en esta jurisdicción no hay más de un monestario in hay pueblo en la provincia que pueda sufrir más, porque son pobres, no hay hospital ninguno en todo este distrito si no es uno en esta Villa que mando hacer el muy Excelente Señor Don Martin Enríquez virrey y capitán general deste reino."
25. On the architectural elements of the sixteenth century mission complexes, see Kubler, *La arquitectura mexicana*; Robert J. Mullen, *Dominican Architecture in Sixteenth-Century Oaxaca* (Tempe: Arizona State University Press, 1975); Roberto Meli, *Los conventos mexicanos del siglo XVI: Construcción, ingeniería estructural y conservación* (México, D.F.: Editorial Miguel Ángel Porrúa, 2011).
26. Yolanda Lastra and Alejandro Terrazas, "Interpretación del posible actividades agrícolas prehispánicas a partir del análisis del chichimeco Jonaz," *Anales de Antropologuita* 40, no. 2 (2006): 165–87.
27. René Acuña, ed., *Relaciones geográficas del siglo XVI: Michoacán* (México, D.F: UNAM, 1987), 69.
28. Jackson, *Conflict and Conversion*, 47–50.
29. Ibid., 48.
30. Ibid., 20–21.
31. On early Augustinian missions in Mexico, see ibid., 45.
32. Ibid., table 5, 43.
33. Luis García Pimentel, ed., *Relación de los obispados de Tlaxcala, Oaxaca y otros lugares en el siglo XVI (*México, D.F.: Private Publication, 1904), 128–30.
34. Jackson, *Conflict and Conversion*, Table 5, 43.
35. García Pimentel, *Relación de los obispados*, 132.
36. Ibid., 130–32.
37. Ibid., 144.

38. Ibid., 133, 141.
39. Ibid., 136.
40. Del Paso y Troncoso, *Papeles de la Nueva España: Tomo I*, 299–300.
41. Jackson, *Conflict and Conversion*, 175–76.
42. Jackson, "The Chichimeca Frontier and the Evangelization of the Sierra Gorda," 61–63.
43. Lino Gómez Canedo, *Sierra Gorda: Un típico enclave misional en el centro de Mexico (siglos XVII–XVIII)* (Querétaro: Provincia Franciscana de Santiago, 2011), 183.
44. Ibid., 52–53.
45. Ibid., 53–54.
46. "Relación de la Villa y Monasterio de San Felipe (1571)," in García Pimentel, *Relación de los obispado*, 122–24.
47. Ibid., 123.
48. Ibid., 122.
49. On the Dominican doctrinas, see Mullen, *Dominican Architecture*; Robert H. Jackson, "Dominican Missions in Mexico: Sixteenth to Eighteenth Century," *Boletin Journal of the California Missions Studies Association* 31, no. 1 (2015): 114–29.
50. Acuña, *Relaciones Geográficas del Siglo XVI: Mexico Tomo Primero*, 97–103.
51. Gerardo Lara Cisneros, *El cristo viejo de Xichú: Resistencia y rebelión en la Sierra Gorda durante el siglo XVIII* (México, D.F.: Dirección General de Culturas Populares, 2007), 83.
52. Gómez Canedo, *Sierra Gorda*, 54–55. A 1688 document recorded the presence of the first Dominicans in the Sierra Gorda: "Alejandro Mathias de Urrutia, Cadereyta, September 4, 1688, Testimonio sobre la presencia franciscana en Cadereyta desde 1640 y su apostolado en la región de la Sierra Gorda," in Gómez Canedo, *Sierra Gorda*, 163–64.
53. Lara Cisneros, *El cristo viejo de Xichú*, 83.
54. Gómez Canedo, *Sierra Gorda*, 55.
55. Ibid., 179.
56. Lara Cisneros, *El cristo viejo de Xichú*, 64. A 1739 document mentioned the Dominican mission at Ranas that no longer existed at the time. "Pedro Navarrete, O.F.M., to Juan Bermejo, O.F.M., San Francisco de Mexico, August 12, 1739," in Gómez Canedo, *Sierra Gorda*, 174.
57. Ibid., 195.
58. Ibid., 87–93.
59. Ibid., 174.
60. José Antonio Perez, O.F.M., provincial of the Province of the Santo Evangelio, reported on the demise of La Nopalera mission in a letter written in Mexico City on July 29, 1739. In ibid., 169.
61. Lino Gómez Canedo, "La Sierra Gorda a fines del siglo XVIII: Diario de un viaje de inspección a sus milicias," *Historia Mexicana* 21, no. 1 (July–September, 1976): 148.

62. For the late eighteenth-century debate on the continued reliance of missions on the frontier, see Robert H. Jackson, *Race, Caste, and Status: Indians in Colonial Spanish America* (Albuquerque: University of New Mexico Press, 1999), 59–62.
63. Ciudad Real, O.F.M., *Relación breve y verdadera*, 1:451. Ciudad Real noted of the convent at Alfajayucan that it had a single nave church with a vaulted roof that had been built in this style because of the heat in the Mezquital Valley and threat of attacks from Chichimecas.
64. Jackson, *Conflict and Conversion*, 25.
65. Lara Cisneros, *El cristo viejo de Xichú*, 65–66.
66. Ciudad Real, O.F.M., *Relación breve*, 1:462–63.
67. Ibid., 1:461–62.
68. Acuña, *Relaciones geográficas del siglo XVI: Michoacán*, 68.
69. Ibid., 63.
70. Del Paso y Troncoso, *Papeles de la Nueva España: Tomo I*, 32–33.
71. Ibid., 68.
72. Ibid., 55, 59, 67.
73. Ciudad Real, *Relación breve*, chapter LXX.
74. Ibid., 1:492.
75. Lara Cisneros, *El cristo viejo de Xichú*, 139–42.
76. Ciudad Real, *Relación breve*, 1:223. Ciudad Real also noted that the Otomí defended the community with bows and arrows and put their women in the church for safety during the many Chichimeca attacks.
77. Acuña, *Relaciones geográficas del siglo XVI: Michoacán*, 60.
78. Felipe Duran Sandoval, "El papel de los franciscanos en la fundación de la alcaldía mayor de San Luis Potosi," in Arturo Vergara Hernández, ed., *Arte y sociedad en la Nueva España* (Pachuca: UAEH, 2014), 104–5.
79. Ibid., 105.
80. Gómez Canedo, *Sierra Gorda*, 164.
81. Ibid., 50.
82. Ibid., 175.
83. Ibid., 58–59.
84. Ibid., 68.
85. Ibid., 77.
86. Ibid., 184.
87. Ibid., 183.
88. Ibid., 91.
89. Ibid., 68.
90. Ibid., 204, 209.
91. Ibid., 92.
92. José Artes de Velasco, O.F.M., "Razón de las Misiones que el Colegio de San Fernando tiene en Sierra Gorda, alias Sierra Madre, y el estado que al presente tienen," in ibid., 220.

93. José Artes de Velasco, O.F.M., Querétaro, June 26, 1744, in Gómez Canedo, *Sierra Gorda*, 203–6.
94. José Artes de Velasco, O.F.M., "Razón de las Misiones que el Colegio de San Fernando tiene en Sierra Gorda, alias Sierra Madre, y el estado que al presente tienen," in Gómez Canedo, *Sierra Gorda*, 220.
95. Gerardo Lara Cisneros, "La domesticación del cristianismo en la Sierra Gorda, Nueva España, siglo XVIII," in Jackson, *Evangelization and Culture*, 180.
96. Gómez Canedo, *Sierra Gorda*, 195–96.
97. Lastra and Terrazas, "Interpretación," 172.
98. Ibid., 173.
99. Cecilia Rabell, "Matrimonio y raza en una parroquia rural: San Luis de la Paz, Guanajuato, 1715–1810," *Historia Mexicana* 41, no. 1 (1992): 5.
100. Ibid., 5–6.
101. Claudia Parrellada, "El Paraná Español: Ciudades y misiones jesuíticas en Guaira," in *Missoes: Conquistando almas e territorios* (Curitiba: Governo do Paraná, 2009), 133–34.
102. For a useful overview to the Jesuit missions among the Guaraní, see Ganson, *The Guaraní under Spanish Rule*.
103. Rafael Carbonell de Masy, S.J., Teresa Blumers, and Norberto Levinton, *La reducción jesuítica de Santos Cosme y Damián: Su historia, su economía y su arquitectura, 1633–1797* (Asunción: Markografik, 2003), 30.
104. Ibid., 45.
105. Ibid., 82.
106. Norberto Levinton, "La significación urbana del pueblo jesuítico de Yapeyú (1627–1817)," in Bartomeu Melía, *Historia inacabada futuro incierto* (Asunción: Centro de Estudios Paraguayos "Antonio Guasch," 2002), 296.
107. Ibid., 302.
108. Carta Annua de Corpus Christi, 1702 AC #929.
109. Francisco Burges, S.J., Procurador General de la Provincia de Paraguay, sin lugar, 1705, AGI, expediente 76-5-7, Charcas 381.
110. Ernesto Maeder, *Una Aproximación a las Misiones guaraníticas* (Buenos Aires: Universidad Católica Argentina, 1996), 50.
111. On the expansion of the Paraguay mission frontier into the Banda Oriental after 1680, see Robert H. Jackson, "Patrones demográficos de una frontera en conflicto: Las siete misiones orientales de la provincia jesuítica de Paraguay, 1680–1830," unpublished paper presented at the Seminário Internacional: Indígenas, Misionários e Espanhois o Parana no Contexto da Bacia do Prata, Seculos XVI e XVII, Paraná, October 15–17, 2008.
112. Levinton, "La significación urbana," 302–3.
113. On the population of the individual Guaraní missions, see Jackson, *Demographic Change and Ethnic Survival*.

114. An untitled and undated tribute census for Yapeyú, probably from 1759, divided the population between the original groups and those transferred from San Francisco Xavier. The tribute census is found in AGN, Sala 9-17-3-6.
115. Pablo Pastells, S.J., *Historia de la Compañía de Jesús en la Provincia del Paraguay*, 9 vols. (Madrid: self-published, 1912), 6:12–22, 24–26, 48–49.
116. Ibid., 6:48.
117. For a general study of the Chaco missions and the social and political organization of the Chaco groups including the Abipones, see Saeger, *The Chaco Mission Frontier*.
118. Carlos Page, *Las otras reducciones jesuíticas: Emplazamiento territorial, desarrollo urbano y arquitectónico entre los Siglos XVII y XVIII* (Saarbrücken, Germany: Editorial Académica Española, 2012), 323–40.
119. Estado De La Reducción De San Gerónimo De Abipones, En El Año 1758. AGN, Sala 9-10-6-10.
120. Anua de la Reducción De S Gerónimo De Abipones, desde 1 de Enero de 1761 hasta 1 de el mismo mes de 1762, AGN, Sala 9-10-6-10.
121. The carta anua recorded a total population of 728 for San Jerónimo and 284 for San Fernando, which would give a total of 1,012 for the two missions.
122. Littre Annuae Provincia Paraguarie Anno 1756–1762, ARSI.
123. Annua de la Reduc[io]n de S[a]n Ignacio de Tovas. Ano 1764, BNAGN, Sala 9-10-6-10.
124. Anua del Pueblo de S. Xavier de la Nación Mocobi del Ano de 1755, BNAGN, #8467/9.
125. Ganson, *The Guaraní under Spanish Rule*, 48
126. Anua del Colegio de Tarija 1761, in Carlos Page, ed., *El Colegio de Tarija y las misiones de Chiquitos según las Cartas Anua de la Compañía de Jesús* (Raleigh, N.C.: Lulu Press, 2010), 199.
127. Littre Annuae Provincia Paraguarie Anno 1735–1743, ARSI, in Page, *El Colegio de Tarija y las misiones de Chiquitos*, 92.
128. Ibid., 92–95.
129. Anua del Colegio de Tarija 1761 in Page, *El Colegio de Tarija y las misiones de Chiquitos*, 199.
130. Littre Annuae Provincia Paraguarie Anno 1756–1762, ARSI.
131. On the nineteenth century Franciscan Chiriguano missions, see Langer, *Expecting Pears from an Elm Tree*.
132. Littre Annuae Provincia Paraguarie Anno 1714–1720, in Javier Matienzo, Roberto Tomicha Charupá, Isabelle Combes, and Carlos Page, compilers and editors, *Chiquitos en las anuas de la Compañía de Jesús (1691–1767)* (Cochabamba: Instituto de Misionologia, 2011), 114–17.
133. Roberto Tomicha Charupá, *La primera evangelización en las reducciones de Chiquitos, Bolivia (1691–1767)* (Cochabamba: Editorial Verbo Divino, 202), 517.
134. Littre Annuae Provincia Paraguarie Anno 1689–1899, in Page, *El Colegio de Tarija y las misiones de Chiquitos*, 33.
135. Littre Annuae Provincia Paraguarie Anno 1743–1750, in ibid, 318–19.

136. Numeración annual de Chiquitos, in ibid., 338.
137. Tomicha Charupá, *La primera evangelización*, 517.
138. Ibid., 536–37, 547, 549.
139. Ibid., 557–59.
140. Carta Anua (1700–1713) in Matienzo, Tomicha Charupá, Combes, and Page, *Chiquitos*, 47.
141. Juan Bautista Xandra, S.J., San Rafael, August 1, 1712, Anua del Pueblo de San Ráphael de los Chiquitos Año mil setecientos onze y doze, BNAGN #6968/1.
142. No author, no date, Anua del Pueblo de San Miguel. Año de 1735. BNAGN, #6468/12.
143. Carta Anua (1714–1720) in Matienzo, Tomicha Charupá, Combes, and Page, *Chiquitos*, 116.
144. Daniel J. Santamaría, "Fronteras indígenas del oriente boliviano. La dominación colonial en Moxos y Chiquitos, 1675–1810," *Boletín Americanista* 36 (1986): 197–228.
145. Carta Anua (1735–1742) in Matienzo, Tomicha Charupá, Combes, and Page, *Chiquitos*, 237.
146. Jackson, "Demographic Patterns on the Chiquitos Missions of Eastern Bolivia," 220–48.
147. The standard study of the Moxos missions remains David Block, *Mission Culture on the Upper Amazon: Native Tradition, Jesuit Enterprise, and Secular Policy in Moxos, 1660–1880* (Lincoln: University of Nebraska Press, 1994).
148. "Católogo de las Reducciones de las Misiones de los Mojos en esta Provincia de Perú de la *Compañía* de Jesús 1748," in Pastells, *Historia de la Compañía de Jesús*, 7:746–47.
149. Jackson, *Demographic Change and Ethnic Survival*, 22–23.
150. Ibid., 101–2.
151. Ibid., 17.
152. Julia Sarreal, "Caciques as Placeholders in the Guaraní Missions of Eighteenth-Century Paraguay," *Colonial Latin American Review* 23, no. 2 (2014): 224–51.
153. Jackson, *Demographic Change and Ethnic Survival*, 53–58.
154. Sean McEnroe suggests that effective co-governance existed on the northern frontier of Mexico, along with a military structure. However, the author documents the cabildos established by Tlaxcalan colonies established on the northern frontier. The Tlaxcalan colonies enjoyed special privileges granted by the Crown in 1591 when the first 400 Tlaxcalan families were sent to colonize beyond the sedentary frontier, and their system of self-governance was based on the central Mexican *pueblos de indios*. Missionaries on the northern frontier did not grant native peoples congregated on the missions the same political autonomy. See Sean F. McEnroe, "A Sleeping Army: The Military Origins of Interethnic Civic Structures on Mexico's Colonial Frontier," *Ethnohistory* 59, no. 1 (2012): 109–39. The Spanish also mobilized residents of missions on the north Mexican frontier for military service, but a formal military structure did not exist on the north Mexican mission communities. For a study of the use of native auxiliaries, see Oakah Jones, *Pueblo Warriors and Spanish Conquest* (Norman: University of Oklahoma Press, 1966).

155. Gibson, *The Aztecs under Spanish Rule*, 166–93.
156. Sarreal, "Caciques as Placeholders."
157. Joaquín Meade y Sainz y Tapaga, *La Huasteca Queretana* (México, D.F.: Imprenta Aldina, 1951), 406–7.

Chapter 2

1. Jackson, *Demographic Change and Ethnic Survival*, 115.
2. Ibid., 114–15.
3. Quoted in Hans Roth and Eckart Kuhne, "Esta nueva y Hermosa iglesia: La construcción y restauración de las iglesia de Martin Schmid," in Eckart Kuhne, ed., *Las misiones jesuíticas de Bolivia: Martin Schmid 1694–1772: Misionero, músico y arquitecto entre los Chiquitos* (Santa Cruz de la Sierra: Cumbre de las Américas, 1996), 89.
4. Ramón Gutiérrez da Costa and Rodrigo Gutiérrez Vinuales, "Territorio, urbanismo y arquitectura en Moxos y Chiquitos," in Pedro Querejazu, ed., *Las misiones jesuíticas de Chiquitos* (La Paz: Fundación BHW, 1995), 347–52.
5. Ibid., 347–52.
6. Roth and Kuhne, "Esta nueva y Hermosa iglesia," 91–95.
7. Ibid., 94.
8. Ibid., 94.
9. Jackson, *Conflict and Conversion*, 195; Meade y Sainz y Tapaga, *La Huasteca Queretana*, 405.
10. Gómez Canedo, *Sierra Gorda*, 223–35, 245.
11. Finbar Kenneally, O.F.M., trans. and ed., *Writings of Fermín Francisco de Lasuen*, 2 vols. (Washington, D.C.: Academy of American Franciscan History, 1965), 1:14–33.
12. For an analysis of the evolution of the California mission building complexes, see Jackson and Castillo, *Indians, Franciscans, and Spanish Colonization*, 137–68. There are sixteen references in the documentary record of the first construction of neophyte housing. Eleven were from ten years or more following the establishment of a mission.
13. Robert H. Jackson, "Los agustinos, la frontera chichimeca, y la evangelización de la Sierra Gorda 1550–1770: Plan urbano, arquitectura y resistencia indígena," *Toltecáyotl* 1 (2012): 56–57.
14. Ibid., 57; David McLaughlin and Rubén G. Mendoza, *The California Missions Sourcebook* (Scottsdale: Pentacle Press, 2012), 40.
15. For a discussion of the baptism controversy, see Jackson, *Visualizing the Miraculous, Visualizing the Sacred*.
16. Ibid., 11–20.
17. Ibid., 72.
18. Tavárez, *The Invisible War*, 49–52; Jackson, *Visualizing the Miraculous, Visualizing the Sacred*, 67–71.
19. Tavárez, *The Invisible War*, 29.
20. Ibid., 28.

21. Louise Burkhart, "Solar Christ."
22. Burkhart, *The Slippery Earth*.
23. Tavárez, *The Invisible War*, 28.
24. Ibid., 28.
25. Louise Burkhart, "Little Doctrine."
26. Tavárez, *The Invisible War*, 29.
27. Jackson, *Conflict and Conversion*, 87–103.
28. Ibid., 102–8.
29. Ibid., 108–14.
30. Tavárez, *The Invisible War*, 29.
31. Ibid., 28–29.
32. For an example of the text of a passion play, see Louise Burkhart, *Holy Wednesday: A Nahua Drama from Early Colonial Mexico* (Philadelphia: University of Pennsylvania Press, 1996).
33. An illustration from the Crónica de Michoacán depicts a catechism class and the commonly held belief of the missionaries that they were engaged in a war with Satan. During the catechism process, demons attempt to seduce the neophytes. However, once baptized the demons disappear, which signals the victory of the missionaries. See Jackson, *Conflict and Conversion*, 4–5.
34. Robert Ricard, *The Spiritual Conquest of Mexico: An Essay on the Apostolate and the Evangelizing Methods of the Mendicant Orders in New Spain, 1523–1572* (Berkeley: University of California Press, 1974). In addition to the sources already cited, see Miguel León Portilla, *Los antiguos mexicanos a través de sus crónicas y cantares* (México, D.F.: Fondo de cultura económica, 2005); Lockhart, *The Nahuas after the Conquest*; James Lockhart, *Nahuas and Spaniards: Postconquest Central Mexican History and Philology* (Stanford: Stanford University Press, 1991); Matthew Restell, *The Maya World: Yucatec Culture and Society, 1550–1850* (Stanford: Stanford University Press, 1999); Matthew Restell, Lisa Sousa, and Kevin Terraciano, *Mesoamerican Voices: Native Language Writings from Colonial Mexico, Yucatan, and Guatemala* (Cambridge: Cambridge University Press, 2005); Kevin Terraciano, *The Mixtecs of Colonial Oaxaca: Ñudzahui History, Sixteenth through Eighteenth Centuries* (Stanford: Stanford University Press, 2004); Robert Haskett, *Indigenous Rulers: An Ethnohistory of Town Government in Colonial Cuernavaca* (Albuquerque: University of New Mexico Press, 1991); Rebecca Horn, *Postconquest Coyoacan: Nahua-Spanish Relations in Central Mexico, 1519–1650* (Stanford: Stanford University Press, 1997); Sarah Cline, *Colonial Culhuacan, 1580–1600: A Social History of an Aztec Town* (Albuquerque: University of New Mexico Press, 1986); Sarah Cline and Miguel León Portilla, eds., *The Testaments of Culhuacan* (Los Angeles: UCLA Latin American Center Publications, University of California, Los Angeles, 1984), among others.
35. For a detailed analysis of the persistence of pre-Hispanic practices, see Tavárez, *The Invisible War*.

36. Ibid., 187–89.
37. Ibid., 35; Jackson, *Conflict and Conversion*, 77.
38. Quoted in Tavárez, *The Invisible War*, 43.
39. Quoted in ibid., 43.
40. Wake, *Framing the Sacred*; Jackson, *Visualizing the Miraculous, Visualizing the Sacred*.
41. Jackson, *Visualizing the Miraculous, Visualizing the Sacred*, 107–10.
42. Ciudad Real, O.F.M., *Relación breve y verdadera*, 1:144.
43. Ibid., 139.
44. Tavárez, *The Invisible War*, 32.
45. Wake, *Framing the Sacred*, 201–2.
46. For a recent discussion of the different interpretations of the mural program, see Jackson, *Visualizing the Miraculous, Visualizing the Sacred*, 97–107.
47. Eleanor Wake first offered this interpretation of the mural program. See her *Framing the Sacred*, 249–51. For an example of the concept of the flowery paradise in Náhuatl devotional literature, see Louise Burkhart, "Flowery Heaven: The Aesthetic of Paradise in Nahuatl Devotional Literature," *Res: Anthropology and Aesthetics* 21 (1992): 88–109.
48. Matienzo, Tomicha Charupá, Combes, and Page, *Chiquitos*, 211.
49. Ibid., 252, 253, 355.
50. Juan Fernández, S.J., *Relación historial de las misiones de indios chiquitos que en el Paraguay tienen los padres de la Compañía de Jesús* (Asunción: A. de Uribe y compañía, 1896), 85.
51. Matienzo, Tomicha Charupá, Combes, and Page, *Chiquitos*, 291.
52. Jackson, *Conflict and Conversion*, 209–10.
53. Quoted in ibid., 184. The original quote in Spanish reads, "Una cuadrilla de demonios feísimos, con terribles semblantes, y descompasados movimientos del cuerpo: unos con cara de tigres, otros de dragones, y cocodrilos, y algunos con apariencias de tan monstruosas, y terribles formas, que no sufria el ànimo mirarlos: echaban todos por la boca, y por las otras partes del cuerpo, llamas de color negro, y espantoso, y gritando, y discurriendo de una parte a otra, remedaban las danzas, y bailes de los indios, hasta que agarrándose del pobre neófito, que estaba todo temblando, creyendo que aquella fiesta era por él, hicieron gran fiesta, gritando: Él, él es, Xarupá nuestro amigo, que antiguamente era nuestro devoto, y usaba de los hechizos, y maleficios, que enseñábamos a sus abuelos."
54. Matienzo, Tomicha Charupá, Combes, and Page, *Chiquitos*, 222, 224.
55. Ibid., 265.
56. Jackson, *Visualizing the Miraculous, Visualizing the Sacred*, 152–58.
57. Matienzo, Tomicha Charupá, Combes, and Page, *Chiquitos*, 212.
58. Ibid., 271.
59. Ibid., 213.
60. Ibid., 298.

61. Ibid., 265, 302.
62. Jackson, *Demographic Change and Ethnic Survival*, 44.
63. Lucas Cabeza de Vaca, O.S.A. to José de Escandón, Xalpa, January 23, 1743, in Ruiz Zavala, *Historia de la provincia agustiniana del Santísimo Nombre de Jesús de México*, 2 vols. (México, D.F.: Editorial Porrúa, 1984) 1:530–31.
64. José Francisco de Landa, Mexico City, July 11, 1743, in Ruiz Zavala, *Historia*, 1:536.
65. Ibid., 1:538.
66. Ibid., 1:544.
67. Ibid., 1:535.
68. Ibid., 1:544.
69. Ibid., 1:544.
70. George Wharton James, ed., *Francisco Palou's Life and Apostolic Labors of the Venerable Father Junípero Serra Founder of the Franciscan Missions of California* (Pasadena, Calif.: Private Printing, 1913), 34–35.
71. Ibid., 35.
72. María Teresa Muñoz Espinosa and José Carlos Castañeda Reyes, "'Los Bailes': Un santuario para el culto de la fertilidad en la Sierra Gorda de Querétaro, Mexico," *Arqueología* 40 (Enero–Abril, 2009): 153–77.
73. Quoted in ibid., 172.
74. Ibid.
75. Lara Cisneros, "La domesticación del cristianismo," 180–86. María Teresa Muñoz Espinosa and Juan Carlos Castañeda Reyes, "La diosa Chacum, un numen de la fertilidad de la Sierra Gorda queretana," *Arqueología* 38 (Mayo–Agosto, 2008): 51–64.
76. Rose Marie Beebe and Robert Senkiewicz, *Junípero Serra: California, Indians, and the Transformation of a Missionary* (Norman: University of Oklahoma Press, 2015), 92–93. The authors translated the 1752 letter from Serra to the inquisition dated September 1, 1752 that brought the allegations of what the Franciscan identified as demon worship.
77. Jackson, *Visualizing the Miraculous, Visualizing the Sacred*, 107–22.
78. José Ortés de Velasco, O.F.M. to Juan Figueras, O.F.M., Querétaro, December 5, 1746, in Gómez Canedo, *Sierra Gorda*, 213.
79. The series of reports on the missions from 1758 described this practice. See, for example, Joachín Fernández, O.F.M., Concá, October 11, 1758, "Razón del estado que ha tenido y tiene esta Missión del glorioso principe Señor San Miguel de Concá," in Gómez Canedo, *Sierra Gorda*, 225.
80. Juan Ramos de Lora, O.F.M., and Antonio Paterna, O.F.M., Tancoyol, October 13, 1758, "Razón individual y verídica de el estado de esta Missión de la Virgen Santísima de la Luz de Tancoyol," in Gómez Canedo, *Sierra Gorda*, 227.
81. For a study of Franciscan studies of Otopame languages, see Joaquín García-Medall, "Los franciscanos y el estudio de las lenguas otomangueanas en Nueva España (s. XVIII)," *Catalogación y estudio de las traducciones de los franciscanos españoles*,

http://www.traduccion-franciscanos.uva.es/archivos/3.Garcia-Medall.Lenguas%20indigenas.pdf (accessed November 4, 2016). See also Otto Zwartjes, ed., *Las Gramáticas Misioneras de Tradición Hispánica (siglos XVI–XVII)* (Amsterdam: Ediciones Rodopi B.V., 2000), in particular Yolanda Lastra, "El arte de la lengua Otomí de Fray Pedro de Cáceres," 97–106.

82. Miguel León-Portilla, *Catecismo náhuatl en imágenes* (México, D.F.: Cartón y Papel de Mexico, SA, 1979). Also see Louise Burkhart, "Little Doctrine." Burkhart argues for a later date for the so-called Testerian manuscripts.
83. Jackson, *Visualizing the Miraculous, Visualizing the Sacred*, 150–58.
84. Gómez Canedo, *Sierra Gorda*, 153–58.
85. Gerardo Lara Cisneros, Personal Communication, February 23, 2015.
86. Quoted in Lara Cisneros, *El cristo viejo de Xichú*, 76.
87. Julián Knogler, S.J., "Relato sobre el país y nación de los Chiquitos en las Indias Occidentales o América del sud y las misiones en su territorio. Redactado para un amigo," in Werner Hoffman, *Las misiones jesuíticas entre los chiquitanos* (Buenos Aires: Fundación para la educación, la ciencia, y la cultura, 1979), 126–27.
88. Ibid., 128–29.
89. Santamaría, "Fronteras indígenas del oriente boliviano," 208–9.
90. Ibid., 212.
91. Ibid., 217. See also Cynthia Radding de Murietta, "From the Counting House to the Field and Loom: Ecologies, Cultures, and Economies in the Missions of Sonora (Mexico) and Chiquitania (Bolivia)," *Hispanic American Historical Review* 81, no. 1 (2001): 45–87.
92. Ibid., 33–34.
93. Santamaría, "Fronteras indígenas," 210–13, 216–18.
94. Cynthia Radding de Murietta, "Republicas dentro de la Republica de Bolivia: Los pueblos Chiquitos en los primeros escenarios de una nueva orden política," *Boletín Americanista* 60, no. 1 (2010): 53.
95. Meade y Sainz y Tapaga, *La Huasteca Queretana*, 408.
96. Joachín Fernández, O.F.M., Concá, October 11, 1758, "Razón del estado que ha tenido y tiene esta Missión del glorioso príncipe Señor San Miguel de Concá," in Gómez Canedo, *Sierra Gorda*, 221–26.
97. Juan Enrique Ponce Olguín, "San Francisco de Tilaco: Su reorganización como misión franciscana en el siglo XVIII," unpublished thesis for the licenciatura, Universidad Autónoma de Querétaro, 2015, 73–74.
98. The series of reports on the missions from 1758 described the mission economy. Gómez Canedo, *Sierra Gorda*, 221–35.
99. María Teresa Álvarez Icaza Longoria, "Un cambio apresurado: La secularización de las misiones de la Sierra Gorda (1770-1782)," *Letras Históricas* 3 (Otoño–Invierno 2010): 28–30.

Chapter 3

1. "Francisco Burges de la Compañía de Jesús, Procurador de la Provincia de Paraguay," AGI, Charcas 381.
2. Carbonell de Masy, Blumers, and Levinton, *La reducción jesuítica*, 136.
3. "Razón de la visita que hizo el ilustrísimo y reverendísimo Señor don Fray Pedro Fajardo, Obispo de Buenos Aires, el ano de 1718," in Pastells, *Historia de la Compañía de Jesús*, 6:172–77.
4. Levinton, "La significación urbana," 302–3.
5. An untitled and undated tribute census for Yapeyú, probably from 1759, divided the population between the original groups and those transferred from San Francisco Xavier. The tribute census is found in AGN, Sala 9-17-3-6.
6. Arlindo Rubert, *Historia da Igreja no Rio Grande do Sul* (Porto Alegre: EDIPUCRS, 1998), 22.
7. Annua Reductionum Anni 1717, AGN, Sala 9-6-9-6; Annua Reductionum Anni, 1720, AGN, Sala 9-6-9-6; Annua Enumeratio Doctrinarum 1724, AGN, Sala 9-6-9-6.
8. Mercedes Avellaneda, *Guaraníes, criollos y jesuitas: Luchas de poder en las Revoluciones Comuneras del Paraguay Siglos XVII y XVIII* (Asunción: Editorial Tiempo de Historia, 2014), 224–26.
9. Jackson, *Demographic Change and Ethnic Survival*, appendix 1, appendix 4.
10. Ibid., 62.
11. Avellaneda, *Guaraníes*, 228–29.
12. Quoted in ibid., 230.
13. Quoted in ibid., 231.
14. Carbonell de Massy, S.J., *Estrategias*, 377.
15. Francisco María Raspart, Los Santos Mártires del Japón, August 15, 1735, "Padrón de los tributarios de est Reducción de los Santos Mártires del Uruguay," AGN, Sala 9-17-3-6; Ventura Suárez, los Santos Cosme y Damián, August 16, 1735, "Padrón del Pueblo de S. Cosme y Damián que se hizo este presente año de 1735," AGN, Sala 9-17-3-6.
16. Jackson, *Demographic Change and Ethnic Survival*, appendix 1, appendix 4.
17. Ibid., 66.
18. Littre Annuae Provincia Paraguaria Anno 1735–1742, in Matienzo, Tomicha Charupá, Combes, and Page, *Chiquitos*, 222.
19. Estado del pueblo de San Javier [1739], in ibid., 263.
20. Estado del pueblo de San José [1744], in ibid., 310.
21. Jackson, *Demographic Change and Ethnic Survival*, 63.
22. Expediente so[br]e la epidemia de Viruelas que acometió a los Pueblos de S[an] Joseph y Apóstoles, AGN, Sala 9-8-3-52 (hereinafter cited as EEV).
23. Ibid.
24. Ibid.

25. I suggested this "kinder and gentler" form of mission organization in a previous study. See Jackson, *Demographic Change and Ethnic Survival*, 58.
26. For a discussion of the Franciscan system on the California missions and its relationship to demographic patterns, see Jackson, *Indian Population Decline*; Jackson and Castillo, *Indians, Franciscans, and Spanish Colonization*.
27. The reconstruction of the population and vital rates of Santa Rosa mission is based on manuscript censuses from the Archivo General de la Nación in Buenos Aires (AGN), the Archivo Nacional de Paraguay in Asunción (ANP), and the Archivo General de las Indias in Sevilla, Spain (AGI). For the years 1711, 1714, 1715, 1716, 1717, 1720, 1724, 1728, 1731, 1733, 1735, 1736, 1738, 1739, 1740, 1741, 1744, 1745, 1746, 1747, 1748, 1749, 1750, 1752, 1753, 1754, 1755, 1756, 1757, 1759, 1760, 1762, 1763, 1764, 1765, and 1767 from AGN, Sala 9-7-2-1, 9-6-9-6, 9-6-9-7, 9-6-10-6; "Empadronamiento de las Treinta Pueblos de Misiones, por el Coronel Don Marcos de Larrazabal," 1772 AGN, Sala 9-18-8-4; censuses for 1797 from AGN, Sala 9-18-6-5; for 1798 from AGN, Sala 9-18-2-4; 1799 AGN, Sala 9-18-2-5; tribute censuses for the individual missions for 1801 from AGN, Sala 9-17-3-6. Census for 1724 from ANP. For 1702 from Francisco Burges, S.J., No Place, No Date [1705], "Francisco Burges de la Compañia de Jesús, Procurador de la Provincia de Paraguay," AGI, Charcas 381. See also Jackson, *Missions and the Frontiers of Spanish America*, 463–76; Santa Rosa Baptismal Register, Santa Rosa Parish Archive, Santa Rosa, Paraguay.
28. Ernesto Maeder, *Una Aproximación*, 50.
29. The Littre Annuae 1714–20 simply mentioned that there was an epidemic in 1718 but provided little details.
30. "Razón de la visita que hizo el ilustrísimo y reverendísimo Señor don Fray Pedro Fajardo, Obispo de Buenos Aires, el ano de 1718," in Pastells, *Historia de la Compañía de Jesús*, 6:172–77.
31. Santa Rosa Baptismal Register, Santa Rosa Parochial Archive, Santa Rosa, Paraguay.
32. Jackson, "Demographic Patterns in the Jesuit Missions of the Río de la Plata Region."
33. For an overview to the Guaraní uprising, see Ganson, *The Guaraní under Spanish Rule*. For the relocation of the populations of the seven missions located east of the Uruguay River, see Jackson, "Population and Vital Rates," table 1, 405–6.
34. For a general history of Santos Cosme y Damían mission, see Carbonell de Masy, Blumers, and Levinton, *La reducción jesuítica*.
35. Jackson, "Comprendiendo los efectos," 122–29.
36. Jackson, "Population and Vital Rates," 419.
37. Jackson, "Comprendiendo los efectos," 122–29.
38. For a detailed discussion of the workings of the post-expulsion civil administration, see Sarreal, *The Guaraní and Their Missions*.
39. Santa Rosa, abril 17, 1799, "Estado que manifiesta el número total de Almas de que se compone este Pueblo de Sta Rosa del Paraguay," y de las que se hallan prófugas..., AGN, Sala 9-18-2-2.

40. Santa Rosa Baptismal Register, Santa Rosa, Santa Rosa Parochial Archive, Paraguay.
41. Carbonell de Masy, Blumers, and Levinton, *La reducción jesuítica*, 85, 93, 114.
42. Ibid., 92, 111, 130.
43. Ibid., 145.
44. Jackson, *Demographic Change and Ethnic Survival*, 79.
45. The population figure from 1807 comes from a summary of a tribute census prepared by Francisco Martinez Lobato, Candelaria, April 1, 1807, "Estado General que manifiesta el Numero de Personas de todas clases y Tributarios que eccisten en los ocho Pueblos de la comprehension de este Departamento de Candelaria según los Padrones formados en la Revisita Practicada por su Subdeleegado el S[eñ]or D[o]n Francisco Martinez Lobato a principios del año de 1807," ANP. The population of the other exmissions was as follows: Santa Ana 1,340; Loreto 1,130; San Ignacio Miní 910; Corpus 2,270; Jesús 1,039; Trinidad 937; Ytapúa 2,109.
46. Jackson, *Demographic Change and Ethnic Survival.*, 165.
47. Ibid., 50.
48. Ibid., 73–76.
49. Jackson, "The Post-Jesuit Expulsion Population," 161.
50. Ibid., 20.
51. Jackson, "Demographic Patterns on the Chiquitos Missions," 225.
52. Ibid., 253–54.
53. Jackson, *Demographic Change and Ethnic Survival*, appendix 3, appendix 7.
54. Ibid., 20, 260.
55. Ibid., 260.
56. María Teresa Álvarez Icaza Longoria, "Un cambio apresurado: la secularización de las misiones de la Sierra Gorda, (1770–1782)," *Letras Históricas* 3 (Otoño–Invierno 2010), 9–45.
57. Ibid., 25.
58. Robert H. Jackson, "The Guaycuros, Jesuit and Franciscan Missionaries, and José de Gálvez: The Failure of Spanish Policy in Baja California," *Memoria Americana: Cuadernos de Ethnohistoria* 12, (2004): 221–33.
59. Gómez Canedo, *Sierra Gorda*, 95–105.
60. José Ortés de Velasco [1748], "Razón de las misiones que el Colegio de San Fernando tiene en Sierra Gorda, alias Sierra Madre, y el estado que al presente tienen," in Gómez Canedo, *Sierra Gorda*, 215–20.
61. Gómez Canedo, *Sierra Gorda*, 137.
62. Ibid., 124.
63. Ibid., 131.
64. Juan Ramos de Lora, O.F.M., and Antonio Paterna, O.F.M., Tancoyol, October 13, 1758, "Razón individual y verídica de el estado de esta Missión de la Virgen Santísima Luz de Tancoyol," in Gómez Canedo, *Sierra Gorda*, 226–29.

65. José Campos, O.F.M., and Miguel de la Campa, Landa, October 14, 1758, "Razón individual y verídica de el estado de esta Missión de la Puríssima Concepción de Agua de Landa," in Gómez Canedo, *Sierra Gorda*, 230.
66. Juan Crespi, O.F.M., and Antonio Cruzado, O.F.M., Tilaco, October 13, 1758, "Razón del estado que ha tenido y tiene esta Missión de N.S.P. San Francisco del Valle de Tilaco, de indios Pames," in Gómez Canedo, *Sierra Gorda*, 232.
67. José Herrera, Xalpa, October 14, 1758, "Razón individual y verídica de el estado de esta Missión de Santiago de Xalpan de indios Pames, sita en la Sierra Gorda," in Gómez Canedo, *Sierra Gorda*, 234.
68. Jackson, *Indian Population Decline*, 65.
69. Ibid., 18.
70. Ibid., 71.
71. Jackson, *Demographic Change and Ethnic Survival*, 150.
72. Meade, *Huasteca*, 408–13, 425–31.
73. Ibid., 403–4.
74. Jackson, *Conflict and Conversion*, 166–67.
75. Meade, *Huasteca*, 422–23.
76. Jackson, *Demographic Change and Ethnic Survival*, 101–3, 225.
77. "Testimonio de los autos originales de la visita y empadronamiento que en virtud de Real Cedula de su Majestad (que Dios guarde) hizo el señor doctor Francisco Xavier de Palacios, Oidor y Alcalde de Corte de esta Real Audiencia de los Charcas, de los pueblos de las santas misiones de los indios de la nación nombrada chiquitos," AGI, Charcas 291.
78. Jackson, *Demographic Change and Ethnic Survival*, 140–43.
79. Ibid., 133–43.

Conclusions

1. Jackson, *Indian Population Decline*, 166.
2. Ibid., 166.
3. Ibid., 166.
4. See Jackson, *Demographic Change and Ethnic Survival*, 125–60.
5. Jackson, *Indian Population Decline*, 169.
6. Ibid., 169.
7. Ibid., 115.
8. Robert H. Jackson, "The Design Element on the Façade of the Jesuit Church of Nuestra Senora de la Asuncion Opodepe (Sonora): The Persistence of Pre-Hispanic Religious Beliefs?" *Kiva Journal of Southwestern Archaeology and History* 80, no. 3–4 (March–June, 2015): 393–408.
9. Ganson, *The Guaraní under Spanish Rule*, 75.
10. Jackson, *Visualizing the Miraculous, Visualizing the Sacred*.

11. On the Augustinian missions beyond the Chichimeca frontier, see Jackson, *Conflict and Conversion*.
12. On the organization of the California mission system, see Robert H. Jackson, "Population and the Economic Dimension of Colonization in Alta California: Four Mission Communities," *Journal of the Southwest* 33 (1991): 387–439; Robert H. Jackson, "The Changing Economic Structure of the Alta California Missions: A Reinterpretation," *Pacific Historical Review* 61, no. 3 (1992): 387–415; Robert H. Jackson, "Agriculture, Drought, and Chumash Congregation in the California Missions (1782–1834)," *Estudios de Historia Novohispana* 19 (1999): 69–90; and Robert H. Jackson and Edward Castillo, *Indians, Franciscans, and Spanish Colonization*.
13. See Jackson, *Indian Population Decline;* Jackson and Castillo, *Indians, Franciscans, and Spanish Colonization;* Jackson, *Demographic Change and Ethnic Survival*, 143–53.

Selected Bibliography

Archival Sources

Archivo General de las Indias, Sevilla, Spain.
Archivo General de la Nación, Buenos Aires, Argentina.
Archivo Nacional de Paraguay, Asunción, Paraguay.
Saint Albert's College, Oakland, California.
Santa Rosa Parish Archive, Santa Rosa, Paraguay.

Published Sources

Acuña, René, ed. *Relaciones geográficas del siglo XVI: Antequera. Tomo primero.* México, D.F.: UNAM, 1984.
———, ed. *Relaciones geográficas del siglo XVI: México. Tomo primero.* México, D.F.: UNAM, 1984.
———, ed. *Relaciones geográficas del siglo XVI: Michoacán.* México, D.F: UNAM, 1987.
Altman, Ida. *The War for Mexico's West: Indians and Spaniards in Nueva Galicia, 1524–1550.* Albuquerque: University of New Mexico Press, 2010.
Álvarez Icaza Longoria, María Teresa. "Un cambio apresurado: La secularización de las misiones de la Sierra Gorda (1770–1782)." *Letras Históricas* 3 (Otoño–Invierno, 2010): 19–45.
Avellaneda, Mercedes. *Guaraníes, criollos y jesuitas: Luchas de poder en las Revoluciones Comuneras del Paraguay Siglos XVII y XVIII.* Asunción: Editorial Tiempo de Historia, 2014.
Bazant, Jan. *The Alienation of Church Wealth in Mexico: Social and Economic Aspects of the Liberal Revolution, 1856–1875.* Cambridge: Cambridge University Press, 1971.
Beebe, Rose Marie, and Robert Senkiewicz. *Junípero Serra: California, Indians, and the Transformation of a Missionary.* Norman: University of Oklahoma Press, 2015.

Berdan, Frances, and Patricia Anawalt, eds. *The Codex Mendoza*. Berkeley: University of California Press, 1997.

Berry, Charles. *The Reform in Oaxaca, 1856–76: A Microhistory of the Liberal Revolution*. Lincoln: University of Nebraska Press, 1981.

Block, David. *Mission Culture on the Upper Amazon: Native Tradition, Jesuit Enterprise, and Secular Policy in Moxos, 1660–1880*. Lincoln: University of Nebraska Press, 1994.

Burkhart, Louise. "Flowery Heaven: The Aesthetic of Paradise in Nahuatl Devotional Literature." *Res: Anthropology and Aesthetics* 21 (1992): 88–109.

———. *Holy Wednesday: A Nahua Drama from Early Colonial Mexico*. Philadelphia: University of Pennsylvania Press, 1996.

———. "The 'Little Doctrine' and Indigenous Catechesis in New Spain." *Hispanic American Historical Review* 94, no. 2 (2014): 167–206.

———. *The Slippery Earth: Nahua-Christian Moral Dialogue in Sixteenth-Century Mexico*. Tucson: University of Arizona Press, 1989.

———. "The Solar Christ in Nahuatl Doctrinal Texts of Early Colonial Mexico." *Ethnohistory* 35, no. 3 (1988): 234–56.

Carbonnell de Massy, S.J., Rafael. *Estrategias de desarrollo rural en los pueblos guaraníes (1609–1767)*. Barcelona: Antoni Bosch Editor, 1992.

Carbonell de Masy, S.J., Rafael, Teresa Blumers, and Norberto Levinton, *La reducción jesuítica de Santos Cosme y Damián: Su historia, su economía y su arquitectura, 1633–1797*. Asunción: Markografik, 2003.

Cline, Sarah. *Colonial Culhuacan, 1580–1600: A Social History of an Aztec Town*. Albuquerque: University of New Mexico Press, 1986.

Cline, Sarah, and Miguel León Portilla, eds. *The Testaments of Culhuacan*. Los Angeles: UCLA Latin American Center Publications, University of California, Los Angeles, 1984.

De Burgoa, Francisco. *Geográfica descripción de la parte septentrional del polo ártico de la América y, Nueva Iglesia de las Indias occidentales, y sitio astronómico de esta provincia de predicadores de Antequera Valle de Oaxaca*. 2 vols. México, D.F.: Editorial Porrúa, 1989.

De Ciudad Real, O.F.M., Antonio. *Relación breve y verdadera de algunas cosas de las muchas que sucedieron al padre Fray Alonso Ponce en las provincias de la Nueva España*. 2 vols. Madrid: Imprenta de la Viuda de Caero, 1875.

Deeds, Susan. *Defiance and Deference in Mexico's Colonial North: Indians under Spanish Rule in Nueva Vizcaya*. Austin: University of Texas Press, 2003.

Del Paso y Troncoso, Francisco, ed. *Papeles de Nueva España publicados de orden y con fondos del gobierno mexicano. Segunda serie geografía y estadística. Tomo I: Suma de visitas de pueblos por orden alfabético*. Madrid: Tip. "Sucesores de Rivadeneyra," 1905.

———, ed. *Papeles de Nueva España. Segunda series geográfica y estadística. Tomo IV: Relaciones Geograficas de la Diócesis de Oaxaca*. Madrid: Tip. "Sucesores de Rivadenyra," 1905.

———, ed. *Papeles de Nueva España publicados de orden y con fondos del gobierno mexicano. Segunda serie geografía y estadística. Tomo V: Relaciones Geográficas de la Diócesis de Tlaxcala*. Madrid: Tip. "Sucesores de Rivadenyra," 1905.

De Santa María, O.S.A., Guillermo, *Guerra de los Chichimecas (Mexico 1575–Zirosto 1580)*, critical introduction, paleography, and notes by Alberto Carrillo Cazares. Zamora: El Colegio de Michoacán, 2003.

Dobson, Andrew P., and E. Robin Carper. "Infectious Diseases and Human Population History." *Bioscience* 46, no. 2 (February, 1996): 115–26.

Duran Sandoval, Felipe. "El papel de los franciscanos en la fundación de la alcaldía mayor de San Luis Potosi." In Arturo Vergara Hernández, ed., *Arte y sociedad en la Nueva España*, 85–108. Pachuca: UAEH, 2014.

Fernández, S.J., Juan. *Relación historial de las misiones de indios chiquitos que en el Paraguay tienen los padres de la Compañía de Jesús*. Asunción: A. de Uribe y compañía, 1896.

Flinn, Michael. *The European Demographic System 1500–1820*. Baltimore: Johns Hopkins University Press, 1981.

Galeana Cruz, Elizabeth J. "La iglesia vieja-casa religiosa dominica de Yucundáa y la casa de la cacica e iglesia y convento de San Pedro y San Pablo Teposcolula. Dos ejemplos de sincretismo arquitectónica en la primera mitad del siglo XVI: Mixtecos y dominicos." In Ronald Spores and Nelly M. Robles García, eds., *Yucundáa: La ciudad mixteca y su transformación prehispánica-colonial*, 2 vols. México, D.F.: INAH, 2014.

Ganson, Barbara. *The Guaraní under Spanish Rule in the Río de la Plata*. Stanford: Stanford University Press, 2005.

García-Medall, Joaquín. "Los franciscanos y el estudio de las lenguas otomangueanas en Nueva España (s. XVIII)." *Catalogación y estudio de las traducciones de los franciscanos españoles,* http://www.traduccion-franciscanos.uva.es/archivos/3.Garcia-Medall.Lenguas%20indigenas.pdf (accessed November 4, 2016).

Garenne, Michel, and Monique Lafon. "Sexist Diseases." *Perspectives in Biology and Medicine* 41, no. 2 (Winter 1998): 176–89.

García Pimentel, Luis, ed. *Relación de los obispados de Tlaxcala, Oaxaca y otros lugares en el siglo XVI*. México, D.F.: Private Publication, 1904.

Gautier, Etienne, and Louis Henry. *La population de Crulai, paroisse normande: Étude historique*. Paris: Presses universitaires de France, 1958.

Gibson, Charles. *The Aztecs under Spanish Rule: A History of the Indians of the Valley of Mexico 1519–1810*. Stanford: Stanford University Press, 1964.

Gómez Canedo, Lino. "La Sierra Gorda a fines del siglo XVIII: Diario de un viaje de inspección a sus milicias." *Historia Mexicana* 21, no. 1 (July–September, 1976): 132–49.

———. *Sierra Gorda: Un típico enclave misional en el centro de Mexico (siglos XVII–XVIII)*. Querétaro: Provincia Franciscana de Santiago, 2011.

Gómez Serafín, Susana. *Altepetl de Huaxtepec: Modificaciones territoriales desde el siglo XVI*. México, D.F.: INAH, 2011.

Gutiérrez da Costa, Ramón, and Rodrigo Gutiérrez Vinuales. "Territorio, urbanismo y arquitectura en Moxos y Chiquitos." In Pedro Querejazu, ed., *Las misiones jesuíticas de Chiquitos*, 342–57. La Paz: Foundation BHW, 1995.

Hale, Charles. *Mexican Liberalism in the Age of More, 1821–1853*. New Haven: Yale University Press, 1968.
Haskett, Robert. *Indigenous Rulers: An Ethnohistory of Town Government in Colonial Cuernavaca*. Albuquerque: University of New Mexico Press, 1991.
Herr, Richard. *The Eighteenth-Century Revolution in Spain*. Princeton: Princeton University Press, 1958.
———. *Rural Change and Royal Finances in Spain at the End of the Old Regime*. Berkeley: University of California Press, 1989.
Hoffman, Werner. *Las misiones jesuíticas entre los chiquitanos*. Buenos Aires: Fundación para la educación, la ciencia, y la cultura, 1979.
Horn, Rebecca. *Postconquest Coyoacan: Nahua-Spanish Relations in Central Mexico, 1519–1650*. Stanford: Stanford University Press, 1997.
Jackson, Robert H. "Los agustinos, la frontera chichimeca, y la evangelización de la Sierra Gorda 1550–1770: Plan urbano, arquitectura y resistencia indígena." *Toltecáyotl* 1 (2012): 47–58.
———. "Agriculture, Drought, and Chumash Congregation in the California Missions (1782–1834)." *Estudios de Historia Novohispana* 19 (1999): 69–90.
———. "The Changing Economic Structure of the Alta California Missions: A Reinterpretation." *Pacific Historical Review* 61, no. 3 (1992): 387–415.
———. "The Chichimeca Frontier and the Evangelization of the Sierra Gorda, 1550–1770." *Estudios de Historia Novohispana* 47 (Julio–Diciembre, 2012): 46–91.
———. "A Colonization Born of Frustration: Rosario Mission and the Karankawas." *Journal of South Texas* 17, no. 1 (Spring 2004): 31–50.
———. "Comprendiendo los efectos de las enfermedades del Viejo Mundo en los nativos americanos: La viruela en las Misiones Jesuíticas de Paraguay." *IHS Antiguos Jesuitas en Iberoamérica* 2, no. 2 (2014): 88–133.
———. *Conflict and Conversion in Sixteenth Century Central Mexico: The Augustinian War on and Beyond the Chichimeca Frontier*. Leiden: Brill Academic Publishers, 2013.
———. "Congregation and Depopulation: Demographic Patterns in the Texas Missions." *Journal of South Texas* 17, no. 2 (Fall 2004): 6–38.
———. *Demographic Change and Ethnic Survival among the Sedentary Populations on the Jesuit Mission Frontiers of Spanish South America, 1609–1803: The Formation and Persistence of Mission Communities in a Comparative Context*. Leiden: Brill Academic Publishers, 2015.
———. "Demographic Patterns in the Jesuit Missions of the Rio de la Plata Region: The Case of Corpus Christi Mission, 1622–1802." *Colonial Latin American Historical Review* 13, no. 4 (Fall 2004): 337–66.
———. "Demographic Patterns on the Chiquitos Missions of Eastern Bolivia, 1691–1767." *Bolivian Studies Journal* 12 (2005): 220–48.
———. "The Design Element on the Façade of the Jesuit Church of Nuestra Senora de la Asuncion Opodepe (Sonora): The Persistence of Pre-Hispanic Religious Beliefs?" *Kiva Journal of Southwestern Archaeology and History* 80, no. 3–4 (March–June, 2015): 393–408.

———. "Dominican Missions in Mexico: Sixteenth to Eighteenth Century." *Boletin Journal of the California Missions Studies Association* 31, no. 1 (2015): 114–29.

———. "A Frustrated Evangelization: The Limitations to Social, Cultural and Religious Change among the 'Wandering Peoples' of the Missions of the Central Desert of Baja California and the Texas Gulf Coast." *Fronteras de la Historia* 6 (2001): 7–40.

———. "The Guaycuros, Jesuit and Franciscan Missionaries, and José de Gálvez: The Failure of Spanish Policy in Baja California." *Memoria Americana: Cuadernos de Ethnohistoria* 12 (2004): 221–33.

———. *Indian Demographic Decline: The Missions of Northwestern New Spain, 1687–1840*. Albuquerque: University of New Mexico Press, 1994.

———. *Liberals, the Church, and Indian Peasants: Corporate Lands and the Challenge of Reform in Nineteenth-Century Spanish America*. Albuquerque: University of New Mexico Press, 1997.

———. "Una mirada a los patrones demográficos de las misiones jesuitas de Paraguay. *Fronteras de la Historia* 9 (2004): 129–78.

———. *Missions and the Frontiers of Spanish America: A Comparative Study of the Impact of Environmental, Economic, Political, and Socio-Cultural Variations on the Missions in the Rio de la Plata Region and on the Northern Frontier of New Spain*. Scottsdale, Ariz.: Pentacle Press, 2005.

———. "Missions on the Frontiers of Spanish America." *Journal of Religious History* 33, no. 3 (September, 2009): 328–47.

———. "Patrones demográficos de una frontera en conflicto: Las siete misiones orientales de la provincia jesuítica de Paraguay, 1680–1830." Unpublished paper presented at the Seminário Internacional: Indígenas, Misionários e Espanhois o Parana no Contexto da Bacia do Prata, Seculos XVL e XVll, Paraná, October 15–17, 2008.

———. "Population and the Economic Dimension of Colonization in Alta California: Four Mission Communities." *Journal of the Southwest* 33 (1991): 387–439.

———. "The Population and Vital Rates of the Jesuit Missions of Paraguay 1700–1767." *Journal of Interdisciplinary History* 28, no. 3 (Winter 2008): 401–31.

———. "The Post-Jesuit Expulsion Population of the Paraguay Missions, 1768–1803." *Revista de História Regional* 13, no. 2 (2008): 134–69.

———. *Race, Caste, and Status: Indians in Colonial Spanish America*. Albuquerque: University of New Mexico Press, 1999.

———. *Regional Markets and Agrarian Transformation in Bolivia: Cochabamba, 1539–1960*. Albuquerque: University of New Mexico Press, 1994.

———. *From Savages to Subjects: Missions in the History of the American Southwest*. Armonk: M.E. Sharpe, 2000.

———. "The Virgin of the Rosary at Tetela del Volcán (Morelos), Conversion, the Baptismal Controversy, a Dominican Critique of the Franciscans, and the Culture Wars in Sixteenth Century Central Mexico." In Robert H. Jackson, ed., *Evangelization and Culture Conflict in Colonial Mexico*, 1–29. Newcastle upon Tyne: Cambridge Scholars Publishing, 2014.

———. *Visualizing the Miraculous, Visualizing the Sacred: Evangelization and the "Cultural War" in Sixteenth Century Mexico.* Newcastle upon Tyne: Cambridge Scholars Publishing, 2014.

Jackson, Robert H., and Edward Castillo. *Indians, Franciscans, and Spanish Colonization: The Impact of the Mission System on California Indians.* Albuquerque: University of New Mexico Press, 1995.

James, George Wharton, ed. *Francisco Palou's Life and Apostolic Labors of the Venerable Father Junípero Serra Founder of the Franciscan Missions of California.* Pasadena: Private Printing, 1913.

Jones, Oakah. *Pueblo Warriors and Spanish Conquest.* Norman: University of Oklahoma Press, 1966.

Kenneally, O.F.M., Finbar, trans. and ed. *Writings of Fermín Francisco de Lasuen.* 2 vols. Washington, D.C.: Academy of American Franciscan History, 1965.

Kiracofe, James B. "Architectural Fusion and Indigenous Ideology in Early Colonial Teposcolula: The *Casa de la Cacica*: A Building at the Edge of Oblivion." *Anales del Instituto de Investigaciones Estéticas* 17, no. 66 (Spring 1995): 45–84.

Knogler, S.J., Julián. "Relato sobre el país y nación de los Chiquitos en las Indias Occidentales o América del sud y las misiones en su territorio. Redactado para un amigo." In Werner Hoffman, *Las misiones jesuíticas entre los chiquitanos*, 126–27. Buenos Aires: Fundación para la educación, la ciencia, y la cultura, 1979.

Kowalewski, Stephen, Luis Barba Pingarrón, Gabriela García Ayala, Benjamin A. Steere, Jorge Blancas Vázquez, Marisol Yadira Cortés Vilchis, Leonardo López Zárate, Agustín Ortiz Butrón, Thomas J. Pluckhahn, and Blanca Vilchis Flores. "La presencia azteca en Oaxaca: La provincia de Coixtlahuaca." *Anales de Antropología* 44 (2010): 77–103.

Kubler, George. *La arquitectura mexicana del siglo XVI.* México, D.F.: Fondo de Cultura Económica, 1983.

Kuhne, Eckart, ed. *Las misiones jesuíticas de Bolivia: Martin Schmid 1694–1772: Misionero, músico y arquitecto entre los Chiquitos.* Santa Cruz de la Sierra: Cumbre de las Américas, 1996.

Langer, Erick. *Expecting Pears from an Elm Tree: Franciscan Missions on the Chiriguano Frontier in the Heart of South America, 1830–1949.* Durham, N.C.: Duke University Press, 2009.

Langer, Erick, and Robert H. Jackson, eds. *The New Latin American Mission History.* Lincoln: University of Nebraska Press, 1995.

Langfur, Hal. *The Forbidden Lands: Colonial Identity, Frontier Violence, and the Persistence of Brazil's Eastern Indians, 1750–1830.* Stanford: Stanford University Press, 2006.

———. "The Return of the Bandeira: Economic Calamity, Historical Memory, and Armed Expeditions to the Sertao in Minas Gerais, 1750–1808." *The Americas* 61, no. 3 (2005): 429–61.

Lara Cisneros, Gerardo. *El cristo viejo de Xichú: Resistencia y rebelión en la Sierra Gorda durante el siglo XVIII.* México, D.F.: Dirección General de Culturas Populares, 2007.

———. "La domesticación del cristianismo en la Sierra Gorda, Nueva España, siglo XVIII." In Robert H. Jackson, ed., *Evangelization and Culture Conflict in Colonial Mexico*, 158–94. Newcastle upon Tyne: Cambridge Scholars Publishers, 2014.

Lastra, Yolanda. "El arte de la lengua Otomí de Fray Pedro de Cáceres." In Otto Zwartjes, ed., *Las Gramáticas Misioneras de Tradición Hispánica (siglos XVI–XVII)*, 97–106. Amsterdam: Ediciones Rodopi B.V., 2000.

Lastra, Yolanda, and Alejandro Terrazas. "Interpretación del posible actividades agrícolas prehispánicas a partir del análisis del chichimeco Jonaz." *Anales de Antropologuita* 40, no. 2 (2006): 165–87.

Ledesma Gallegos, Laura. *Génesis de la arquitectura mendicante del siglo XVI en el plan de Amilpas y las cañadas de Morelos*. México, D.F.: INAH, 2012.

León-Portilla, Miguel. *Catecismo náhuatl en imágenes*. México, D.F.: Cartón y Papel de Mexico, 1979.

———. *Los antiguos mexicanos a través de sus crónicas y cantares*. México, D.F.: Fondo de cultura económica, 2005.

Levinton, Norberto. "La significación urbana del pueblo jesuítico de Yapeyú (1627–1817)." In Bartomeu Melía, *Historia inacabada futuro incierto*. Asunción: Centro de Estudios Paraguayos "Antonio Guasch," 2002.

Lockhart, James. *The Náhuas after the Conquest: A Social and Cultural History of the Indians of Central Mexico, Sixteenth through Eighteenth Century*. Stanford: Stanford University Press, 1992.

———. *Náhuas and Spaniards: Postconquest Central Mexican History and Philology*. Stanford: Stanford University Press, 1991.

Maeder, Ernesto. *Una aproximación a las misiones guaraníticas*. Buenos Aires: Universidad Católica Argentina, 1996.

Matienzo, Javier, Roberto Tomicha Charupá, Isabelle Combes, and Carlos Page, comp. and eds. *Chiquitos en las anuas de la Compañía de Jesús (1691–1767)*. Cochabamba: Instituto de Misionologia, 2011.

McEnroe, Sean F. "A Sleeping Army: The Military Origins of Interethnic Civic Structures on Mexico's Colonial Frontier." *Ethnohistory* 59, no. 1 (2012): 109–39.

McLaughlin, David, and Rubén G. Mendoza. *The California Missions Sourcebook*. Scottsdale, Ariz.: Pentacle Press, 2012.

Meade y Sainz y Tapaga, Joaquín. *La Huasteca Queretana*. México, D.F.: Imprenta Aldina, 1951.

Meli, Roberto. *Los conventos mexicanos del siglo XVI: Construcción, ingeniería estructural y conservación*. México, D.F.: Editorial Miguel Ángel Porrúa, 2011.

Morasch Taylor, Sara. "Art and Evangelization at the Sixteenth-Century Convento of Santiago Apóstol at Cuilapan, Mexico." Unpublished PhD dissertation, Bryn Mawr College, 2006.

Mullen, Robert J. *Dominican Architecture in Sixteenth-Century Oaxaca*. Tempe: Arizona State University Press, 1975.

Muñoz Espinosa, María Teresa, and José Carlos Castañeda Reyes. "'Los Bailes': Un santuario para el culto de la fertilidad en la Sierra Gorda de Querétaro, Mexico." *Arqueología* 40 (Enero–Abril, 2009): 153–77.

Navarrete Linares, Federico. *Los orígenes de los pueblos indígenas del valle de México: Los altépetl y sus historias*. México, D.F.: UNAM, 2011.

Parrellada, Claudia. "El Paraná Español: Ciudades y misiones jesuíticas en Guaira." In *Missoes: Conquistando almas e territorios*, 130–39. Curitiba: Governo do Paraná, 2009.

Page, Carlos. *El Colegio de Tarija y las misiones de Chiquitos según las Cartas Anuas de la Compañía de Jesús*. Raleigh, N.C.: Lulu Press, 2010.

———. *Las otras reducciones jesuíticas: Emplazamiento territorial, desarrollo urbano y arquitectónico entre los Siglos XVII y XVIII*. Saarbrücken, Germany: Editorial Académica Española, 2012.

Pastells, S.J., Pablo. *Historia de la Compañía de Jesús en la Provincia del Paraguay*. 9 vols. Madrid: self-published, 1912.

Pennington, Renee. "Did Food Increase Fertility? An Evaluation of !Kung and Herero History." *Human Biology* 64, no. 4 (1992): 497–501.

Ponce Olguín, Juan Enrique. "San Francisco de Tilaco: Su reorganización como misión franciscana en el siglo XVIII." Unpublished thesis for the licenciatura, Universidad Autónoma de Querétaro, 2015.

Querejazu, Pedro, ed. *Las misiones jesuíticas de Chiquitos*. La Paz: Fundación BHW, 1995.

Rabell, Cecilia. "Matrimonio y raza en una parroquia rural: San Luis de la Paz, Guanajuato, 1715–1810." *Historia Mexicana* 41, no. 1 (1992): 3–44.

Radding de Murrieta, Cynthia. "From the Counting House to the Field and Loom: Ecologies, Cultures, and Economies in the Missions of Sonora (Mexico) and Chiquitania (Bolivia)." *Hispanic American Historical Review* 81, no. 1 (2001): 45–87.

———. *Landscapes of Power and Identity: Comparative Histories in the Sonoran Desert and the Forests of Amazonia from Colony to Republic*. Durham, N.C.: Duke University Press, 2005.

———. "Republicas dentro de la Republica de Bolivia: Los pueblos Chiquitos en los primeros escenarios de una nueva orden política." *Boletín Americanista* 60, no. 1 (2010): 51–66.

———. *Wandering Peoples: Colonialism, Ethnic Spaces, and Ecological Frontiers in Northwestern Mexico, 1700–1850*. Durham, N.C.: Duke University Press, 1997.

Restell, Matthew. *The Maya World: Yucatec Culture and Society, 1550–1850*. Stanford: Stanford University Press, 1999.

Restell, Matthew, Lisa Sousa, and Kevin Terraciano. *Mesoamerican Voices: Native Language Writings from Colonial Mexico, Yucatan, and Guatemala*. Cambridge: Cambridge University Press, 2005.

Ricard, Robert. *The Spiritual Conquest of Mexico: An Essay on the Apostolate and the Evangelizing Methods of the Mendicant Orders in New Spain, 1523–1572*. Berkeley: University of California Press, 1974.

Roller, Heather Flynn. *Amazonian Routes: Indigenous Mobility and Colonial Communities in Northern Brazil*. Stanford: Stanford University Press, 2014.

———. "Colonial Collecting Expeditions and the Pursuit of Opportunities in the Amazonian Sertao, ca. 1750–1800." *The Americas* 66, no. 4 (2010): 435–67.
Roth, Hans, and Eckart Kuhne. "Esta nueva y Hermosa iglesia: La construcción y restauración de las iglesia de Martin Schmid." In Eckart Kuhne, ed., *Las misiones jesuíticas de Bolivia: Martin Schmid 1694–1772: Misionero, músico y arquitecto entre los Chiquitos*, 89–102. Santa Cruz de la Sierra: Cumbre de las Américas, 1996.
Rubert, Arlindo. *Historia da Igreja no Rio Grande do Sul*. Porto Alegre: EDIPUCRS, 1998.
Ruiz Zavala, O.S.A., Alipio. *Historia de la provincia agustina del Santísimo Nombre de Jesús de México*. 2 vols. México, D.F.: Editorial Porrúa, 1984.
Saeger, James. *The Chaco Mission Frontier: The Guaycuruan Experience*. Tucson: University of Arizona Press, 2000.
Sales, O.P., Luis. *Observations on California, 1772–1790*. Edited and translated by Charles N. Rudkin. Los Angeles: Dawson's Bookshop, 1956.
Santamaría, Daniel. "Fronteras indígenas del oriente boliviano. La dominación colonial en Moxos y Chiquitos, 1675–1810." *Boletín Americanista* 36 (1986): 197–228.
Sarreal, Julia. "Caciques as Placeholders in the Guarani Missions of Eighteenth-Century Paraguay." *Colonial Latin American Review* 23, no. 2 (2014): 224–51.
———. *The Guaraní and Their Missions: A Socioeconomic History*. Stanford: Stanford University Press, 2014.
Sepúlveda y Herrera, María Teresa. *La Matrícula de Tributos Arqueología Mexicana Edición Especial 14*. México, D.F.: Editorial Raices, 2010.
Spores, Ronald, Nelly Robles García, Laura Diego Luna, Laura Lizeth Roldán López, and Ixtchel Guadalupe Ruiz Ríos. "Avances de investigación de los entierros humanos del sitio Pueblo Viejo de Teposcolula y su contexto arqueológico." *Estudios de Antropología Biológica* 13 (2007): 285–305.
Spores, Ronald. "Yucundáa: Su etnohistoria y consideraciones de relaciones arquitectónicas y patrones de urbanismo con España." In Ronald Spores and Nelly M. Robles García, eds., *Yucundáa: La ciudad mixteca y su transformación prehispánica-colonial*, 2 vols. México, D.F.: INAH, 2014.
Tavárez, David. "Idolatry as an Ontological Question: Native Consciousness and Juridical Proof in Colonial Mexico." *Journal of Early Modern History* 6, no. 2 (2002): 114–39.
———. *The Invisible War: Indigenous Devotions, Discipline, and Dissent in Colonial Mexico*. Stanford: Stanford University Press, 2011.
———. "The Passion According to the Wooden Drum: The Christian Appropriation of a Zapotec Ritual Genre in New Spain." *The Americas* 62, no. 3 (2006): 413–44.
Terraciano, Kevin. "The Colonial Mixtec Community." *Hispanic American Historical Review* 80, no. 1 (February, 2000): 1–42.
———. *The Mixtecs of Colonial Oaxaca: Ñudzahui History, Sixteenth through Eighteenth Centuries*. Stanford: Stanford University Press, 2004.
Tomicha Charupá, Roberto. *La primera evangelización en las reducciones de Chiquitos, Bolivia (1691–1767)*. Cochabamba: Editorial Verbo Divino, 2002.

Vergara Hernández, Arturo, ed. *Arte y sociedad en la Nueva España*. Pachuca: UAEH, 2014.
Vázquez Vázquez, Elena. "Distribución geográfica del Arzobispado de México Siglo XVI Acapistla (Yecapixtla)." *Estudios de Historia Novohispana* 4 (1971): 1-25.
Wade, Maria de Fatima. *Missions, Missionaries, and Native Americans: Long-Term Processes and Daily Practices*. Gainesville: University Press of Florida, 2008.
Wake, Eleanor. *Framing the Sacred: The Indian Churches of Early Colonial Mexico*. Norman: University of Oklahoma Press, 2010.
Warinner, Christina Gertrude. "Life and Death at Teposcolula Yucundáa: Mortuary, Archaeogenetic, and Isotopic Investigations of the Early Colonial Period in Mexico." Unpublished Ph.D. dissertation, Harvard University, 2010.
Weisdorf, Jacob. "From Foraging to Farming: Explaining the Neolithic Revolution." *Journal of Economic Surveys* 19, no. 4 (2005): 561-86.
Wilde, Guillermo. *Religión y poder en las misiones de guaraníes*. Buenos Aires: Editorial Sb, 2009.
Wrigley, Edward, and Roger S. Schofield. *The Population History of England 1541-1871*. Cambridge: Cambridge University Press, 1989.
Zwartjes, Otto, ed. *Las gramáticas misioneras de tradición Hispánica (siglos XVI-XVII)*. Amsterdam: Ediciones Rodopi B.V., 2000.

INDEX

Agiar y Sejas, Francisco, 32
altépetl, 16, 17, 18
apostolic colleges (Franciscan): Pachuca, 41, 42, 90, 125, 142; San Fernando (Mexico City), 4, 8, 9, 10, 15, 22, 42, 43, 85, 87, 107, 124, 125, 136, 138, 140, 142, 143; Santa Cruz de Querétaro, 40, 41
Asunción (Paraguay), 48, 51, 52, 98, 100, 101, 109
auto da fé, 70, 140

Baja California (Mexico), ix, 6, 32, 42, 63, 65, 87, 89, 107, 125, 127, 133, 134, 136, 137, 138, 142
Banda Oriental (Uruguay), 48, 100
Battle of Caibaté, 111
Bazan de Pedraza, Juan Gregorio, 49
bandeirantes, 46, 47
beeswax, 17, 91, 92
Bourbon Reforms, 6, 136
Buenos Aires (Argentina), 98, 100, 103, 110

cabildo, 49, 50, 57, 58
Cachum, 85, 139, 141
cacique, 57, 58, 114, 116, 117
cacicazgo, 49, 57, 99, 102, 114, 115, 116, 117
Canada, 106
capillas posa, 21, 63, 89
cartas anuas, 5, 13, 78, 101
Carvajal, Luis de, 29
casa de la cacica, 20, 22

Charcas, 93
Charles III (1759–1788), 6
Chichimeca, 9, 22, 23, 24, 26, 27, 28, 29, 30, 31, 32, 33, 35, 36, 37, 38, 39, 44, 45, 69, 75, 90, 136, 141
Chichimeca frontier, ix, 3, 6, 8, 9, 13, 15, 16, 22, 24, 25, 27, 28, 29, 30, 32, 35, 36, 38, 44, 45, 46, 50, 69, 87, 139, 141
Chichimeca War, 22, 23, 31, 36, 45, 139
Coahuila-Texas (Mexico), ix, 41, 136
cofradia (confraternity), 82, 88
Coixtlahuaca, 17, 21
Colonia do Sacramento, 47, 48, 111
communal economy, 92, 140
communion, 13, 27, 78, 79, 86
Comunero Rebellion (Paraguay), 100
congregación, 20
crops:
—Chiquitos missions: cacao, 91; corn, 91; cotton, 91; peanuts, 91; rice, 91; sugar cane, 91
—Sierra Gorda missions: bananas, 94; chile, 94; corn, 86, 87, 94; cotton, 94; pinto beans (*frijol*), 87, 94; sugar cane, 94

De la Barreda, Cayetano, 84
De la Fuente y Rojas, Miguel Bernardino, 78
disciplina, 81, 82
dysentery, 105

Ebola, 107
encomienda, 16, 17, 19, 27, 29, 36, 46

195

epidemics: of 1618, 106; of 1697, 120; of 1702, 120; of 1705–1707, 120; of 1722, 120; of 1735–1736, 110, 117; of 1738–1739, 120; of 1743–1745, 120; of 1747, 120
—dysentery: 1739, 105; 1743, 105
—measles: 1545, 20; 1695, 98; 1748–1749, 104
—smallpox: 1718–1719, 97, 98–100, 109, 110, 146; 1738–1740, 103, 104, 110, 113, 122; 1762, 125; 1763–1765, 104, 113, 114, 116, 118; 1777, 119; 1786, 106; 1797–1798, 116
Escandón, José de, 30, 34, 41, 42, 43, 44, 58, 61, 83, 84, 87, 124, 125, 128, 132, 136, 140, 141, 142
excursiones, 54

Fajardo, Pedro, 98, 99, 110, 146
famine, 100, 102, 106
Fernández del Pilar de rama, Gaspar, 124
Francisco Andrés (El Cristo Viejo), 86

Gálvez, José de, 136, 137, 142
Guerrero de Ardilla, Gabriel, 40

Huaxtepec (Oaxtepec, Morelos), 18

Iberá Lake, 101, 102
idolatry, 14, 66, 67, 70, 90, 138, 140
indigenous peoples: Be'ena'a, 21; Chiquita, 54, 56; Chiriguanos, 16, 51, 52; Charrúa, 47, 99; Chontales, 21; Chumash, 128; Culhua-Mexica, 16, 17; Cutades, 54; Guachichiles, 39, 44; Guamares, 30, 31; Guananas, 57; Guaraní, 16, 46, 47, 48, 49, 51, 56, 98, 99, 100, 101, 104, 106, 110, 111, 112, 113, 116, 117, 118, 132, 135, 136, 139; Guarapes, 55; Guarayos, 56; Guaxabanes, 44; Guaycuros, 125, 136, 142; Guenoas, 99; Huastecos, 29; Isistines, 51; Jonaces, 3, 4, 8, 9, 22, 32, 33, 34, 40, 41, 42, 43, 44, 83, 84, 87, 89, 90, 95, 108, 124, 125, 132, 133, 136, 141, 142; Karankawas, 7; Matlazinca, 29; Mazahua, 36; Mixe, 21; Mocobis, 51; Náhuas, 27, 28, 29, 30, 45, 68, 129, 141; Nudzahui, 20; Otomí, 28, 29, 33, 36, 38, 44, 45, 129, 141; Pames, 3, 4, 7, 8, 9, 10, 11, 13, 22, 30, 43, 44, 63, 65, 83, 84, 85, 87, 89, 90, 93, 94, 95, 96, 103, 108, 124, 125, 126, 127, 128, 129, 131, 132, 133, 135, 136, 140, 141; Payaguaes, 52, 55; P'urépecha, 23, 30, 31, 36, 45; Tesus, 30; Tobas, 51; Yaros, 47; Zamucos, 54; Zatienos, 54
Inguiteria (Oaxaca), 17

Labra, Gerónimo de, 34
Labra, Pero Gerónimo de, 39, 40
Landa, José Francisco de, 84

measles, 7, 8, 19, 20, 98, 104, 105, 107, 110, 132
Mezquital Valley, 26, 32, 35
missionaries, by order:
—Augustinian (O.S.A.): Cabeza de Vaca, Lucas, 30, 83, 84, 124; De Aguilar, Antonio, 70; De Santa María, Guillermo, 24, 30, 31; De Trejo, Luis, 128; Medrano, Felipe, 40
—Dominican (O.P.): Durán, Diego, 77; Galindo, Felipe, 32, 33
—Franciscan (O.F.M.): De Aguirre, Francisco, 40; De Ciudad Real, Antonio, 19, 35, 37, 38, 75, 76; De Cosín, Bernardino, 31; De Gante, Pedro, 68; De Heredia, Martín, 125; De Landa, Diego, 140; De Ochoa, Nicolás, 40; De la Fuente, Pedro, 40; De Sahagún, Bernardino, 71, 77; De San Miguel, Juan, 36; De Tastera, Jacobo, 68; De Urinate, Juan, 125; De Valencia, Martín, 67, 140; De Zumárraga, Juan, 66, 140; Ladrón De Guevara, Lucas, 125; Ortes de Velasco, José, 42, 124; Palou, Francisco, 42, 85; Pérez de Mezquia, Pedro, 58; Ponce, Alonso, 35, 38; Serra, Junípero, ix, 29, 42, 85, 86, 108, 134, 136, 137, 142; Soriano, José Guadalupe, 86, 90
—Jesuit (S.J.): Caballero, Lucas, 78, 80; De Arce, José, 52; De Blende, Bartolomé, 52, 55; Leunis, Jean, 82; Lizardí, Julian, 52; Schmid, Martin, 60, 61
missions, by region:
—Baja California (Mexico): San Francisco de Borja, 65; San Francisco Xavier, 137; San José del Cabo, 137; Santa Rosalia de Mulege, 127; Todos Santos, 125, 136
—California (Mexico): San Carlos, 65; San Miguel, 65; Santa Barbará, 65; Santa Cruz, 137
—Central Mexico: Acacingo (Puebla), 18, 19; Acámbaro (Guanajuato), 36, 37, 38; Actopan (Hidalgo), 68, 88; Alfaxayuca (Hidalgo), 35; Apatzeo (Guanajuato), 37; Atlatlauhca (Morelos), 18; Azcapotzalco (Ciudad de México), 31; Celaya (Guanajuato), 37; Chapulhuacán (Hidalgo), 27, 28, 29; Charo (Michoacán), 24; Chichicaxtla (Hidalgo), 27, 28, 29, 139; Cholula (Puebla), 74, 75, 76; Chucándiro (Michoacán), 25;

Index

Copándaro (Michoacán), 25; Coyoacán (Ciudad de México), 31; Cuauhtinchán (Puebla), 75, 76; Cuitzeo (Michoacán), 24, 25; Disinuu (Tlaxiaco) (Oaxaca), 17, 18; Huejotzingo (Puebla), 82; Hueychiapa (Huichapan) (Hidalgo), 35, 36; Huango (Michoacán), 24, 30; Huejutla (Hidalgo), 29; Ixmiquilpan (Hidalgo), 24, 32, 73, 74, 75, 76; Jacona (Michoacán), 24; Malinalco (Edo de México), 76, 78; Maní (Yucatán), 140; Metztitlán (Hidalgo), 26, 27, 29, 71, 72; Mixcoac (Ciudad de México), 31; Molango (Hidalgo), 29; Nexapa (Oaxaca), 21; Oaxtepec (Morelos), 18; Ocuila (Edo de México), 70; Tacubaya (Ciudad de México), 31; Tecali (Puebla), 18, 19, 76; Tecamachalco (Puebla), 18, 19; Tecozautla (Hidalgo), 35; Teitipac (Oaxaca), 20; Tepeaca (Puebla), 18, 19; Tepetitlán (Hidalgo), 35; Tepetlaoxtoc (Edo de México), 31, 67, 69; Tepexi del Río (Hidalgo), 35; Tepeyanco (Tlaxcala), 67; Teposcolula (Oaxaca), 17, 20, 21, 22; Tetela del Volcán (Moreelos), 67; Tetzcoco (Edo de México), 66, 67; Tlachinolipac (Hidalgo), 29; Tlayacapa(n) (Morelos), 18, 71, 72; Totolapan (Morelos), 18; Ucareo (Michoacán), 24; Xilitlán (San Luis Potosi), 27, 28, 29, 124, 128, 129, 141; Xilotepec (Jilotepec) (Edo de México), 35; Yautepeec (Morelos), 18; Yecapixtla (Morelos), 18; Yodzocahi (Yanhuitlan) (Oaxaca), 17, 18, 21; Yodzocoo (Coixtlahuaca), 21; Yucundáa (Teposcolula) (Oaxaca), 17, 18, 20, 21, 22; Yuririapúndaro (Guanajuato), 22, 23, 24
—Chaco Region (South America): Concepción, 50; San Carlos, 50; San Estebán de Lules, 50; San Fernando, 50; San Francisco Xavier de Mocobis, 51; San Ignacio de Tobas, 51; San Jerónimo, 50; San Juan Bautista de Isistines, 51
—Chichimeca (Mexico): Ayo el Chico (Jalisco), 30; Pénjamo (Guanajuato), 30; San Felipe (Guanajuato), 31, 69; Santa María del Río (San Luis Potosi), 39; Valle de Maiz (San Luis Potosi), 39
—Chiquitos (South America): Concepción, 53, 54, 60, 78, 81, 120, 130; San Francisco Xavier, 11, 54, 60, 81, 82, 98, 105, 119–24, 130; San Ignacio, 54, 60; San Ignacio de Boacocas, 54; San Ignacio de Zamucos, 54, 105; San José, 54, 59, 60, 61, 65, 78, 105; San Juan Bautista, 63, 54, 60, 61, 78, 105; San Miguel, 54, 55, 56, 60, 61, 81, 82; San Rafael, 54, 60, 61, 78, 80, 82; Santa Ana, 54, 60; Santiago, 54, 60; Santo Corazón de Jesús, 54
—Chiriguano (South America): Concepción, 51, 52; Rosario, 51, 52; San Jerónimo, 52; Valle de las Salinas, 51
—Moxos (South America): Desposorios de la Virgen María, 56; San Miguel, 56; San Nicolás, 56; San Simón, 56; Santa Rosa, 56
—Paraguay (Argentina, Brazil, Paraguay, South America): Candelaria, 47, 98, 103, 115–16; Copacabana, 46; Corpus Christi, 48, 57, 58, 115, 123, 130; Encarnación, 46; Guananas, 46; Inaí, 46; Jesús, 46, 48, 112; Jesús María, 46; Jesús María de los Guenoas, 99, 100; La Asunción (La Cruz), 99, 104, 115; Loreto, 46, 48, 102, 110, 113, 114, 115, 123; Los Ángeles, 46; Nuestra Señora de la Fé, 48, 100, 109, 112, 115; San Antonio, 46; San Francisco de Borja, 48, 99, 100, 112; San Francisco Xavier, 46, 49, 57, 99, 111, 115, 122, 123; San Ignacio Guazú, 46, 48, 99, 100, 103, 109, 112, 115; San Ignacio Miní, 46, 48, 115; San José, 46, 48, 98, 103, 106, 111, 115; San Juan Bautista, 48, 104, 112, 118, 123; San Lorenzo Mártir, 48, 58, 120; San Luis Gonzaga, 48, 99, 102, 104, 112, 118; San Miguel, 48, 115; San Nicolás, 48, 102, 104, 115; San Pablo, 46; Santa Ana, 48, 58, 99, 115, 123; Santa María, 46; Santa María la Mayor, 49, 99, 102, 104, 111, 113, 115; Santa Rosa, 11, 48, 49, 50, 57, 58, 98, 100, 108–14; Santiago, 99, 104, 112, 115; Santo Ángel Custodio, 48, 102, 112, 118; Santo Tomás, 46; Santos Cosme y Damián, 47, 98, 102, 112, 113, 115; Santos Mártires del Japón, 49, 98, 99, 102, 111, 115, 116–19; Santo Tomé, 112, 115; Trinidad, 99, 103, 112, 139; Yapeyú, 47, 49, 57, 98, 99, 115; Ytapúa, 48, 99, 100, 103, 106, 112, 115
—Sierra Gorda (Mexico): Ahuacatlán (Querétaro), 32, 34; Arnedó (Guanajuato), 90; Cadereyta (Querétaro), 33, 34, 39, 42; Cerro Prieto (Hidalgo), 42; Concá (Querétaro), 44, 61, 62, 84, 94, 95, 124, 125, 127; Deconi (Querétaro), 40; Jiliapa(n)/Xiliapa (Hidalgo), 35, 42, 90; Las Adjuntas (Hidalgo), 42; La Nopalera (Querétaro), 32, 34, 40, 141; Maconi (Querétaro), 32, 34, 40; Minas de Xichú (Guanajuato), 32; Pacula (Hidalgo), 30, 41, 42, 43,

missions, by regions, Sierra Gorda *(continued)* 84, 124; Palmar (Querétaro), 40; Peña Miller (Querétaro), 34; Pinal de Amoles (Querétaro), 34; Ranas (Querétaro), 34, 40, 90; San José del Llano/San José de Vizarrón (Querétaro), 32, 34, 40, 42, 84, 124; San Juan del Río (Querétaro), 33; San Luis de la Paz (Guanajuato), 44–45, 84; San Miguel de Palmillas/San Miguel de (las) Palmas/San Miguel Palmillas (Querétaro), 32, 34; San Pedro Tolimán (Querétaro), 33, 37, 84; Soriano (Querétaro), 32, 33, 34, 38, 84; Tancoyol (Querétaro), 11, 12, 35, 44, 63, 64, 94, 95, 124, 125, 126, 128, 129, 130, 131; Tetlá (Querétaro), 40; Tilaco (Querétaro), 11, 28, 44, 58, 61, 63, 64, 86, 89, 90, 94, 125, 126, 128, 129, 130, 131, 141; Tolimán (Hidalgo), 37, 40, 42, 43, 125, 142; Tonatico (Querétaro), 35; Xalpa (Jalpan) (Querétaro), 29, 30, 35, 43, 44, 61, 62, 84, 86, 94, 95, 108, 124, 125, 126, 139, 140; Xichú de Indios (Guanajuato), 38, 86, 90; Zimapán (Hidalgo), 32, 37, 42, 125, 139
—Sonora: Guevavi-Tumacacori (Arizona), 127; Opodepe (Sonora), 87, 139
—Tarima (South America): San Estanislao (Paraguay), 51; San Joaquín (Paraguay), 51
Mixcoatl, 70, 71

Neolithic Revolution, 7
Nezahualcoyotl, 66
nomadic peoples, 8, 22, 38, 45, 124, 125, 127, 129, 130, 131, 132, 133
nonsedentary indigenous populations, 3, 4, 6, 7, 8, 10, 15, 22, 23, 46, 50, 96, 97, 104, 131, 134, 135, 138, 141, 142

Oaxaca (Mexico), 14, 17, 20, 21, 32, 67, 70
Ometochtzin, Carlos (Don Carlos), 66

Paraná River, 46, 47, 100, 112, 115
peyote (Rosa María), 86
plague hospital, 106, 107
Province of Paraguay (Jesuit Jurisdiction), 15, 46, 51, 105
Pulque, 69, 71, 72

República de Españoles, 16
República de indios, 16
reservado (tribute category), 102
Río de la Plata Region, ix, 9, 16, 47, 49, 105
Rio Grande do Sul (Brazil), 46, 47, 99, 111, 112, 113, 115, 116

Río Tebicuary, 100
Romero, Francisco, 94

San Javier de Pinocas (*Estancia*), 91
Santa Fe (Argentina), 98, 101
Santa Cruz de la Sierra (Bolivia), 78, 91, 93, 98, 105, 132
santo entierro, 81, 82, 88
Sao Paulo, 16, 47
Satan, 69, 78, 81
sedentary indigenous populations, 3, 4, 6, 7, 8, 10, 13, 15, 22, 23, 27, 28, 29, 30, 36, 38, 45, 46, 50, 87, 90, 96, 97, 124, 127, 128, 130, 131, 132, 134, 135, 136, 138, 139, 141
Seven Years War (1755–1763), 112
shaman, 86, 90
Sierra Alta (Hidalgo), 25, 29
Sierra Mixteca (Oaxaca), 17, 20, 67, 70
smallpox, 7, 19, 20, 49, 97, 98, 99, 100, 101, 103–7, 109, 110, 113, 115, 116, 118, 119, 122, 123, 125, 132, 135, 137
solar/solares, 94
Sonora (Mexico), ix, 5, 6, 44, 87, 134, 136, 139
suma de visitas, 17, 29, 36
swidden agriculture, 5, 8, 52, 91

tapia, 50
tecpan, 71, 72
Tehuantepec (Oaxaca), 21
tepache, 84
Tezcatlipoca, 71, 73, 75, 76
Tláloc, 70
tlatoani/tlatoque, 67, 76, 140
Treaty of Madrid (1750), 107, 111, 112
Treaty of San Ildefonso (1777), 111
tributaries, 16, 17, 28, 102, 103, 116
tribute, 4, 11, 16, 17, 18, 20, 29, 36, 57, 58, 92, 102, 117, 140

Uruguay River, 46, 47, 48, 49, 99, 102, 103, 107, 111, 112, 115, 116, 117, 118

Villapando, Joachín de, 34, 40
visual catechism, 68

War of Spanish Succession (1701–1713), 53, 54

Xarupá, Lucas, 80, 81
Xipe Tótec, 71, 72

Zahui, 70
Zika (virus), 107

www.ingramcontent.com/pod-product-compliance
Lightning Source LLC
Chambersburg PA
CBHW032252150426
43195CB00008BA/428